Literary Taste, Culture and Mass Communication

Volume 11

THE WRITER AND POLITICS

Literary Taste, Culture and Mass Communication

Volume 11

THE WRITER AND POLITICS

edited by

Peter Davison/Rolf Meyersohn/Edward Shils

CHADWYCK-HEALEY CAMBRIDGE
SOMERSET HOUSE TEANECK, NJ

Chadwyck-Healey Ltd
20 Newmarket Road
Cambridge CB5 8DT
ISBN 0 85964 046 9

Somerset House
417 Maitland Avenue
Teaneck, NJ 07666
ISBN 0 914146 54 8

Library of Congress Cataloging in Publication Data
Main entry under title:

The writer and politics

(Literary taste, culture and mass communication v. 11
Bibliography: p
1. politics and literature — Addresses, essays, lectures, I. Series.

ACL. L79 vol. 11 (PN51) 301.16′ls   77-90620

British Library Cataloguing in Publication Data

Literary Taste, culture and mass communication.
Vol. 11: The writer and politics.

1. Arts and society — Addresses, essays, lectures
I. Davison, Peter II. Meyersohn, Rolf
III. Shils, Edward Albert IV. Writer and politics

700   NX180.S6

Printed in England

Contents

Introduction

Divisions in a series such as this cannot and should not be hard and fast. This volume brings together a number of articles concerned with the writer and politics, but inevitably it overlaps aspects of the relationship of the writer and society included in volume 10. Furthermore, authors who have appeared in earlier volumes might well also have been represented here: Ralph Fox (volumes 3 and 9), and Christopher Caudwell (volumes 3 and 5), both killed fighting against Franco in the Spanish Civil War; George Orwell, who is represented in volumes 3 and 10 (twice) and who also fought in Spain; André Malraux (represented in volume 5), who flew against Franco and whose *L'Espoir* (Paris 1937, translated by Stuart Gilbert and Alastair Macdonald as *Man's Hope*, New York 1938, in Britain as *Days of Hope*) is the outstanding novel of the Civil War; Claud Cockburn, whose introduction to *Bestseller* is reprinted in volume 12, but who in the Spanish Civil War was the London *Daily Worker*'s correspondent, and, on the other side, Wyndham Lewis (in volume 4) who until about 1939 supported the Nationalists against the Republicans. The way in which such contributions are spread through the series, even though they are not concerned specifically with the Spanish Civil War, may suggest how deeply concerned were so many writers with literature and its relationship to society and how, in a particular event, this concern was given practical expression — by creative work, for example in *Poems for Spain* (London 1939) edited by Stephen Spender and John Lehmann (both of whom are represented in this volume); or by direct participation, by fighting and even dying.

Martin Turnell in his 'The Writer and Social Strategy' (volume 6) traces the way that the artist has shifted from a position in which he aims to 'glorify the existing order' (vol. 6, p. 325) to one in which he tries to change society. Inevitably that means for some writers direct commitment and even the attempt to remain detached assumes political significance in such circumstances. Of course, as Katharine Bail Hoskins points out very clearly in her excellent study, *Today the Struggle: literature and politics in England during the Spanish Civil War* (Austin 1969), 'the excursion into political action of almost all the writers considered in this study was no more than that, a temporary excursion' (p. xiv), but the effects of such an excursion are long-lasting. (Note, incidentally, the use of the word 'excursion' and the comment on 'excursions of authors into the arena of politics' in Charles King's 'The Author and Politics' (p. 68) referring to R.H. Mottram's 'Can the Author Keep Out of It?' (p. 61).) Direct political concern may produce very bad art — O'Casey's *The Star Turns Red* comes to mind — but emotions

stirred in Europe by the Spanish Civil War, in Britain by Suez, and in
America (and to some extent in Australia) by Vietnam, cannot but have
profound and pervasive effects on writers in less explicit ways than in, say,
Orwell's *Homage to Catalonia*, Gustav Regler's *The Great Crusade* (New York
1940, with a preface by Ernest Hemingway), John Osborne's *The
Entertainer*, or the Royal Shakespeare Company's production, *US*.

The volume begins with a broad survey of the relationship of artistic
creativity to political dynamics. It is followed by analyses of radio and film
propaganda — placed here as a reminder that what is one author's committed
concern can easily slip into being read by others as propaganda. The
majority of the articles in this volume are, however, much more intimately
concerned with writing and politics. Sixteen of them were first published in
the 1930s and they debate whether, as Joseph Wood Krutch puts it, 'The
real business of literature is . . . not propaganda at all but the communication
of an aesthetic experience, and the most striking characteristic of an
aesthetic experience is a certain disinterestedness' (p. 47); or that the novel
is the most effective form of propaganda (and Gerald Gould cites *Uncle
Tom's Cabin* — but, as the cliché goes, compare and contrast Montagu
Slater's 'The Purpose of a Left Review' and Stephen Spender on 'Writers and
Manifestoes'), or argue, as does Harriet Monroe that 'the deliberate
propagandist rarely achieves art, and the artist, though possessed by a cause,
can rarely become a successful propagandist' (p. 88); or suggest how the
writer might aid the Republican cause in Spain: 'how can [writers] help
through their own trade?' as John Lehmann asks (p. 159). The last
contribution of the 1930s is Charles Henry Salter's essay, 'Poetry and
Politics'. This was the Chancellor of Oxford University's Prize Essay for
1939. It includes an early assessment of W.H. Auden's and Stephen Spender's
'Complete break with tradition', and comments on their using 'the word
Revolution, with ecstasy, about their own trade' (pp. 170—171).

The next four items are, by contrast with those that have preceded
them, drawn from three decades, beginning with James T. Farrell's
discussion of politics and the writer (1945); continuing with two short
articles under the general heading 'From Engagement to Indifference', seen
from British and American points of view; and concluding with a 'review' by
Stephen Spender published in 1967. This is a review of a particular book
about two young men who died in Spain, Julian Bell (a nephew of Virginia
Woolf) and John Cornford,[1] a review of their attitudes and their short lives,
and a review of 'the disgrace' attaching to the 'low dishonest decade of the
thirties in England' (p. 216). The volume concludes with a short debate

---

1   The Humanities Research Center, University of Texas at Austin, has recently
     (1978) mounted an exhibition on the Spanish Civil War and the catalogue compiled
     by Paul Patrick Rogers lists Pat Sloan's *John Cornford: a Memoir* (1938). The
     annotation states that Cornford was the first Englishman to be killed in the war.
     The first English volunteer to be killed was a woman, Felicia Brown, in Aragon in
     August 1936 (item 79).

published in 1962—63 on romanticism, socialism, and poetry, arising from an article published in *New Left Review* by Gabriel Pearson. Stanley Mitchell argues that 'There is a real sense in which the bourgeois socialist poet of the twentieth century does not belong to a stable community with unquestioned values' and he goes on to suggest that movements which have included Brecht, Mayakovsky, and Aragon, are forms of twentieth century Romanticism (p. 273). In looking back to an early period of Romanticism in which 'many actually took part in revolutionary movements or regarded themselves as political figures' (p. 274), Mitchell reasserts the strength of a heritage in which literature is seen as being an agent for political change — but see the reference to Kurt Tucholsky in Further Reading.

PETER DAVISON

Further Reading

There is a very good section on Propaganda in *Handbook of Communication* ed. I. de Sola Pool and others (Chicago 1973), pp. 844–870, in which Paul Kecskemeti reviews the literature and provides a good bibliography. Allan M. Winkler assesses the nature and practice of American propaganda in *The Politics of Propaganda: the office of war information, 1942–45* (New Haven 1978).

Further reading on writers and politics is, roughly speaking, of three kinds: creative work expressive of that relationship, direct or indirect; analyses and histories of the subject; and autobiographies, which often combine the first two categories. The titles that follow include examples of each kind but the list is obviously not intended to be exhaustive; some of the specialized studies contain bibliographies, of course.

Two of the outstanding novels of the Spanish Civil War (those by Malraux and Regler) are mentioned in the Introduction and so is *Poems for Spain*. Ernest Hemingway's *For Whom the Bell Tolls* is paradoxically 'the' Spanish Civil War novel without being, in the end, a novel of the Spanish Civil War. Arthur Koestler's experiences as a prisoner of the Nationalists in Spain under sentence of death served as the source of much that is profoundly telling in his *Darkness at Noon* (1940), although the subject of that novel is the Stalin purges.

Edward Upward's *In the Thirties* (1962) was described by Stephen Spender as 'the most truthful picture of life in that decade' and it 'describes the experience of a young poet who becomes a Marxist and joins the Communist Party of Great Britain' (Author's Note). Orwell's *Coming Up for Air* (1939) describes a Britain of the Spanish Civil War period in which the prospect of more general war is on the horizon: 'War is coming. 1941, they say'. In the preceding year, Orwell's bitter account of life as a volunteer in Spain, *Homage to Catalonia*, was published. Malcolm Lowry's *Under the Volcano* (1947) has among its references to the Spanish Civil War a discussion about 'going to fight for Spain . . . and poor little defenceless China!' The Consul loudly describes Tolstoy's categorization of such volunteers: 'All of them, you see, misfits, all good for nothing, cowards, baboons, meek wolves, parasites, every man jack of them, people afraid to face their own responsibilities, fight their own fight, ready to go anywhere, as Tolstoy well perceived—'. Or were they, as Hugh suggests, 'an expression of the whole soul of the Russian people'? (ch. 10). Claud Cockburn's *In Time of Trouble: an autobiography* (London 1957), is particularly valuable,

being written by someone who survived the war physically and with his
political faith intact.

A useful, general introductory book is *Britain in the Nineteen Thirties*
by Noreen Branson and Margot Heinemann (London 1973). This not only
provides much background material, including such details as wages in the
period, but also has chapters on 'Leisure and the Rise of the Mass Media',
and 'The Radical Trend in Culture'. In 'Attitudes to the Outside World', it
gives a brief account of the response in Britain to the Spanish Civil War (pp.
337–343).

The study of literature and politics in England during the Spanish Civil
War mentioned in the Introduction, *Today the Struggle* by Katharine Bail
Hoskins, is particularly good. Although from the same university as *The
Spanish Civil War: an exhibition*, compiled and annotated by Paul Patrick
Rogers (1978), it is modestly omitted from that catalogue's short-list of
'Later Assessments'. The pride of place there being given to Herbert L.
Matthews, *The Yoke and the Arrows* (New York 1957). The catalogue has
not only interesting illustrations but some succinct and pointed comments.
The Foreword lists locations of other collections of Spanish Civil War material
in the United States. A study of British poets of the Civil War in Spain is
given in *A Poet's War* by Hugh D. Ford (Philadelphia 1965). The Scottish
nationalist poet, Hugh MacDiarmid, has written, under his real name of
Christopher M. Grieve, *Lucky Poet: self-study in literature and political ideas,
being the autobiography of Hugh MacDiarmid* (London 1943). A general
study of *The Writer and Politics* is provided by George Woodcock (London
1948).

The Theatre of Commitment was very active in America and Britain in
the Thirties and, of course, saw the rise of Bertol Brecht. Eric Bentley's essay,
'The Theatre of Commitment' (*Commentary*, 1966) is reprinted in his
collection of essays of that title (London 1968). Elmer Rice's autobiography,
Minority Report (1963) gives a vivid account of the theatre in America,
especially in the twenties and thirties. The Federal Theater Project,
particularly The Living Newspaper, have been well written-up. First must be
mentioned Hallie Flanagan's *Arena: the history of the Federal Theater*
(1940). Random House published three Federal Theater scripts in 1938
(including *Triple-A Plowed Under* and *Power*). Jane de Hart Mathews gives a
history of the project in *The Federal Theater, 1935–39: plays, relief, and
politics* (Princeton 1967) and there is a section of illustrations, including the
famous set for *One Third of a Nation*. A broader and more recent study is
Malcolm Goldstein's *The Political Stage: American drama and theater of
the Great Depression* (New York 1974). This also has a section of pictures.

Two issues of the British journal, *Theatre Quarterly*, are particularly
useful in the context of this volume. Arthur Arent (the author of *Power*)
writes on 'The techniques of the Living Newspaper' in no. 4 (1971), an
article which originally appeared in *Theatre Arts*, 1938. There is also in this

number an account of 'The early years at Unity', the avowedly political London theatre that opened its doors in 1936. Issue 9 (1973) has an article by Ewan MacColl on street theatre in the Lancashire of the thirties (with Joan Littlewood); an assessment of the Living Newspaper; and previously unpublished Living Newspaper scenes and scenarios.

The Left Book Club has also been well written-up in, for example, Julian Symon's *The Thirties: a dream revolved* (1960); Stuart Samuels, 'The Left Book Club', *Journal of Contemporary History*, 1 (1966), 65–86; and J. Lewis, *The Left Book Club: an historical record* (1970). Among the many books published by the Left Book Club was Joseph Freeman's *An American Testament: a narrative of rebels and romantics* (London 1938), which describes the inter-war years in America from the point of view of an editor of *New Masses*. The use of 'romantic' in the sub-title might be noted in the light of the use of that word in the Pearson-Craig-Mitchell debate. *The Left Heresy in Literature and Life* by Harry Kemp, Laura Riding, and others (London 1939) is described by Katharine Hoskins as an 'ill-tempered, oversimplified, and dogmatic attack on the bad temper, oversimplification, and dogmatism of the Left' which 'contains some telling arguments' (p. 96, fn 49). Allen Tate's 'The Function of the Critical Quarterly' (1936), in his *Essays of Four Decades* (1970) might be read in conjunction with Montagu Slater's 'The Purpose of a Left Review'.

In *Power and Consciousness*, edited by Conor Cruise O'Brien and William Dean Vanech, (London and New York 1969), there is a fine essay by Noam Chomsky, 'Objectivity and Liberal Scholarship'. This draws on the abuse of language at the time of the Spanish Civil War and Vietnam. Though it is directed especially at historians, it is of much wider interest.

Perhaps nothing in modern times so graphically reminds us of the fate of the committed writer and his work as the condemnation which greeted Kurt Tucholsky's and John Heartfield's *Deutschland, Deutschland über alles* (Berlin 1929). In his Afterword to the American translation (by Anne Halley, Amherst 1972), Harry Zohn succeeds in setting the record straight. He quotes Tucholsky as answering his own question, 'What May Satire Do?' with 'Everything' (p. 241). But, as authors from Defoe to Tucholsky have discovered, politics and literature make uneasy bed-fellows and misunderstanding comes very readily. Yet, without a sense of commitment in times of uncertainty, literature can so easily be spineless. So little could satire effect the changes Tucholsky believed necessary that, as Zohn quotes him, he sought 'the truest of all democracies, the democracy of death' by taking poison (p. 244).

PETER DAVISON

Literary Taste, Culture and Mass Communication

Political Dynamics and Artistic Creativity
Vytautas Kavolis

from

Sociology and Social Research, 49, 1965.

Reprinted by permission of the author and *Sociology and Social Research*.

POLITICAL DYNAMICS AND ARTISTIC CREATIVITY*

VYTAUTAS KAVOLIS
Dickinson College
Carlisle, Pennsylvania

ABSTRACT

Two types of sociopolitical processes have been related to historical fluctuations in artistic creativity. In both types, artistic creativity tends to be stimulated by disturbances of political latency; inhibited during the periods of most intensive goal-directed action; maximized in the phase of social-emotional integration normally following such periods; and again reduced in the subsequent phase of latency. These fluctuations appear to be due to changes (a) in the social utility of art as an integrative facility, and (b) in the allocation of social resources to artistic action. It is suggested that the first factor determines, to some degree, the qualitative level of artistic achievement, and the second factor, the amount of art production.

Hauser's observation that "artistic excellence . . . is not definable in sociological terms"[1] may be correct as it stands, but it can be demonstrated that social trends may either stimulate or inhibit qualitative artistic growth.

The present paper constitutes an attempt to organize some of the accumulated evidence on dynamic political correlates of creativity in the visual arts into a theory consonant with art-historical data and relevant to general sociological theory. It is not assumed that all political factors conducive to artistic creativity have been identified or that the present theory is in its final form. It is intended as a theoretical baseline against which exceptions may be tested, with a view toward either further refinement or rejection of the theory.

PRELIMINARY ASSUMPTIONS

The variable to be measured—artistic creativity—is defined as referring to an increase in the quality of art production in any definable sociohistorical unit and/or the culmination(s) of artistic attainment of such a unit, as judged by the reasonably general consensus of artists and art critics which tends eventually to emerge as "historical judgment."[2]

Historical fluctuations in artistic creativity, as previously defined, will be interpreted in terms of the phase-cycles theory of Parsons and Bales.[3]

A variant of this theory, derived in part from small-group research but redefined so as to be more applicable to large-scale historical processes, can be summarized as follows:

(1) Any social system faces a number of basic functional problems. The most important of these are: adaptation to the external environment, organization of the legal-institutional machinery for goal attainment, integration of the adaptive and organizational solutions into the social-emotional structure of the community, and finally the reduction of tension previously accumulated in dealing with adaptive, organizational, and integrative problems.

(2) Social systems produce only limited amounts of social resources (including wealth, power, cultural symbolism, and cathectic interest) and, furthermore, may be able to use only a variable part of them for problem solving.

(3) Consequently, basic system problems tend to be dealt with in a somewhat irregular cyclical manner. Major emphasis is placed on one type of problem, to the relative neglect of others, at any particular time. As the system approaches solution of any one of its functional problems, social resources are increasingly recommitted, in a specific sequence, to previously neglected problems.

In problem-solving processes, the normal sequence appears to be adaptation, goal attainment, integration, and tension reduction. At the end of a relatively pure type of sequence, an approximation to an equilibrium should be attained. In this phase, the social system (particularly if the process takes place on a historical scale) should be structurally different from what it was during the relative equilibrium with which the sequence had started, because reactions to the disturbance of the initial state have been incorporated into the organization of the social system, which has therefore "evolved" beyond its original state. However, the end state is processually similar to the initial state, in that the sense of having solved the basic functional problems reduces the readiness to commit resources to problem-solving action.[4]

In terms of this theory, it is hypothesized that artistic creativity will tend to be stimulated in the phase of social-emotional integration[5] normally following that of intense goal-directed action; and inhibited, to varying degrees, in the other phases of any type of large-scale social process. The purpose of the present paper is to apply this general theory to two kinds of sociopolitical processes, focusing around warfare and political consolidations.

WARFARE AND ARTISTIC CREATIVITY

One type of political process necessitating the maximum commitment of resources to goal-directed action is warfare. A very general correlation between periods of warfare and those of artistic creativity has been noted, mostly in the Asian civilizations, by Mukerjee[6] and, in the European context, by Sorokin.[7] When a more exact historical analysis is possible, it tends to suggest that artistic creativity is maximized not during, but immediately after, the periods of most intensive political action,[8] and, furthermore, only if a developed artistic tradition is present to begin with.

As a possibly paradigmatic case, consider the sevententh century efflorescence of Dutch art. "Most of the artists of the seventeenth century were born when Holland was at war with Spain and fighting for her very existence."[9] The peak of creativity followed the conclusion of the truce of 1609 by which the Netherlands achieved recognition of national independence.[10] But the "births of superior talent ceased at 1640."[11] And, as Holland began to decline as a world power, "late in the seventeenth century Dutch painting once again became susceptible to French influence. . . ."[12]

Cases of gratifying victories followed by artistic revivals, particularly in monumental art, can be cited almost at random. The "booty of war" repeatedly nourished Egyptian creativity.[13] Assyrian sculpture "followed the fortunes of the empire. . . ."[14] The golden age of Athens was initiated by the victory of 480 B.C. The early success of the Crusades is followed by the age of cathedral building, approximately 1100 to 1270 A.D.[15] In Renaissance Italy, local victories were celebrated by great works of art. In France and Spain, the periods of military glory have preceded those of artistic renown.[16] Presumably, victory in warfare facilitates artistic creativity by releasing social resources from political to other kinds of action. However, such released resources are channelized to artistic creativity only to the degree to which art is culturally valued. Thus, military victories did not stimulate artistic creativity in Sparta.

As might be expected, a radical defeat, particularly if entailing prolonged conquest by a foreign power, has frequently led either to the destruction of a civilization or an immediate decline in artistic excellence (which may be followed by a revival of creativity after the conquerors have amalgamated with the conquered).[17] Defeat by invading peoples was followed by destruction, for example, of the Assyrian, Minoan, Mycenaean, Phrygian, Sassanian, and the ancient American civilizations.[18] Artistic decline set in after the collapse of the Old Kingdom in Egypt; the Athenian defeat during the Peloponnesian wars; the conquest of Ceylon by Rajaraja in the eleventh century and the Indian invasion of 1213; the Norman invasions of the ninth century, which ended the Carolingian renaissance; the Mongol invasions of the Near East in the thirteenth century; and the two conquests of Constantinople in 1204 and 1453.[19]

However, a number of cases suggest that artistic creativity, especially in small-scale art, may also be stimulated by moderate defeats, which are neither completely disruptive of the social system nor associated with permanent occupation by an invading power. Spain's defeat by Napoleon seems to have contributed to the creative growth of Goya. The ultimate downfall of the Corsican was followed by a stronger revival of French painting than occurred during his years of glory. Again in France, the post-defeat "decade 1870-1880 is by far [the] best period" of the Impressionists.[20] The shock of defeat in the Russo-Japanese war of 1904-5 may have had an emancipating effect on artistic developments in Russia, during the only decade in which Russian painting had a pioneering significance.[21] And the disaster of World War I has certainly not dampened the creative ardor of the German expressionists.

In accounting for such cases, it is suggested that a moderately disruptive defeat may have an artistically stimulating effect by upsetting a previous state of political latency. Latency is the condition of the social system in which it most closely approaches the only theoretically conceivable state of equilibrium, and is characterized by a tension reduction orientation. A tension reduction orientation in a social system is likely to produce in its participants, or to be caused by, a generalized feeling that the basic functional problems of the system have been essentially solved and therefore do not require any intensive commitment of social resources to them. This implies, among other things, a reduced perception of the need for socioemotional integration, and thus for art in its function as an integrative facility.[22] Insofar as a disturbance of latency increases the felt need for integration, it should increase the importance of art for society, as one source of supply of the symbolic means by which recent disturbances could be articulated into the social-emotional structure of the community. The increased social utility of art should imbue the action of art creation with a stronger sense of seriousness of purpose, with a greater urgency, and thus to make for higher artistic achievements.

On the assumption that a prolonged period of relative peacefulness is likely to set up a movement within the social system toward latency, it is possible to construct an approximation to a quantitative test of the hypothesis that political latency has artistically inhibiting effects. For the purposes of measurement, prolonged peacefulness is defined as referring to a period of at least a hundred-years duration, during which warfare is less intensively waged than either before or afterwards (if there is a subsequent increase in warfare at all). Two of Sorokin's indices of the intensity of warfare will be used: (1) the estimated number of casualties, and (2) the duration of warfare, in both cases estimated by twenty-five year periods.[23] In the following discussion, data will be presented on the only periods in Sorokin's tables which both indices agree in identifying as those of prolonged peacefulness, in the above sense.

In Greece, a decline in warfare occurred during the third and particularly the second centuries B.C. Towards the end of this period, a reduction in artistic creativity is evident in mainland Greece and, somewhat later, in the Greek-speaking eastern Mediterranean area as a whole. In Rome, warfare declined in the first and second centuries A.D. A reduction in artistic creativity began in the second half of this period. In Spain, a long-range decrease in warfare began in 1651 or 1676 (depending on which index is used) and continued until the Napoleonic wars. Then, until the twentieth century, Spain was relatively peaceful. This whole period was marked by reduced artistic creativity. The only significant exception is Goya, whose best period is associated with the Napoleonic wars. In Holland, a long-range reduction in warfare started in 1651 (or 1726)[24] or 1676. Approximately after 1680, artistic creativity also began to decline. In Austro-Hungary, prolonged peacefulness is indicated for 1776 (or 1750) to 1900. This period, particularly the nineteenth century, conforms to the expectation of reduced creativity in the visual arts. In all three modern cases, there was a revival of creativity, chronologically associated with increasing domestic and international disturbances, in the twentieth century. Thus, whenever the two indices of warfare are in agreement, the periods of prolonged peacefulness are associated with reductions in artistic achievement. In spite of the somewhat arbitrary definition of political latency and the imprecision of the data on both variables, the findings can be taken as supporting the hypothesis that artistic creativity tends to be inhibited during the latency phase.

However, when a disturbance of political latency becomes a continuous condition affecting the social order with great intensity, in what might be regarded as a prolonged goal-attainment phase, artistic creativity is likely to decline. Prolonged periods of unsatisfying warfare—of "wars more exhausting than remunerative, and leading from dominance to stalemate,"[25] as Kroeber has characterized the wars of Louis XIV, may not allow sufficient accumulations of social resources that could be devoted to the creation of art; "and such conflicts as the Hundred Years War in France and the Thirty Years in Germany produced general misery and retardation of artistic development."[26]

POLITICAL CONSOLIDATION AND ARTISTIC CREATIVITY

The basic problem in the goal-attainment phase is to achieve "control over parts of the situation in the performance of goal-oriented tasks."[27] Within the political process, this analytical phase can be empirically located, most clearly, during periods of institutionalization of socio-political cohesiveness, after its disturbance by disorder, struggle, or fragmentation. Such periods, with qualifications to be noted, tend to be followed by artistic efflorescences of varying magnitudes.

Illustrative cases include: the unification of Sumeria by the third Ur dynasty; the "burst into vivid life" of Chinese painting during the Han dynasty, after the consolidation of the empire by Ch'in in 221 B. C.; a second outburst of creativity following the consolidation under the T'ang dynasty, 618-907; and a third, following the S'ung reunification in 960. One may also cite the artistic revivals consequent upon the emergence of national dynasties in Ceylon in 150 B. C. and 1153 A. D.; in Gupta India in 320 A. D.; and in Safavid Persia; the Frankish and Saxon consolidations antecedent to the Carolingian renaissance and the Othonian efflorescence; and the centralization effected by the Macedonian dynasty (867-1056) which inaugurated the late blossoming of Byzantine art during the eleventh and twelfth centuries. The establishment of effective feudal orders has been followed by artistic efflorescences in Chou China (ninth to seventh centuries B. C.), in thirteenth-century Europe, and in fifteenth-century Japan.[28] "Around 1550 or 1600 . . . the other west European countries drew abreast of Italy in . . . the arts, and the sciences, after having consolidated themselves into organized nation-states."[29] The artistic after-effects of the establishment of the Netherlands as an independent state have been noted before.

The large-scale cycle initiated by a ground-breaking event of political organization may require, in a complex historical constellation, a century or more for its artistic effects to become fully felt. It took two centuries from the conquest of Persia by the Mongols in the thirteenth century to the fifteenth-century artistic flowering under the Timurid princes. It took approximately one century from the importation of the Norman tradition of miniature painting, after the conquest of 1066, to the remarkable achievements of English pictorial art during the twelfth century;[30] from the final unification of Spain, between 1469 and 1492, to the greatest period of Spanish painting, 1580-1660; and from the establishment of the Latin-American republics to the first significant developments in their art after 1910. The length of time required to reach the integrative phase of the long-range cycle initiated by state-founding action, or a complete absence of such a phase before the beginning of a political decline, or possibly the lack of a developed native tradition of high art, may explain the several cases of imperial consolidation (Mongol, Turk, Lithuanian) which have not significantly invigorated artistic creativity.[31]

Inconsistently, "the simultaneous appearance of 'empires' after 1300, both in Mesoamerica and in the central Andes,"[32] seems to have been associated with a decline in artistic creativity in the Inca empire[33] and an increase in the Mexico of the Aztecs.[34] The Inca decline may in part be accounted for by a continued extreme commitment of social resources to political and economic action.[35] From this point of view, the degeneration of art in the Soviet Union and Nazi Germany may be susceptible of explanation by the same general principle as the decline in the Inca empire. Does it seem unreasonable to suggest that the Aztecs, after the establishment of their hegemony, seem to have shared an "integrative" orientation with thirteenth-century France and with fifteenth-century Italy,[36] in contrast to the "organizational" emphasis characteristic of the Inca as well as of the modern totalitarian states?

The Inca-Aztec difference in religious orientation may also have been to some degree responsible for the differential effect of imperial consolidation on artistic creativity. Roger Fry explains the "fantastic inventiveness" of both Aztec and Gothic art as possibly due to "the tension of spirit produced by this perpetual terror of supernatural forces" which, he thinks, may have had a "stimulating effect on their creative power."[37] The Inca, "a pragmatic people," appear to have had a more craftsman-like approach to art.[38] It has been demonstrated elsewhere that religious tensions tend to contribute to artistic creativity.[39]

That, in dealing with historical as constrasted with small-group processes, a consideration of cultural programs must be added to the categories of the phase cycles theory to make valid analyses possible, is indicated by a strategic Chinese case. After the expulsion of the Mongols in 1368, "the new Chinese dynasty of Ming did its best in every sphere of activity to restore its past . . . and to resume history from the point it had reached . . . in 907;"[40] "they decided to take as their models the T'ang, who before them had been the last sovereigns of a united China."[41]

A national consolidation on the basis of such a reactionary program did not invigorate the arts; and a "decadence of sculpture" set in.[42] Thus to provide an adequate stimulation to artistically creative capacities, a political consolidation may have to permit a considerable scope for innovative exploration in cultural expression. More generally, the several cases just considered imply that the general cultural program of a political consolidation may mediate, or even determine, its impact on artistic creativity.

Cases may be cited in which the obverse of political consolidation—a process of state disintegration—appears to have contributed to a decline in artistic creativity. The "finest era" of Chinese art ended when "a rebellion by An Lu-Shan" so weakened the empire that "effective centralized control of administration could never be fully restored. . . ."[43] In Japan, the great period of Amidist art ended at the beginning of the civil war between the clans of Taira and Minamoto, in the middle of the twelfth century. In Africa, "too often material insecurity, fear of plunder or the raids of slave hunters have by provoking the disintegration of the society, also killed the art of the people."[44]

However, the "turmoil" of the Five Dynasties period, 907-960, did not prevent a "full flowering of Chinese landscape painting." A suggested explanation of this somewhat unusual case is that

> the division of the country prevented the expression of . . . energy through normal political channels. (Artistically cultivated) men, who would normally have devoted themselves to the service of the country, found themselves unemployed and turned to the arts.[45]

This response to the suspension of political action would not be possible, because of lacking technical competence, for the political elites of almost any other society. Furthermore, it presupposes considerable economic prosperity. Again, after the division of China caused by the Manchurian invasion of the twelfth century, "the Sung empire, henceforth restricted to South China (1127-1276), very rapidly recovered its prosperity," "and Hangchow, the new imperial capital . . . during the last quarter of the twelfth century . . . produced the greatest Chinese landscapists of all time."[46] In this case, a reconsolidation of a fragment of the state after partition was combined with economic prosperity. State disintegration was not total and did not preclude a sizable allocation of social resources to artistically creative action, while the disturbance of political latency may have increased the need for art as an integrative facility. All of this occurred in a culture with a highly developed native artistic tradition.

It is significant, however, that while imperial consolidations frequently encourage developments in monumental art, in the two Chinese cases it was principally small-scale art that was stimulated. It was primarily interest rather than wealth or organized power that could, under the circumstances, be allocated as resources for artistically creative action.

All artistic efflorescences subsequent to political consolidations have, of course, eventually subsided. To what extent this is the effect of a transition to the latency phase in the political process, it is at present difficult to determine. In this type of a long-range political-action cycle, the latency phase is particularly hard to identify. Illustratively, however, one may point to the exhaustion of the Gothic around 1270 and the decline of both Dutch and Spanish painting after 1680 as probably reflecting, to some degree, the adverse effects of political latency on artistic creativity.

THEORETICAL INTERPRETATION

It has been observed that artistic creativity tends to increase in periods following those of intensive goal-oriented action in the political sphere (warfare or political consolidations). This tendency may be theoretically accounted for by the increased salience of the integrative problem in such periods. A high salience of the integrative problem is assumed to increase the social utility of art,[47] which may be thought of as the degree to which art contributes positively to the maintenance and further development of the social system.

When the integrative phase of the sociopolitical process is greatly prolonged, it apparently tends, in the relative absence of other disturbances, to pass over into the latent tension reduction phase, in which all basic problems of the political system (including the integrative) are felt to have been essentially solved. In this phase, quality art seems to have less social utility, and artistic stagnation is more likely to occur.

The main reasons why artistic peaks do not tend to occur during the periods of most intensive political action seems to be the lack of resources which could be diverted from urgent adaptive and organizational tasks and allocated to integrative action. In the latency phase, however, the reduction in creativity occurs in spite of the possibility, frequently actualized in such periods (as in mainland Greece during and immediately after the Hellenistic period), of committing social resources on a large scale to artistic action. This suggests that the social utility of art may not necessarily be closely correlated with the empirical allocation of social resources to artistic creativity.

If artistic creativity increases during periods of moderate disturbance of latency and during those of re-equilibration after radical disturbances, it may be hypothesized that the salience of the integrative need in the social system determines, to some degree, the qualitative *level* of artistic achievement. If, during intensive political action and after catastrophic defeat, social resources cannot be made available to artistically creative action, then, regardless of the integrative need, high-quality art cannot be created. Thus the availability of social resources constitutes a limiting factor with regard to artistic creativity. But that the availability of social resources does not by itself guarantee a high-level artistic achievement is suggested by the tendency for artistic creativity to decline in the latency or tension-reduction phase, when most extensive resources can be allocated to artistic action. It is therefore hypothesized that the degree to which social resources are committed to artistic action determines primarily the amount of art production, and affects its quality only in the limiting cases in which the allocation of resources to artistic action declines below the minimum level necessary to sustain an organization of art production at all. (Such declines may be caused either by an "economic" deficiency of resources in the social system, or by a "cultural" decision, as in Sparta, not to allocate existing resources to artistically creative action.)

The present analysis suggests that high artistic achievements do not reflect stable equilibria in the social system, but must be regarded either as spontaneous cultural projections of ongoing processes of social re-equilibration, or as products of a more or less organized effort to increase the supply of symbolic facilities for social integration, or both. Whichever the interpretation, high-quality art seems to be more energetically created in a political system which, after a serious disturbance of equilibrium, is moving toward a new integration (on a larger, smaller, or the same geographical basis), than in one in which an adequate equilibrium is widely felt to have been attained, or in one which is in the midst of an intense disturbance of equilibrium (or for other reasons lacks the social resources required for effective reintegration).

CONCLUDING OBSERVATIONS

Political phase cycles may cut across other types (economic, religious, communal) of phase cycles, and the effect of the former on artistic creativity may be modified or offset by the combined effects of the latter. Artistic creativity is presumably maximally stimulated when the integrative phases of several types of phase cycles coincide or overlap. It is also assumed that a tradition of high art must be present for any sociological factor to have an artistically stimulating effect.

In spite of these complexities, the present survey suggests that political phase cycles are among the factors responsible for historical variations in the level of artistic attainment. To be sure, the present theory has been derived from illustrative comparisons and measurements based on somewhat uncertain estimates, and must be tested by detailed study of individual cases before it can be regarded as adequately validated. Its theoretical framework, however, has been found workable in parallel studies on the economic and religious backgrounds of artistic creativity.[48]

The paradigm presented is not a substitute for detailed historical analysis, for, as the present study has demonstrated, several additional factors (such as cultural programs) impinge upon the paradigmatic model and must be considered, particularly in accounting for exceptional cases.

FOOTNOTES

* Presented at the 1964 annual meeting of the Pennsylvania Sociological Society. The author is Associate Professor and Chairman of the Department of Sociology-Anthropology at Dickinson College, Carlisle, Pennsylvania. Comments by Allan I. Ludwig are gratefully acknowledged.

[1] Arnold Hauser, *The Philosophy of Art History* (New York: Alfred A. Knopf, 1959), 8.

[2] In the following paragraphs is presented a somewhat improved revision of the working assumptions formulated in Vytautas Kavolis, "Economic Correlates of Artistic Creativity," *The American Journal of Sociology,* 70 (November, 1964), 332-33.

[3] Talcott Parsons and Robert F. Bales, "The Dimensions of Action Space," in Talcott Parsons, Robert F. Bales, and Edward A. Shils, *Working Papers in the Theory of Action* (New York: The Free Press, A Division of the Macmillan Co., 1953), 63-109; Talcott Parsons and Neil J. Smelser, *Economy and Society* (New York: The Free Press, A Division of The Macmillan Co., 1956), 242-43.

[4] Since system movement toward integration, or the tension reduction phase, is in reality constantly interrupted by beginnings of new cycles, it is the movement toward or away from integration, rather than an integrated state, that constitutes the normal condition of society. When the system approaches integration most closely, it may indeed be least capable of surviving, in a competitive environment, since "deactivation" of human resources presumably occurs upon the attainment of what can be felt as a *relative* integration.

[5] Cf. Talcott Parsons, Robert F. Bales, and Edward A. Shils, "Phase Movement in Relation to Motivation, Symbol Formation, and Role Structure," in Parsons *et al., Working Papers, op. cit.,* 190. On some empirical observations supporting this expectation, and suggesting intervening variables, see Thorstein Veblen, *The Theory of the Leisure Class* (New York: The Modern Library, 1931), 373; and Eric Hoffer, *The True Believer: Thoughts on the Nature of Mass Movements* (New York: The New American Library, 1958), 140.

[6] Radhakamal Mukerjee, *The Social Functions of Art* (Bombay: Hind Kittabs Ltd., 1951), 27-28.

[7] Pitirim A. Sorokin, *Social and Cultural Dynamics,* Vol. III (New York: American Book Co., 1937), 365.

[8] This is implicit in Sorokin's earlier observation that a "correlation between the war periods and the extraordinary number of the great men of genius born in such a period, or immediately after it, seems to exist . . ." Pitirim Sorokin, *Contemporary Sociological Theories* (New York: Harper & Bros., 1928), 351.

9 Adriaan J. Barnouw, *The Pageant of Netherlands History* (New York: Longmans, Green and Co., 1952), 263.

10 During the Thirty Years war, "the fine arts (also) flourished in Holland." But the Netherlands were less involved in this war than in their own struggle for independence. Furthermore, the devastation of Germany gave a relative advantage, in this period, to the Netherlands. George Edmundson, *History of Holland* (Cambridge: The University Press, 1922), 186, 199, 201.

11 A. L. Kroeber, *Configurations of Culture Growth* (Berkeley: University of California Press, 1944), 368.

12 *Encyclopedia of World Art* (New York: McGraw-Hill Book Co., 1959), hereafter cited as *EWA*, V, 436.

13 *EWA*, II, 105; IV, 669.

14 A. L. Kroeber, *op. cit.*, 245.

15 Cf. André Malraux, *The Metamorphosis of the Gods* (Garden City, N. Y.: Doubleday & Co., 1960), 266.

16 A. L. Kroeber, *op. cit.*, 700, 702, 709.

17 Cf. René Grousset, *Chinese Art and Culture* (New York: Grove Press, Inc., 1959), 117, 169, André Grabar and Carl Nordenfalk, *Romanesque Painting from the Eleventh to the Thirteenth Century* (New York: Skira, 1958), 113, 141.

18 *EWA*, I, 871; A. L. Kroeber, *op. cit.*, 689; *EWA*, I, 886-87; Herbert Read, *The Meaning of Art* (Baltimore: Penguin Books, 1961), 81; *EWA*, I, 231.

19 *EWA*, IV, 653; A. L. Kroeber, *op. cit.*, 694; *EWA*, II, 105; III, 331; V, 526; Richard Ettinghausen, *Arab Painting* (Lausanne: Skira, 1962), 142; *EWA*, II, 812, 819.

20 Maurice Serullaz, *French Painting, The Impressionist Painters* (New York: Universe Books, Inc., 1960), 55.

21 Camilla Gray, *The Great Experiment: Russian Art 1863-1922* (New York: Harry N. Abrams, Inc., 1962), 61.

22 The hypothesis that art has socially integrative functions tends to be supported by empirical observations suggesting that artistic interest is associated with role deviance, role discomfort, and role change. Vytautas Kavolis, "A Role Theory of Artistic Interest," *The Journal of Social Psychology*, 60 (June, 1963), 33-35.

23 P. A. Sorokin, *Dynamics, op. cit.*, Vol. III, 293, 295, 301, 319, 328, 331. For estimates of peaks of artistic creativity, see Pitirim A. Sorokin, *Society, Culture, and Personality: Their Structure and Dynamics* (New York: Harper & Bros., 1947), 549-50. The estimates of artistic peaks for Spain and Holland are my own, since Sorokin does not present any.

24 There was a short increase in warfare during the 1700-1725 quarter-century, according to the estimated casualties index.

25 A. L. Kroeber, *op. cit.*, 702.

26 Adolph Seigfried Tomars, *Introduction to the Sociology of Art* (Mexico City: Privately Printed, 1940), 376.

27 Parsons *et al.*, *op. cit.*, 64.

23 P.A. Sorokin, *Dynamics, op. cit.*, Vol. III, 293, 295, 301, 319, 328, 331. For Universal Books, Inc., 1958), 18; R. Grousset, *op. cit.*, 170; P. A. Sorokin, *Society, Culture, and Personality, op. cit.*, 549; *EWA*, II, 802, 810; III, 331; H. Read, *op. cit.*, 82; A. L. Kroeber, *op. cit.*, 671; Rushton Coulborn, *ed., Feudalism in History* (Princeton, New Jersey: Princeton University Press, 1956), 372-73.

29 A. L. Kroeber, *A Roster of Civilizations and Culture* (Chicago: Aldine Publishing Co., 1962), 91.

30 Richard N. Frye, *Iran* (New York: Henry Holt & Co., 1953), 55, 57; Grabar and Nordenfalk, *op. cit.*, 113, 141.

31 A. L. Kroeber, *Configurations, op. cit.*, 791-92.

32 George Kubler, *The Art and Architecture of Ancient America: The Mexican, Maya, and Andean Peoples* (Baltimore: Penguin Books, 1962), 21.

33 *Ibid.*, 22, 272-73; J. Alden Mason, *The Ancient Civilizations of Peru* (Harmondsworth, Middlesex: Penguin Books, 1957), 231.

34 G. Kubler, *op. cit.*, 22; G. C. Vaillant, *The Aztecs of Mexico* (Harmondsworth, Middlesex: Penguin Books, 1956), 164.

[35] G. Kubler, *op. cit.,* 272-73, 322. The Aztec "empire" had a looser political structure, an indication of a less intensive commitment of social resources to goal-oriented action.

[36] Cf. Vytautas Kavolis, "Community Integration Cycles and Artistic Creativity," unpublished manuscript.

[37] Roger Fry, *Last Lectures* (Boston: Beacon Press, 1962), 88.

[38] "The art of the Inca period was . . . technically excellent, under perfect control, but uninspired and aesthetically the poorest of the several major traditions developed in Peru." J. A. Mason, *op. cit.,* 231.

[39] Vytautas Kavolis, "Religious Dynamics and Artistic Creativity," unpublished manuscript.

[40] René Grousset, *The Rise and Splendour of the Chinese Empire* (Berkeley: University of California Press, 1953), 256.

[41] R. Grousset, *Chinese Art and Culture, op. cit.,* 291.

[42] *Ibid.,* 290.

[43] P. C. Swann, *op. cit.,* 51.

[44] Denise Paulme, *African Sculpture* (New York: The Viking Press, 1962), 19.

[45] P. C. Swann, *op. cit.,* 51. The stress on "privatism" in contemporary American society may be contributing to artistic creativity in a somewhat similar manner.

[46] R. Grousset, *op. cit.,* 261.

[47] Cf. note 22.

[48] V. Kavolis, "Economic Correlates," *op. cit.*

Studies in Radio and Film Propaganda
R.K. Merton and P.F. Lazarsfeld

from

Social Theory and Social Structure by
R.K. Merton. The Free Press, New York, 1968.

STUDIES IN RADIO AND
FILM PROPAGANDA*

T HIS IS A REPORT on certain studies of domestic propaganda in radio and motion pictures. Having said this, let us define the term propaganda and let us make the definition hold throughout our discussion. We understand by propaganda any and all sets of symbols which influence opinion, belief or action on issues regarded by the community as controversial. These symbols may be written, printed, spoken, pictorial or musical. If, however, the topic is regarded as beyond debate, it is not subject to propaganda. In our society, the belief that 2 and 2 make 4 cannot, in this sense, be propagandized any more than the moral conviction that mother-son incest is evil. But it is still possible to propagandize the belief that our victory in war is not inevitable; that the poll tax runs counter to certain conceptions of democracy; that it would be unwise, during wartime, to provide citizens with as much fuel oil and gasoline as they wish; that one religious system has greater claim to our allegiance than another. Given a controversial issue, propaganda becomes possible and, it would seem, almost inevitable.

Another general remark. In many quarters, propaganda is often identified with lies, deceit or fraud. In our view, propaganda has no necessary relation to truth or falsity. An authentic account of the sinkings of American merchant ships in time of war may prove to be effective propaganda inducing citizens to accept many deprivations which they would not otherwise accept in good spirit. If we succumb to the view that propaganda and falsity are one, we are well on the way to nihilism. Let us recognize also that an attitude of uncritical distrust may develop as a defense against the acceptance of deprivation or against a barrage of facts and information which invite fear, discomfort or the abandonment of cherished beliefs.

But it is long since time to halt discussions of propaganda in the large; discussions which have all the fascination of speculation uncontrolled by empirical inquiry. To bring certain problems of propaganda

---

* In collaboration with Paul F. Lazarsfeld.

into clear focus, we must turn to propaganda in the particular, and develop definite procedures for testing our interpretations. It is not that general discussions of propaganda are necessarily invalid; it is only that they tend to outrun our funded knowledge. They are big with the bigness of vacuity.

Possibly this paper errs in the opposite direction. We intend only to report some of the studies conducted in World War II by the Columbia University Bureau of Applied Social Research under the supervision of Dr. Herta Herzog and the authors. One characteristic of these studies is their concern with the ascertainable effects of particular propaganda documents. Another characteristic is their technial orientation; they constitute one basis for advising the writers and producers of this propaganda. The research must be such as to implement immediate decision and action. A dozen years before he fled to Samoa, Robert Louis Stevenson was unwittingly describing the very type of situation which confronts research students operating within the framework of political action:

> This is no cabinet science, in which things are tested to a scruple; we theorize with a pistol to our head; we are confronted with a new set of conditions on which we have not only to pass judgment, but to take action, before the hour is at an end.

The present report, then, deals with research conducted "with a pistol to our head." Our object is to plead that you not pull the trigger.

MODES OF PROPAGANDA ANALYSIS

In one sense, detailed propaganda analysis is not a new development. For at least the past generation, the effects of films, radio programs and newspaper materials have been studied. Until recently, however, these studies have dealt with the over-all effects of the propaganda material as a whole. These researches—for example, those of L. L. Thurstone—have consequently confined their general results to observations of this order:

> An anti-Negro film, "The Birth of a Nation," increased anti-Negro sentiment among tested audiences.
> The film, "Streets of Chance," which portrayed a gambler "as an interesting, likeable character," for some unascertained reason led to an increased condemnation of gambling.
> The film, "All Quiet on the Western Front," led to more marked reactions against war among groups of school children than did the film "Journey's End."

You will notice that such research tells us little about the specific features of the propaganda which provoked these effects. But this is the very question with which the script-writer and the producer are concerned. If they are to benefit from propaganda research, it must be directed toward discovering the typical effects of definite and specific aspects of propaganda as well as its over-all effects. What is the character of effective propaganda under given conditions? In this report, we shall examine samples of recent studies in which definite features of propaganda are linked with definite types of response.

Before turning to methods of analyzing propaganda effects, we should seek to dispel one common illusion. It is clear that, in general, writers of propaganda cannot know how audiences will respond to their material merely by relying on intuition or by observing their own reactions. Several examples, the first of which is educational rather than propagandistic, will illustrate what unexpected responses the writer may elicit.

A skilled writer had drafted the instructions for the use of the second war ration book in as lucid a fashion as he could. Psychological consultants assisted him in the task. Trained interviewers presented the instructions to housewives and observed their reactions. On the basis of these observations, a second draft of instructions was prepared. This also was tested by interviewing, and a modified third draft was finally adopted. A central objective was that of making it clear that ration stamps of different values could be added to reach a given number of points.

It was assumed that since most people have had experience with postage stamps, an analogy might profitably be used in the instructions. Who would have anticipated from the vantage point of his armchair that this simple analogy would elicit comments such as these:

> I didn't realize that you had to mail them.

> There doesn't seem to be any place to stick them.

This trivial example of the unexpected response merely reflects a breakdown in communication. Other illustrations are provided by films which emphasize the cruelty and immorality of the Nazis. Episodes which ostensibly indicate that the Nazis are entirely unconcerned with common human decencies are at times appraised by audiences in purely technical terms: they are taken as illustrations of Nazi efficiency. The emotional and moral implications intended by the producers of these films are overlooked by the audience.

Much the same pattern of the unexpected response is found in radio materials. A talk on X-rays was broadcast under the auspices of a medical society, as part of a campaign seeking to promote "proper" use of health services by members of the community. The speaker, a noted radiologist, attempted to dissuade his listeners from turning to unlicensed practitioners (quacks) for X-ray examinations and treatments. In an effort to make his persuasion effective, he repeatedly stressed "the dangers in the use of and in the making of X-ray examinations." The radiologist's good intentions elicited unexpected anxieties. Some members of the audience—who, in any case, would not have consulted quacks—expressed their newly acquired fears:

It left people not wanting X-rays. It sounded so dangerous. The doctor uses lead and wears gloves. People wouldn't even want to get an X-ray after that. They'd be scared away.

I would feel that maybe it would hurt. From hearing about currents and so on I would think that it would be at least unpleasant.

The pattern of the unanticipated response raises several basic questions. How can we analyze propaganda films, radio and print, in such a way that we can determine what is likely to produce given effects? The procedures for achieving this end have come to be known as *content-analysis*. There are further questions. How can we ascertain responses actually elicited by propaganda? How far can we account for discrepancies between anticipated and actual responses? Can we build a fund of experience and interpretation which will enable us more fully to anticipate responses to various types of propaganda, thus minimizing or precluding undesirable responses by appropriate modification of the propaganda before it is released? Procedures designed to answer these questions we shall call *response-analysis*.

And now we turn to what we consider our main task: to report our experience in the analysis of various types of propaganda during a period of two years. Perhaps by focusing on problems actually encountered in these studies, we can make clear some of the procedures of content- and response-analysis which have been developed.

CONTENT-ANALYSIS

The propaganda document—a pamphlet; film or radio program—is first scrutinized to determine the probable types of responses to its various components, aspects, or to the document-as-a-whole. It may be assumed, perhaps, that anyone who examines the propaganda material will know its content. But this is far from being the case. Content-analysis requires certain procedures, based on clinical experience and funded in psychological or sociological theory, in order to discern the probable responses to the content. Mere impressionism is not enough. The content of a 15-minute radio program or of an hour film can be adequately appraised only through systematic procedures. Just as we need a field glass to perceive an object in the far distance, so we need devices, at times surprisingly simple devices, to perceive a flow of experience which endures over an extended period of time. These devices vary from the one extreme of counting the frequency of certain *key symbols* to the other extreme of determining the *structure* of the propaganda-as-a-whole or of an entire propaganda campaign.

Let us consider a few examples of the simplest type: symbol-analysis.

A radio series of morale programs contained approximately 1000 symbols denoting the United Nations (or its constituents, other than the United States) and the Axis (distributively or collectively). Upon examination of the frequency of these respective sets of symbols in twelve programs, several uniformities emerge which reflect a structure of the programs that runs counter to the manifest intent of the producers. In all but one of the programs, the frequency of United Nations symbols is positively correlated with those pertaining to the Axis: an increase or decrease in the one set of symbols is associated with an increase or decrease in the other. This brought to the fore a significant pattern in these morale programs. Interest in the United Nations is largely confined to their role in the war vis-à-vis the Axis: they are seldom mentioned in any other connection. So far as this morale series is concerned, the United Nations appear to be "foul-weather friends": interest is primarily manifested in them as allies helping to fight the Axis, and not as allies with whom we have sympathetic ties, irrespective of the war. The programs deal with them, not as societies, but only as nations exhibiting military prowess and courage. We salute the heroic dead of the Russians and rejoice that they are enemies of Hitler. We eulogize the British who have so long held the fortress Britain against the Nazis. Or we mourn the fate of the occupied nations and, again, interest in these nations is limited to their experience at the hands of the enemy. Because these are the motifs expressed in allusions to the United Nations, we find the observed association between the frequency of symbols referring to the United Nations and to the Axis. It should be noted that the analysts, and possibly the producers, of this radio series would not have detected this underlying structure had the symbol counts not called it to their attention.

This series of programs also made extensive use of the personification stereotype in referring to the enemy: about 25 per cent of all symbols denoting the enemy refer to Hitler, Mussolini, Goering, *etc.*, whereas only four per cent of references to the United Nations and 11 per cent of those to the United States consist of personifications. This use of simplified personalized stereotypes presents the enemy as consisting essentially of a small band of evil men and implies that once these men are destroyed, all will be well. This kind of personification proves to be all too acceptable to listeners, since it accords with common simplistic ideas; for example, the parallel notion that we must fight crime primarily by punishing criminals and not by preventive measures.

Moreover, we have found that varying distributions of terms used to designate the enemy in documentary films are reflected in the comments of interviewees who have seen these films. Thus, if the single satanic figure, Hitler, or the entire German people, rather than the Nazis, are most frequently identified as the enemy by the film commentator, this is reflected in the pattern of audience responses. We need only remember reactions to the war-guilt clause in the Versailles treaty to realize that the issue has considerable political importance. Current propaganda may be inadvertently ignoring the Fascist or Nazi character of the enemy and thus building up a reservoir of misdirected ill will for the post-war period.

Another example is provided by a pamphlet concerning Negroes. The main themes of the pamphlet were two: It is true that Negroes continue to suffer from discrimination but, none the less, they have made great progress in our democratic society which has enabled many Negroes to achieve individual success and to contribute to the community. In contrast, Hitler has always expressed contempt for colored peoples and, should he win the war, all gains of the Negro would be wiped out. The content of the pamphlet can thus be classified in two categories: material pertaining to "Negro gains and achievements in a democracy," and to "deprivations threatened by a Hitler victory." There were 189 paragraphs and captions. 84 per cent of these dealt with present gains and 16 per cent with potential losses under Nazism. To the producers of the pamphlet, this evidently seemed a reasonable distribution of emphasis on the two themes.

But the pamphlet contained two types of presentation. One was an article by a prominent Negro writer; the other, a series of attention-fixing photographs with short captions. Further thematic analysis found that the photograph-captions and the article presented the two themes in completely different proportions. Some 73 per cent of the items in the article referred to losses under Hitler and 27 per cent to gains in a democracy, whereas 98 per cent of the photographs and captions referred to gains and only two per cent to the Hitler threat.

Now it so happens that a majority of the population, and particularly the Negro population with its lower educational level, generally prefer photographs and captions to a detailed text. They are more likely to look at the former than the latter. The photographs, in this case, almost wholly neglected the theme of Negro losses in the event of a Nazi victory. As a result, the pamphlet largely missed its mark. Certain attitudes of Negroes were tested both before and after they read the pamphlet. Most of the readers experienced pride and a higher ego-level as a result of this testimonial to the achievements and contributions of the race. But the pamphlet failed to canalize special motives for Negroes to push the fight against Nazism in their own interest, since readers had largely overlooked the essential message.

However cursorily, these two examples illustrate ways in which ordinary counts of key-symbols and thematic analysis enable us to discover inadvertent errors of the propagandist. They also serve as a guide to interviews with persons exposed to the propaganda. There are other types of content-analysis which can be briefly summarized:[1]

1. *Symbol-counts:* Consist of identifying and counting specified key-symbols in communications. This merely indicates, in a restricted fashion, the symbols which have been at the focus of attention of audiences. The count of references to the enemy in film commentaries illustrates this type.[2]

2. *One-dimensional classification of symbols:* This is a slight elaboration of the previous type. Symbols are classified according to whether they are employed, broadly speaking, in positive ("favorable") or negative ("unfavorable") contexts. Thus, Britain may be described in + terms (victorious, democratic, courageous) or in − terms (defeated, caste-ridden, perfidious). This type of analysis is a first step in determining the most effective distributions of symbols for reaching a given result. It may serve to check the often ineffectual practice of dealing in black-and-white contrasts. When applied to enemy propaganda, this kind of analysis provides one basis for gauging the relative security or insecurity of the enemy.[3]

3. *Item-analysis:* Classification of segments or sections of the propaganda (*e.g.*, scenes in a film; songs in a radio program; photographs in a pamphlet). This requires selection of significant and insignificant items on the basis of a psychological theory of "attention-value." Will these items tap central or peripheral interests of the audience? How will these items be interpreted by different types of audiences? In several analyses of films, it was possible to predict scenes and sequences which would be at the center of attention of audiences.

4. *Thematic analysis:* Classification of the explicit and implicit (symbolic) themes in propaganda material. This, as distinct from item-analysis, deals with the supposed cumulative significance of a series of items.[4]

5. *Structural analysis:* Concerned with the interrelations of the various themes in propaganda. These relations may be *complementary* (enemy is cruel, we are merciful); *integrated* (enemy is cruel, deceitful, aggressive, irreligious); *interfering* (when themes work at cross-purposes; *e.g.*, theme of Nazi strength produces anxiety.)[5]

6. *Campaign analysis:* Deals with the interrelations of different documents all of which are designed for a general over-all purpose. Whereas structural analysis deals with the relations *within* a single propaganda document, cam-

---

1. A thorough examination of the procedures of content analysis is now available: Bernard Berelson, *Content Analysis in Communications Research* (Glencoe, Illinois: The Free Press, 1951). See also H. D. Lasswell, "A provisional classification of symbol data," *Psychiatry*, 1938, 1, 197-204; Douglas Waples et al., *What Reading Does to People.* Appendix B, (Chicago, 1940); N. C. Leites & I. de Sola Pool. On content analysis. Experimental Division for the Study of Wartime Communications. Document No. 26. September, 1942.

2. See, for example, H. D. Lasswell, "The world attention survey," *Public Opinion Quarterly*, 1941, 3, 452-462.

3. For example, studies by Hans Speier & Ernst Kris, Research Project on Totalitarian Communication, at the New School for Social Research; an unpublished symbol-analysis of the "This Is War" radio series. Bureau of Applied Social Research, Columbia University.

4. For example, a study by Gregory Bateson of a Nazi propaganda film. See, also, Siegfried Kracauer, *Propaganda in the Nazi War Film* (New York: Museum of Modern Art Film Library, 1942).

5. For example, Kracauer, *op. cit.;* also film studies by the Bureau of Applied Social Research.

paign analysis deals with the relations of a series of such documents. Problems of sequence, duration, relative emphasis, timing, as well as the relations mentioned under structural analysis, are involved.[6]

From this summary, we see that a major task of content-analysis is to provide clues to probable responses to the propaganda. But this is not enough. We must see whether these anticipated responses actually occur, whether the content-analysis is essentially valid. This requires interviews with members of audiences; interviews of a special type, which we shall call the "focused interview."[7]

Incidentally, there is interaction between analyses of propaganda content and focused interviews with readers and listeners. A prior content-analysis is indispensable for helping to guide the interview and experience in interviewing sharpens your eye for more adequate content-analysis.

RESPONSE-ANALYSIS

Interviews designed to discover actual responses to propaganda seem, at first sight, a simple task. But in actual experience, it is not so at all. Use of the customary interviewing techniques does not suffice to obtain the needed information. Most people find it difficult to express their reactions to a film or radio program in terms which will be of use to the writer or producer or social scientist.

We have found that respondents fall into two broad classes. If they are highly articulate, they will usually express their advice on how the film "should be presented" or how the radio program "should be revised" to increase its effectiveness. They seek to act as professional critics or consultants, and this is precisely what we do not want. Interview tactics have had to be devised for the purpose of avoiding such consultant attitudes on the part of interviewees and of making it possible for them to report their own immediate responses to the propaganda.

For other subjects who find it difficult to report their responses at all, special interview techniques have been developed to enable them to render their experiences articulate. The entire interview is focused in terms of the propaganda material which is being tested. The interviewer's remarks do not direct attention toward definite aspects of the propaganda. They merely facilitate the respondents' reports of their own centers of attention and of their own reactions to those items which are significant for them. If the figure be permitted, the interviewer provides the respondent with a flashlight which illumines the traces of the film or radio program or printed material in the respondent's mind. It is only after the interviewees have fully reported their reactions to the aspects of the propaganda which they experienced most vividly that the inter-

---

6. For example, studies of political campaigns, public utility propaganda campaigns, bond drives, etc.

7. R. K. Merton, M. Fiske and P. L. Kendall, *The Focused Interview*.

viewer rounds out the discussion by checking these hypotheses derived from content-analysis which have not yet been considered in the interview. The entire interview is recorded verbatim by stenotypists. This permits a later intensive analysis of just which aspects of the propaganda elicited certain types of response.

In general, we may say that a focused interview is valuable according to the extent that it achieves the following objectives:

1. Determines the effective aspects of the propaganda to which the audience has responded.
2. Determines the many-sided nature of these responses in considerable detail.
3. Enables us to test whether the responses which we expected on the basis of content-analysis have actually occurred.
4. Discovers wholly unanticipated responses; that is, responses which were anticipated neither by the writer nor by the content-analyst.

Although all of these objectives of the interview are important, it is the last which is of special practical importance. You will remember our examples of the Negro pamphlet and of the radio talk on X-rays. These were intended to indicate to you that without a content- and response-analysis to aid him, the propagandist sometimes cannot see the forest for the trees. We should suggest, further, that often the propagandist cannot see the thorns for the rose. If a propagandist wishes to convey an idea or create a given impression, he must do it by words, illustrations or other symbols. Once his pamphlet, play, radio program or script is out in the world, it is for the audience to understand him as they will. The story is told of a missionary who pointed to a table and repeatedly said "table" until his audience of non-literates could repeat the word. After some time, he was dismayed to learn that some non-literates referred to a tree as "table," because both were brown. Others called dogs "tables" since both had four legs. In short, each listener had selected some aspect of the complex object, which for the missionary was so well designated as a whole by the word "table." In the same way, it is instructive to see how often the effects of propaganda can be totally unexpected.

The Boomerang Effect

The case we want to consider here is derived from the previously mentioned test of a health program. This had wide implications, should the government seek to maintain the educational and propagandistic functions which it has assumed in an effort to maintain morale during the war. Having had the experience of accepting some measure of government supervision, the American population may prove more receptive to the promotion of public health, nutrition and educational activities in the post-war period.

In this instance, it will be remembered, a representative of a county medical society broadcast a talk on X-rays. He stressed the precautions needed to prevent X-ray burns; he indicated that the local government protects the citizen by a system of licensing X-ray operators and by inspecting equipment; he emphasized the specialized training required to attain competence in this field. The speaker was evidently seeking to prevent his listeners from falling into the hands of quacks who have neither competence nor integrity. Professionally concerned with this problem, he apparently did not realize that his listeners had not accumulated experience comparable to his own. He neglected to integrate the problem into the experience-world of his audience.

It is well known from related fields of investigation that listeners cannot readily assimilate information and attitudes if these are not integrated with their backlog of experience. Had the physician described the procedures used by quacks for obtaining clients, or had he indicated how they might readily be recognized or, even, if he had presented figures on the presumed number of unlicensed operators in this field, his listeners might have assimilated his views and attitudes. Since he did not, he seemed to be pounding at open doors.

He talked about licensed doctors but he didn't make it too clear. He never said what would happen to you if an unlicensed person did it.

As a result, listeners began to doubt the importance and, at times, the reality of the issue. The physician talked, as it were, into a psychological void which the listeners had somehow to structure for themselves. They had been told of the complexity of X-ray apparatus, and they used this newly acquired information to look at the problem in their own way.

I don't think the warning is justified at all. Just anyone can't have an X-ray machine. General Electric probably wouldn't sell the equipment to anybody without a license.
I couldn't conceive that anybody without a license would dare to buy such expensive machinery for about $10,000 only to be caught the next day by somebody who found he didn't have his license.

Possibly intending to meet this problem, the speaker went on to extol the merits of the specialist in general terms. A content-analysis found 63 references in 14 minutes to the conceptions of authority, licensing, and specialization. Since the talk raised issues which it failed to clarify, it led to a *boomerang effect*. The listener became more and more impatient and in the end challenged the X-ray expert himself.

There are a good many cases where there is a licensed man and he doesn't use the X-ray just right.
You can get an automobile license but that doesn't prove you can drive. In the same way these people can get a license but that doesn't prove they are competent.

The program stressed the value of proper training for X-ray specialists. But it assumed, erroneously, that listeners had the mental set necessary to identify licensing with appropriate skills. Consequently, the whole emphasis of the speaker led first to impatience, then to disbelief and finally to distrust.

Under certain conditions, then, people respond to propaganda in a fashion opposite to that intended by the author. In the course of our tests, we have found various types of such boomerangs, some of which may be mentioned here. The foregoing "specialist" boomerang illustrates a familiar type: *it results from an erroneous psychological appraisal of the state of mind of the audience.* Propaganda will not produce the expected response unless its content corresponds to the psychological wants of the audience. It is necessary, therefore, to have a continuing flow of intelligence information concerning prevalent attitudes and sentiments in the population, if propaganda is not to invite boomerangs. It is at this point that the familiar types of opinion polls and other mass observation studies are linked with detailed propaganda analysis.

We know, for instance, from public opinion polls that a large proportion of Americans believed, at a time when it was not remotely the case, that we had the largest army, the greatest production of war materials and had contributed most to victory over the Axis. Therefore, films which seek to emphasize the contributions of our allies must be especially designed not to feed this ethnocentrism. If we want to show what the British or the Russians or the Chinese have accomplished, sequences dealing with lend-lease aid or other American contributions must specifically and explicitly indicate the limits of such assistance. Otherwise, we shall find the indicated type of boomerang-effect, where a neglected psychological set of the audience deflects the film to ends other than those for which it was intended.

A second type of boomerang-effect is probably part of the irreducible minimum of boomerang-responses. *It arises from the dilemma confronting the writer who must address his propaganda to a psychologically heterogeneous audience, i.e., the members of which are in different states of mind on the given issue.* Material which is effective for one segment of the audience may produce opposite effects among another segment which is socially and psychologically different.

Let us take a case in point. A radio morale program, broadcast shortly after Pearl Harbor, contained two dominant themes. The first stressed the power and potentiality of the United Nations, being intended to combat defeatism. The second emphasized the strength of the enemy in an effort to combat complacency and over-confidence. The problem is clear enough. Is it not possible that emphasis on our strength will reinforce the complacency of those who are already complacent? And correlatively, that references to enemy strength will support the defeatism of those who are already defeatist?[8] To judge from interview materials, this is evidently what happened.

It is no easy task to avoid opposed reactions by different sections of the audience. It is further complicated by shifts and, it would sometimes seem, by mercurial shifts in the "state of the public mind," such that the prevalent outlook is at one time "complacent" and, at another, "acutely pessimistic." Once again, it appears that if "morale propaganda" is to be functionally appropriate to the situation, there must be a continuing intelligence concerning dominant emotional orientations of the population.

A third type of boomerang is perhaps more significant than the others, for it is one which can be largely eliminated on the basis of adequate propaganda analysis. This we may call the *structural boomerang, which results from different themes in the same piece of propaganda working at cross-purposes.* If the propagandist considers *separately* the several themes in his propaganda and ignores their social and psychological interrelations, he may find that his total propaganda document is ineffective in reaching his ends. Structural analysis of the relations between themes is necessary if this is to be avoided.

A hypothetical case, parallel in essentials to instances which have actually emerged in tests, may serve to illustrate the structural boomerang. Several films, produced before American entrance into the war, included two dominant themes, among others. The first of these emphasized the immense cruelty and sadism of the Nazis as well as their threat to our way of life; a theme vividly exemplified by scenes of mistreatment of civilians simply because of their political or religious convictions. In interviews, sequences such as these are found to evoke profoundly aggressive feelings on the part of many in the audience.

But curiously enough, such aggression directed against the Nazis does not necessarily lead a larger proportion of those who have seen these films than of those who have not to express their willingness for this country to enter the conflict. In fact, there may be at times a slight decrease in the numbers of the "film-group" as compared with the "control-group" who wish to intervene in the war. How does this come about?

On occasion, interview material will show that this apparent absence of effect so far as intervention is concerned derives from the fact that another theme in the film works at cross-purposes. This counteracting theme may stress the skill, experience and enormous size of the Nazi army, exemplifying these by detailed and vivid sequences of Nazi fighting men in action. A theme such as this may serve to elicit fears and anxieties about the prospect of Americans coping with armies as formidable as the Nazi, particularly since we had not yet built up our own forces.

----

8. In fact, there is some experimental evidence, however slight, that persons respond selectively in such manner as to reinforce their current attitudes and sentiments.

Thus, it may develop that the Nazi-strength theme which elicits fears may counteract the Nazi-cruelty theme which elicits aggression. Aggressive feelings may thus not be translated into a realistic desire to have this nation enter the conflict. Adequate structural analysis of such films would have indicated the likelihood that one theme in the film would inhibit the very effects deriving from another theme in the same film. Consequently, although each theme may be effective, as it were—the one in exciting hostility, the other in acquainting Americans with the might of the enemy—the net result with respect to willingness to have us intervene in the war may be nil.

This type of case not only illustrates a type of boomerang-response, but also shows how the focused interview enables us to supplement and enrich the value of the traditional controlled experiment, of the type mentioned at the outset of our discussion. The controlled experiment consists in having two closely matched groups of subjects, one of which has been exposed to the propaganda, the other of which has not. Certain attitudes and sentiments of the two groups are tested twice: once, before the experimental group has been exposed to the propaganda; again, at some time after it has been exposed. If the groups are indeed properly matched, differences in attitude between the two groups which are found in the second test can be ascribed to the propaganda. But let us suppose that, for some attitudes, there is no perceptible difference, as was the case with our subjects' attitude toward American intervention in the war. The controlled experiment will not tell us why there is no change. *Its results show only the net effect of the propaganda on this attitude and not the more intricate dynamics of response which led to this net effect.* But, as we have seen, the failure of the film may be due to the fact that two themes, each of which was effective, produced responses which cancelled each other out. The interview material thus enables us to provide a psychological explanation of responses which may not be registered in the experimental results.

A fourth type of boomerang should be briefly discussed, if only because it is so frequently found in propaganda. *This boomerang results from what we may call,* with due apologies to Whitehead, *the fallacy of misplaced exemplification.* Whenever propaganda deals with matters which are familiar at first-hand to the prospective audience, there is the risk that the particular examples chosen will not be considered representative by some in the audience who consult their own experience. The pamphlet dealing with Negroes and the war which we have previously discussed was largely devoted to the social and economic gains of Negroes under American democracy. This theme was exemplified for the most part by photographs of prominent Negroes, of improved housing conditions and the like. Some 40 per cent of a sample of Negroes discounted the entire pamphlet as "untrue," because of the marked discrepancy between their own experience and observations, on the one hand, and these "examples of progress," on the other.

It should be noted that the truth of the examples does not spare them from producing a boomerang response. The reader consults his own immediate experience and if this does not correspond to the examples contained in the document, he rejects these wholeheartedly. The distrust generated by such apparent discrepancies between "fact" and the "propaganda" tends to be generalized and directed toward the document as a whole.

Moreover, boomerang responses diffuse far beyond the persons who experience them initially. In discussing the document with others, the distrustful reader becomes, as it were, a source of contagious scepticism. He predisposes other potential readers toward the same distrustful attitude. Thus, content-analysis and response-analysis, which eliminate such bases for boomerang responses, serve an important prophylactic function.

Our account has perhaps included enough examples of propaganda analysis to help overcome a perennial difficulty with writers and producers of propaganda. The creative writer often cannot accept the notion that what he has conceived as a unique expression of an inspired moment could possibly be improved or even dealt with by what seems to him a rather mechanical testing procedure. But this is all beside the point. It is not assumed that we are getting at the mind of the artificers, the craftsmen, the artists who contrive this propaganda. It is not believed that our prosy analysis recaptures the deft rhetoric and impressive rhythms which enter into its dramatic effectiveness. It is agreed that we cannot readily teach them their craft. Creative ideas, whether expressed in words, sounds or pictures, cannot be manufactured synthetically.[9] But systematic research is needed to see whether propagandists have achieved their aims. Just as researchers cannot write acceptable scripts, so, we are convinced propagandists often cannot gauge the psychological effects of their products without using techniques such as we have described. It might even be conjectured that it is in the nature of this problem that the propagandist is bound to overlook some of the undesired implications of his work.

This may explain the frequency with which our tests uncover inadequacies which, it would seem, should have been anticipated. But, in

---

9. We should thus agree whole-heartedly with the views of Aldous Huxley on essentially this same issue. ". . . the man of letters does most of his work not by calculation, not by the application of formulas, but by aesthetic intuition. He has something to say, and sets it down in the words which he finds most satisfying aesthetically. After the event comes the critic [read: propaganda analyst], who discovers that he was using a certain kind of literary device, which can be classified in its proper chapter of the cookery-book. The process is largely irreversible. Lacking talent, you cannot, out of the cookery-book, concoct a good work of art." "T. H. Huxley as a man of letters," Huxley Memorial Lecture, 1932, 28; also Remy de Gourmont, *La culture des idées*, 1900, 51.

fact, response-analysis is usually indispensable; it uncovers a host of other inadequacies which we cannot now discuss at any length. This extends to modes of presentation. For example, consider the technique fact, response-analysis is usually indispensable: it uncovers a host of which the radio has adapted from the movies, the quick shift of scenes corresponding to montage in visual presentations. We are confident, on the basis of tests, that this technique in general leads to obscurity for the average radio listener. Continuity is lost. They just don't know what it is all about. They lose interest. In much the same way, historical allusions often fall on deaf ears unless they are carefully explained.

Or consider the question of authenticity in the case of documentary films. Propagandists would probably be surprised to learn how often the audience questions the possibility of having an actual film of Hitler in his mountain retreat, or of the mountainous Goering in a conference room. The propagandist knows that it is a clip from a German film, but the audience does not. Distrust is engendered and spreads. In the same way we have found numerous errors of judgment in the use of radio narrators or of officials' speeches which outrun the endurance of the audience.

We have repeatedly emphasized the need for obtaining detailed evidence of responses to propaganda. As an aid toward this end, we have often used a device called the Program Analyzer. The device, so called because it was first used for radio tests, can also be used for any communication, such as a film, which develops along a time-dimension. The purpose of the Program Analyzer may be briefly explained. Interviews on responses to propaganda must of course be postponed until the film or radio program is over, since we do not wish to interrupt the normal flow of the audience's experience. How, then, can we help the audience to recall their responses to particular aspects of the material? Should the interviewer mention specific scenes or episodes, he would be determining the focus of attention. Moreover, the interviewer's description of the scene would also influence the respondent's account of his experience. The Program Analyzer serves to eliminate these limitations.

While watching a film or listening to a radio program, each subject presses a green button in his right hand whenever he likes what is being presented, and a red button in his left hand when he dislikes it. He does not press either button when he is "indifferent." These responses are recorded on a moving tape which is synchronized with the film or radio program. Thus, members of the audience register their approval or disapproval, *as they respond to the material.* Reasons for and details of these reactions are later determined by the type of focused interview to which we have referred.

Two advantages of this procedure are clear. In the first place, the audience itself selects the sections of the material which are significant enough to be made the object of a detailed interview. Each listener presents, as it were, a general running account of his own reactions by classifying the material into three groups: the items which affect him positively, negatively, or neutrally.

Secondly, the responses recorded on the tape can be cumulated for the audience as a whole to obtain a general "curve of response." This curve lends itself to statistical treatment, enabling us to determine the main sources of favorable and unfavorable response. Above all, it provides, together with prior content-analysis, an extremely useful guide to the focused interview.

TECHNOLOGICAL PROPAGANDA OR
THE PROPAGANDA OF FACTS

This discussion has perhaps served its major purpose. It may have given you some conception of procedures used in the psychological analysis of propaganda. Now let us turn to some general conclusions which we have reached in the course of our work.

One of the most conspicuous responses which we observed in our tests is the pervasive distrust of propaganda exhibited by many people. Propaganditis has reached epidemic proportions. Any statement of values is likely to be tagged as "mere propaganda" and at once discounted. Direct expressions of sentiment are suspect. Comments such as the following are typical of the ubiquitous man in the street when he believes that others seek to sway him:

I just think it's too sappy to put over on an adult mind. To me it gave the opposite kind of a reaction than it was supposed to give me. I suppose they wanted to make you feel full of patriotism, but I think it gave me the opposite reaction.

And then at the end—whistling "The Star-Spangled Banner." Everybody believes in the flag, but they don't like it waved in front of their faces.

This distrust of sentiment will not surprise you. There appears to have been relatively little fanfare during the war. As the psychoanalyst, Ernst Kris, has put it, referring to our enemies as well as ourselves, "men went to war in sadness and silence."[10] Or, in the words of a subject in one of our tests:

In this present situation, we haven't seen the boys marching as we did in 1917. We haven't got the feeling of the situation.

What implications does this lack of collective outbursts of enthusiasm have for the propagandist who seeks to rally all support to the war effort?

Our observations suggest that such distrust is levelled primarily against propaganda which obviously seeks to sway or stir people by general appeals to sentiment. Efforts to excite diffuse emotions are dis-

---

10. It is interesting that, basing his discussion on quite different propaganda materials, Ernst Kris has independently come to much the same conclusions. See his instructive paper "Some problems of war propaganda," *The Psychoanalytic Quarterly* 1943, 12, 381-399.

counted. But this is only a partial scepticism. The same audiences which set up defenses against fervent appeals to patriotic sentiments show a readiness to accept the implications of another type of propaganda, which we may tentatively call *technological propaganda* or *the propaganda of facts.*

Again let us begin with observations made in the course of our own studies. We observed at once a central interest in *detailed circumstantial facts.* Facts are in the saddle. The following comment by a subject in one of our tests reflects this attitude:

A great many people [*sic*] don't like that rah-rah sort of patriotism that stirs you up. I [*sic*] like factual things.

This desire for specific, almost technological information, sometimes takes on naive forms, as can be seen from the following remark on a documentary film which stressed the strength of the Nazis:

I was really surprised. I mean I don't believe everything I have read in the papers. But what you actually see with your own eyes and is authentic, you have to believe.

One of the most effective scenes in the aforementioned radio morale program described in great detail how the speed of a convoy is not necessarily determined by the speed of the slowest boat. Wrapped in this layer of technical information was an effective implication that men in the merchant marine willingly sacrifice themselves for the common good. The moral contained in the facts—"surely my sacrifices do not match theirs"—could be accepted by those who would reject a direct appeal of the same type. Films showing battle scenes or bombings prove effective if they focus on the details of the operations rather than stressing the direct propaganda "message" for the audience. *The fact, not the propagandist, speaks.*

We may now ask: why the prevalent interest in "facts"? What are the functions of this interest? *The concrete incident, rich in circumstantial detail, serves as a prototype or model which helps orient people toward a part of the world in which they live. It has orientation-value.* For large sections of the population, the historical events which they experience are wholly bewildering. Nations which are enemies one day are allies the next. The future seems dark with despair or bright with promise. Many have not the time or capacity to understand the trends and the forces behind them, yet they sense how closely these are bound up with their lives. All this accentuates a powerful need for orientation. Concrete facts take on the role of models in terms of which more complicated events can be explained and understood.

Illustrations of this are numerous. Thus, one episode in a radio morale program made a notable impression on the audience: during the last war, Franklin Delano Roosevelt, then Assistant Secretary of the

Navy, accompanied a submarine crew on a trial run, immediately after a series of submarine disasters. This proved far more satisfying and effective than to be told directly of the courage and past experience of our President. It had an *integrating*, explanatory function.

He showed he wasn't a coward; that if the men were willing to go down, he was willing to go; and he's the best man to be president because he's been through the thing himself, and because of the things he's done.

So, too, when films indicate specifically the virtual absence of armored divisions in England after Dunkirk, this type of fact will effectively integrate a variety of discrete points. It will be mentioned repeatedly in interviews. It helps to crystallize, so to speak, the ingenuity and courage of the British in the face of such odds. It proves effective where direct evaluations of the British would evoke scepticism and doubt. *Facts which integrate and "explain" a general course of events comprise one important component of the propaganda of facts.*

We can make another general observation about the propaganda of facts. We have observed that a certain type of fact which contains the desired propaganda implications appears to be most effective. This is the *"startling fact,"* of the type exploited by "believe it or not" columns and by quiz programs. This is effective for at least three reasons. In the first place, it has great *attention-value*. The startling fact stands out as a "figure" against the "ground." Secondly, such tidbits of information have *diffusion-value*. They readily become part of the currency of conversation and small-talk ("Did you know that . . ."). The propagandistic implications of these are thus often transmitted by word of mouth. Finally, these integrating startling facts have *confidence-value*. They are "cold," as idiom so aptly puts it. They are not likely to elicit the distrust which is so widely latent in the population.

The propaganda of facts has yet another characteristic which marks it off from propaganda which seeks to persuade by clarion calls and direct exhortation. The propaganda of facts does not seek so much to tell people where to go, but rather shows them the path they should choose to get there. It preserves the individual's sense of autonomy. *He* makes the decision. The decision is voluntary, not coerced. It is by indirection, not by prescription, that the propaganda of facts operates. It has *guidance-value*. The cumulative force of facts carries its own momentum, so to speak. It is virtually a syllogism with an implicit conclusion—a conclusion to be drawn by the audience, not by the propagandist. To take a case in point: a pamphlet was recently issued by a war agency, directed to the families of men in the armed service, for the purpose of persuading them not to repeat the contents of letters received from abroad. Little emphasis was placed on the theme that careless words cost lives and ships. Instead, the bulk of the pamphlet was devoted to a detailed description of the methods used by the enemy to construct their total information from bits and patches gathered by agents on different occasions and in different places. Tests showed that the pamphlet succeeded in driving the story home, by permitting the reader to draw the inevitable conclusions from this circumstantial array of facts. The voluntary drawing of conclusions has little likelihood of the aftermath of disillusionment which so often follows upon the propaganda of exhortation. The hammerlike blows of frenzied oratory may produce present acquiescence and later recriminations; autonomous decisions under the cumulative pressure of facts do not exact this price.

Interestingly enough, it appears that our enemies have also discovered the power of technological propaganda. This type of propaganda, as any other tool, may be abused as well as used. The pseudo-facts may supplant the fact. Several observers have commented on the Nazi "stage-managing" of reality. It is reported, for example, that prior to the invasion of Belgium, a German officer made an apparently forced landing in Belgium. On his person were found plans for an invasion quite unlike that actually intended. Or again, there is the case of the first night bombing of Berlin. It is said that the Nazis planted reports of great destruction in Berlin in Swiss and Swedish newspapers, accrediting them to the English. These accounts were rebroadcast over the German domestic radio and the local population was invited to look at the actual damage and see for themselves that the reports were untrue. In this way, probably, many people could not escape the conclusion that the British had lied. The effect of this type of self-indoctrination was probably considerably greater than if the German radio had directly denounced the veracity of the British.

In passing, it might be remarked that the logic of the propaganda of facts is not far removed from the logic of progressive education. It is typical in progressive schools that the teacher does not indicate what the children are to do and believe but rather creates situations which lead them to decide for themselves the conduct and beliefs which the teacher considers appropriate.

Your own experience will demonstrate that the propaganda of facts is not a "new" conception. We are concerned only with formulating this idea in terms which may be of some value in planning morale programs. Widespread distrust and scepticism pushed to the extreme of cynicism are corrosive forces. But, since they are here, they must be considered. If propaganda is restricted wholly to exhortation, it runs the risk of intensifying distrust. The propaganda of facts can be utilized to supplant cynicism with common understandings.

Nor do we suggest that exhortations are wholly a thing of the past. Common values and common attitudes still need to be established among a considerable part of the population if propaganda is to prove effective. But our observations may be useful to those of us who are concerned with a constructive post-war era. We should not wait until post-war problems press in upon us before we recognize that a re-integration of societies must, to some extent, draw upon the instrument of propaganda.

And, finally, we should not exaggerate the role of propaganda. In the long run, no propaganda can prevail if it runs counter to events and forces underlying these events, as the fascists have begun to discover. Propaganda is no substitute for social policy and social action, but it can serve to root both policy and action in the understandings of the people.

Literature and Propaganda
Joseph Wood Krutch

from

English Journal, vol. 22, no. 10, 1933.

LITERATURE AND PROPAGANDA

JOSEPH WOOD KRUTCH

I

Ten years ago the young writers of America were vigorously defending the freedom of the artist. Their opponents were those conventionally minded persons who complained that the new literature was, in various ways, unwholesome, and to them the poets and novelists were replying that it was not their business to teach, but only to reveal and create. They were determined, they said, to divest themselves wholly of all preconceived notions, to present life as they saw it, and to let the chips fall where they might. Didacticism had been the curse of American literature, and the one thing they had resolved not to be was didactic.

Today the question of the relation between literature and propaganda has come to the front in a new form. A goodly portion of contemporary writing youth has adopted notions more or less colored by communist dogma, and it is busy with the production of novels, plays, and poems deliberately designed for the purpose of expressing political and social convictions. These young men are not, to be sure, on the side of the conventions, but they have taken up the position once maintained only by the conventional. They do, that is to say, insist that it is the business of literature to teach and they have nothing but scorn for any art which professes to be detached or neutral.

Perhaps most of these young men have done more talking than writing, and John dos Passos is the only one to produce a novel which has found any wide acceptance. Nevertheless, the influence of their opinion is very great. Mike Gold in the pages of the *New Masses* and V. F. Calverton in various books and articles have hammered persistently away with sufficient effect to win many converts to their attitude, and the much-touted "Marxian approach to literature" is the subject of the liveliest contemporary literary debates. "Humanism," which had its brief hour a year or two ago, is pretty thoroughly dead, but any general discussion of the arts is pretty certain to come around, rather sooner than later, to a consideration of "the Marxian position."

Now it is not very easy to define exactly what this position is. So far as I know there is no extended official statement of it and the communist, when pushed into a corner, is very likely to declare that he does not really mean what he seems to have been implying. Nevertheless his position may be summed up somewhat as follows: All religions, science, philosophies, and arts are determined by economic factors. The most important economic reality today is the class struggle and therefore all human activities are influenced by this class struggle. The so-called disinterested pursuit of truth or beauty is a bourgeois delusion when it is not a bourgeois hypocrisy. Everyone is defending the interests of his class, and if he pretends to be neutral or to be concerning himself with matters which have nothing to do with the class struggle, he is, in reality, merely a cowardly defender of the capitalist oppression.

Sometimes the communist will admit that a piece of bourgeois literature may have purely technical excellences, and sometimes he will call a work like Proust's *Remembrance of Things Past* great because, so he says, Proust was unconsciously giving a true picture of the social structure. But the general tendency of his attitude is narrow, dogmatic, and intolerant. The value of a work of art depends upon the effectiveness with which it teaches and, since there is only one thing worth teaching, upon the effectiveness with which it promotes the class struggle.

Now I have no intention of discussing the Marxian philosophy as a whole. No sensible man would deny the influence of economic conditions upon many things, but to maintain that thought, art, and science are nothing but economically conditioned phenomena seems to me to fly in the face of all human experience. Keats did not write the "Ode to a Grecian Urn" because he was born over a stable. It is neither a defense of capitalism nor an attack upon it. It simply has nothing to do with either, and a part of its value lies just in the fact that it can be equally valuable to the son of a millionaire and the son of a ditch-digger.

What I do want to discuss is the more general contention that literature must teach something; that its value lies in the effectiveness with which it teaches. Is or is not propaganda, of some sort and for something, its *raison d'être?*

II

The first thing which one will have to notice is that a good three-quarters of all the attempts to define the function of literature have resulted in the conclusion that it does teach. The early Christian church rejected the literature of Greece and Rome because it did not see how that literature could help to make men better Christians. And when the Renaissance discovered the delights of literature again and felt the need to justify its interest, the rhetoricians elaborated what is called the theory of "the sugar-coated pill of philosophy." Poetry, they said, is a form of instruction which goes down easily, and this thought of theirs has survived even to the present day. You may find it charmingly stated in English in Sidney's *Defense of Poetry*, and it bobs up again time after time. Sometimes feeble protests have been made against it; more often it has been simply disregarded as, one may imagine, Shakespeare disregarded it. Yet the theory not only survives but gets a new birth every time some writer of unusual force adopts it, as Tolstoi did when he wrote "What is Art?" and as Bernard Shaw did when he proclaimed in *The Revolutionist's Handbook* that "Beauty and Pleasure are by-products"—meaning, as he elsewhere explained, that great literature is merely the skilful and impassioned teaching of some moral truth.

To the common man this theory seems, moreover, the only tenable one. He likes "inspiring" poems or novels, and by that he means rhymes or tales which reinforce his own moral or political opinions. Hence the Marxian who insists that literature cannot be good for anything unless it teaches "the truth" is merely following in the footsteps of whole generations of earnest reformers who have insisted that literature is not good for anything unless it helps them to convert the world. When a modern communist says that book cannot be great because it helps no one to become a better communist, he is merely repeating the protest of the religious fanatic who has protested against most of the world-literature because, so he said, it would not help anyone to become a better Christian. Your Marxian, like the Puritan, is obsessed with the idea that man must be saved, and impatient with anything which does not concern itself primarily with a discussion of the ways and means of his salvation.

The real lover of literature does not generally bother to answer these arguments or protests. He has found in the almost infinite variety of the world's great books a source of delight so vivid and direct that he does not need to prove them good. He knows that the authors of these books were men of many minds who could not possibly all agree with one another upon any conceivable moral, political, or religious subject. But he knows also that they have something in common, something which makes each of them recognizable as a great writer, and he knows still further that it is this something which delights him. Obviously it cannot be their teaching because that is too varied, and obviously, therefore, doctrine is not the essence of literature.

Incautious critics have always had an unfortunate tendency to identify literature with some one quality. The result of such a tendency is usually to rule out three-fourths of the world's greatest works, and against that absurdity the man of taste rebels. Nor does it make much difference whether the narrow critic sets up as his criterion the presence of Christian or of Marxian teaching or whether, as is equally often the case, he chooses some other quality. He may prove that Pope is not a great poet because Pope has no "sense of wonder." He may just as easily prove (as Bernard Shaw does) that Shakespeare is not a first-rate poet because Shakespeare took his philosophy from the Elizabethan man-in-the-street. But it makes no difference. Pope continues to give delight to generation after generation, and Shakespeare asserts his greatness too unmistakably for anyone to bother whether or not Shaw has "proved" him to be only a second-rater.

It would, of course, be as foolish to maintain that literature never attempts to teach anything about morals or economics as it is to maintain that it ought to do nothing else. Certain great writers have written great books which profoundly affected the social and political attitude of their readers. Milton would not be Milton if he were not a Puritan and a republican. Nor is there, to come down to the present, any reason why a convinced communist should not write a great novel in which society was pictured from the communist point of view and in which, perhaps, there was some considerable admixture of communist propaganda. But such a novel is not the only kind of great novel possible today, and if it were written it would not be great because of the propaganda it contained.

There, indeed, is the point. Propaganda is not incompatible with literature and no subject is impossible for it. But neither, on the other hand, is either propaganda or any special class of subject matter essential to it. Ten or twelve years ago I was one of those who gave enthusiastic praise to such writers as Sinclair Lewis and Theodore Dreiser. At that time it was necessary to defend their critical treatment of American society from those esthetes who maintained that such realism and such implied "propaganda" were foreign to literature. I maintained then the novelist's right to choose the subject which seemed to him most interesting or important, but I feel bound to add that the right to discuss subjects with social implications is a right and not an obligation. The artist must give us what he can. "Society" is a perfectly proper subject for literature. But so, too, is the individual soul, and it is as absurd to say that a good artist must be a Marxian as it would be to say that he must be a Baptist or a Presbyterian.

Conceivably, of course, he might be either of the three. Most men have some political as well as some religious convictions and these are likely enough to color their vision of the world. But the less such convictions obtrude themselves, the less the artist's account of life is obviously edited and arranged for the purpose of defending these convictions the better. But the very fact, first that Marxism is a narrow creed and, second, that most of its defenders are converts with all the convert's intemperate zeal, makes it a peculiarly dangerous philosophy for the artist to embrace. Propaganda is, I repeat, not incompatible with literature; but it imposes upon any work of art a heavy handicap.

III

So much for the negative side of the argument. It is easy to say what literature is not. It is easy to pick out certain of the qualities which certain great works have and to say "These are accidental, not essential, qualities." But it is not so easy to say what literature *is*, what qualities or attitudes are common to all great books, and give some unity to the apparently infinite variety discoverable in the great poems and novels and dramas of the world's literature. But if literature is not primarily a "sugar-coated pill of philosophy," Marxian or otherwise, some attempt must be made to say what it is and one may best begin, perhaps, by saying that all great literature seems to be interested to some extent at least in experience for its own sake.

Your reformer wants to get something done. Things as they are do not please him and he is determined that somehow or other they shall all be made different. "This," he says, "is no time to fall in love or to find in the meanest flower that blows a thought too deep for tears." Contemplation, enjoyment, and self-realization are all criminal wastes of time, and in so far as a particular great writer has some of the reformer in him he shares this attitude. He wants his book to prove something and teach something; he wants it to change men and to make them change conditions. Hence his work contains a certain element of propaganda and his conscience would not be easy if it did not.

But no artist is pure reformer, or rather, perhaps, no pure reformer can be an artist, because a certain delight in pure experience, a certain ability to see beauty and wring joy from things as they are, is necessary to art. Your artist may be all sorts of things in addition to being an artist. He may be, like Dante, overwhelmed by a sense of the sinfulness of the world or, like Theodore Dreiser, overwhelmed by a sense of the world's social injustice. But just in so far as he is also an artist he will be fascinated by the spectacle, determined to represent it, and capable of making others realize it with the vividness of his own experience.

This, I think, suggests the quality which all great art has and which, indeed, constitutes its art. The opinions and even the visions of the artists may be poles apart. The things they choose to look at and the things they choose to say about what they have seen may be entirely different. But they are interested in looking and interested in saying for the sake of looking and the sake of saying. The world is not merely something to be made over, and sensation or emotion is not merely a stimulus to action. Both are also subjects for contemplation and realization. Like Faust, the artist is overwhelmed by the impulse to say to something seen or felt, "Oh, wait a moment, you are so beautiful!" When he says that he has the impulse to art and when he succeeds in making us say the same thing, then he has created a work of art. From the whole work we may come away, as we come away from some novels, with changed convictions about virtue or justice. On the other hand, we may have been, as is the case with most poems, merely elevated for a moment without having been taught anything at all. But the essential thing is that, incidentally in the novel or primarily in the poem, we have found the possibilities of human life worth while in themselves.

The real business of literature is, therefore, not propaganda at all but the communication of an aesthetic experience, and the most striking characteristic of an aesthetic experience is a certain disinterestedness. In its purest form, this disinterested experience does not stimulate us to any action, and the reformer is quite right in maintaining that it does not promote reform. To read *Hamlet* is not to become any more determined to fight the injustices of the world. To enter in that great tragedy is not to be led to want anything for humanity. Neither is it to be made to want anything for ourselves. The experience is disinterested and complete in itself. Hamlet's life seems its own justification and the privilege of sharing his experience seems enough to make life worth living.

Some natures are undoubtedly almost wholly incapable of such an experience. They belong to the people who must always be doing something or going somewhere. Everything must be a means to something else; nothing can be worth while for its own sake. They live wholly in the future, never in the present, and life seems to them valuable only as a preparation for heaven if they are Christian, or a preparation for communism if they are communists. They are as incapable of undergoing an aesthetic experience as a deaf man would be of enjoying music, and it is no wonder, therefore, that when they hear of a thing called literature they should attempt to explain it in terms of something which they can understand. But their interpretation misses the essential part. They may come to understand certain of its incidental qualities. They may perceive the elements of propaganda, which is often mixed up with literature itself. But they do not really know what it is all about.

It is natural, also, that such people should invent the theory that all our thoughts and emotions are determined by our economic interests. Certainly such interests do influence us very greatly and often when we do not know that we are so being influenced. It is difficult to rise above animal needs and difficult to escape what Spinoza called long ago the "bondage of the passions." Most of our thinking is done because we want something, and it is only rarely that the best of us rise to that distinctly human level where thought and feeling have so detached themselves from their animal origins that they have become pure contemplation. But the person who has really learned to understand literature knows that it is possible to achieve a genuine detachment, and he loves literature because it enables him to rise to that purely human height.

Sometimes he achieves it also in the midst of his own life. Sometimes he gets a genuine aesthetic experience in the midst of the real world and, by freeing himself from his own crude desires and crude prejudices, sees the world through genuinely human eyes. But he knows how rare and how difficult that experience is, and the world of literature is the world which has been created in order that he may there live freely, easily, and continuously upon the level which he can only rarely achieve in the real world. Literature reveals to him the possibility of just that freedom which the theory of economic determinism would deny. Hence it may be said that literature does, after all, teach one thing. It teaches that man can escape from the bondage of his own material interests and take an interest, not personal but impersonal, in the phenomena of life.

IV

Of one thing one may, moreover, be comfortably sure, and that thing is that literature will survive despite the Marxian insistence that it does not and cannot exist. The impulse to art is too fundamental in man not to reassert itself irresistibly; if it could be killed by stupid critics and philosophers it would have been killed long ago. Even through the Dark Ages it was kept alive in cloisters where monks had to invent strange excuses for the interest which their dogma could not justify. Troubadours cultivated it at a time when to be an artist was to be something of an outcast and then, during the Renaissance, it was born again in the bosom of the church. The important thing is not what men say about art or even what they think about it, but the fact that the sternest societies cannot prevent from breaking out here and there that impulse to the detached and delighted contemplation of something for its own sake which is the impulse to literature.

The chances are that "the Marxian approach to literature" is no more than a passing fashion destined to disappear as completely and almost as quickly as the "humanism" which preceded it. But even if it should not—even if, perchance, it is destined to become the official philosophy of a new state—it will still be as impotent to change the real nature of literature or to prevent that nature from asserting itself as the moral and critical dogmas of the past proved themselves in their time. Who would ever guess that *Hamlet* was written at a time when the official opinion of the learned was that art was a sugar-coated pill of philosophy and that the really great English play would have to be written on the model of the unreadable *Gorboduc?* Who cares that so sensible a man as Addison believed his own *Cato* a great play and was joined in that opinion by the leading critics of his time, who proved that it must be a masterpiece because it taught so fine a lesson?

To say this is not to say that the novel of the next ten years may not concern itself a good deal with "society." It is not to say that the best novel of that period may not possibly be written by a communist or even that, mixed up in it, there may not be a good deal of propaganda. But it is to say that if the Marxians produce a great novel it will not be great because it is Marxian. It is also to say that this same not impossible work will be written—if it is written at all—by someone who is not as good or thoughgoing or as orthodox a communist as he may believe himself to be. It will, on the contrary, be the work of someone who has something of the artist left in him. He may believe that he believes that "art is a weapon" and nothing else. He may think that his whole purpose is the practical one of promoting the "class struggle." But the thing which will make his book great is the thing which has made all great books great, namely, a delight in the thing itself, a contemplation of the struggle for its own sake, a determination to pass on to the reader an aesthetic experience.

The Novel: Its Influence in Propaganda
Gerald Gould

from

The Aryan Path, 5, 1934.

Reprinted by permission of *The Aryan Path*.

The question of the place and value of the novel as a means of propaganda for national and humanitarian causes falls naturally into two parts. The novel, after all, is only the particular form, which for various reasons has at the present time superseded most others in popular favour, of the thing which has delighted all ages of mankind—namely, the story. We cannot, in the first stage of our enquiry, put the novel in opposition, for instance, to poetry, because, in poetry and in prose narrative alike, the actual story element has always been a predominating one. We have to remember that hundreds, and even thousands, of years before the novel, as we know it to-day, began to develop, poetry, and specifically narrative poetry, was in high favour. Whether in its epic or in its dramatic form, it filled the place in the life of the ancient Greeks which the novel fills in ours. When Aristotle said that poetry was "more philosophical" than history, he did so for the specific reason that the poet could shape conclusions to establish a moral point, whereas history was bound down to external facts. The phrase which we still so commonly use, "poetic justice," was a legacy of this Aristotelian theory.

It must not be supposed that Aristotle was asking for any sort of crude and convincing adaptation of fact to theory : such, for instance, as we get in the sentimental Victorian tales which reward the good boy with wealth and punish the bad boy with poverty. Aristotle, in common with all the great Greek writers, had grasped, more clearly, perhaps, than it is grasped by most people to-day, the fact that it is impossible to chop up experience, into artificial sections, putting fortune on the one side and character on the other. Character and circumstances play into each other's hands, and help to shape each other in real life, and consequently must do so in fiction, if the fiction is to be convincing.

Sir Philip Sidney, the first English critic to write on literary questions with a profound understanding of general principles, praised narrative poetry for its power to capture and hold the attention ; but already, in Sir Philip Sidney's time, there existed, as a result of the Renaissance, some of those early prose tales in Italian out of which it may be said that the modern novel directly developed. Not, of course, that we could not go even further back, if we wanted to, for origins. There were imaginative prose tales in both

Greek and Latin, long before the Italian *novella* appeared, and it is only for convenience sake that the modern novel is dated from one point rather than another. But the point to establish is that, in all periods of man's development, the story, as such, has had a tremendous appeal.

I have mentioned outstanding instances in the development of Western civilisation: indubitably the same truth holds of the older civilisations of the East. From childhood to old age, both in the life of the individual and in the life of the nation or race, everybody wants to be told stories, of one kind or another; and it is therefore not hard to see why so many people have chosen the story medium as a means of propaganda.

We come now, however, to the second part of our enquiry. Why is it that the old love of poetry has so largely given way to the popularity of prose fiction? I can speak only of my own country and my own time, but certainly nowadays in Great Britain one is both surprised and delighted if one finds anybody with a keen and sustained appreciation of poetry. Many people go through a youthful stage of poetry reading, but in maturer years put aside this interest as if it were one of the idle whims of adolescence. To find a mature person, of ordinary interests and accomplishments, who keeps up an active and vivid interest in poetry to the extent of looking out for new poets, and re-reading the established classics, is extremely rare, even among the most highly educated classes; whereas it may be roughly said that the whole adult population reads novels, and that their popularity increases yearly.

The change from verse to prose, like so many other things in the changes of civilisation, is largely due to an external and mechanical discovery: in this case, the printing press. So long as stories depended upon human memory, and were handed on from one generation to another by word of mouth, the rhythm of verse had definite "survival value": it enabled stories to be remembered easily, and therefore preserved. There is no doubt that the activities of the printing press have gone far to destroy the necessity, and therefore the use, and even the existence, of human memory.

More and more, then, in spite of the competing claims of the wireless, the talking pictures, and so forth, people rely for entertainment and distraction upon the novel. The foregoing historical outline can be summarised in two assertions—the human being, as such, loves a story: the convenient form for the modern human being to indulge this taste is the novel. It may be added that, in Great Britain alone, roughly four thousand new novels are published every year, besides vast numbers of reprints.

The propagandist, then, is faced with this situation—he wants to get his message accepted by the largest possible number of people: how is he to get at his audience? The old simile of the pill and the jam can scarcely be avoided here. The reader may be unwilling to swallow the pill of moral or political reform unless it is disguised for him with a sweet-tasting story to help it down. Even the advertisement writers have long learnt this lesson. When recommending a particular brand of goods, they no longer consider it sufficient merely to assert that the brand is good, or even that it is the best of its kind. The up-to-date advertisement begins at some distance from its actual subject, or, rather, object; it beguiles us with an anecdote or something of the kind, and only when our interest is already roused do we find that we have been led up to appreciation of somebody's patent medicine, or tailoring, or cosmetics.

There is surely no reason to pursue by psychological investigation the natural and universal love of a story. It is so primitive and basic that it can scarcely be explained by anything simpler than itself. Yet, if we need an explanation, it can easily be found in the common desire of the human being to dramatise himself, and to see himself in a nobler posture than he can take up in everyday life, or in circumstances more exciting than his own. The child who is told a fairy tale dreams of being a fairy prince: the boy who reads an exciting adventure story dreams of going on like adventures himself; and this tendency by no means disappears, though it may grow less crude and obvious, with increasing age.

The propagandist, then, will naturally make use of this tendency. When song and dance were the natural communal means of expressing emotion, the preacher of a popular cause would strike his harp-strings and sing what he wanted people to believe. Now, he finds it easier and more expedient to appeal through the written and printed word.

But, it may be said, though all human beings like stories, they like other things as well. Their psychological equipment includes not merely imagination, but reason. Why should the propagandist not go straight to his purpose, and tell us what he wants us to accept through exposition and argument? Of course, in many cases, he does so. Political campaigns are still mostly conducted by direct propaganda, though the political speaker who knows his job by no means neglects the aid of apposite anecdote. But, broadly speaking, we may say that the human reason is not anywhere near so highly developed as the human imagination, and that therefore the appeal of mere bare argument is apt to meet with little response. There have been, it is true, in the history of the world, purely philosophical or sociological documents which have had an enormous influence on historical development. It is commonly said, and with as much truth as such an unqualified statement can be expected to possess, that Rousseau's "Social Contract" sowed the seeds of the French Revolution. Similarly, Burke's essay on that Revolution had great influence on British political thought; and so, later on, had John Stuart Mill's essays on "Liberty" and "The Subjection of Women". But the influence of these propagandist and didactic works is almost wholly indirect. Of every million citizens who have been indirectly influenced by Rousseau's "Social Contract," it would be pretty safe to say that only a few thousand, at the utmost, had ever read the book. Possibly the majority have never even heard of the book. Its influence has been exercised through the acts and words of people who had read other books which took their inspiration, often unintentionally, from the original argument.

How different is the challenge of a work of fancy or imagination! It can become immediately popular. It can pass directly into the hands and minds of the millions. It may be read for the sake of enjoyment; whereas, at the present state of our mental development, most people regard the tackling of an abstract case as a task, and even a hardship. There are those who *do* enjoy political or ethical debate, but they are still in a minority. To make a cause popular, something more colourful must be used.

The outstanding historical example of effective propaganda through fiction is, of course, *Uncle Tom's Cabin*. The average man or woman, at the time when this work appeared, would no doubt have admitted vaguely that slavery was a moral wrong, and that the slave trade could not be carried on without the violation of elementary rights, to say nothing of individual cruelties; but the average man or woman, while admitting this, did not get wrought up about it. Then came along an author who presented the wrongs and cruelties in a concrete and dramatic form, a series of human pictures which moved human feeling. It was no longer a question of slavery in general: it was a question of a particular suffering fellow creature —a mother wickedly parted from her child, or a man brutally flogged to death. Those pictures had a direct effect, as they were meant to have, upon emotion; and emotion is a much stronger force than logic.

It would be impossible to discuss the use of fiction for propaganda in the world of to-day without going into questions which are still controversial, and therefore outside the immediate scope of this essay, which pretends to deal with no more than the bare question of why and how propaganda is best embodied in the story form. I venture to think that even this bare essay may, to a certain extent, prove its point by illustration as well as argument. Readers may have wondered why I began with Aristotle. It is true that he is the earliest, and remains the greatest, of literary critics in the whole of Western civilisation, and that most of our theories on æsthetic points get their ultimate inspiration from his speculations. That might be a good enough reason in itself, but it was not the main one. By beginning more than two thousand years ago, I was enabled, in a sense, to tell a story—to trace through the centuries the history of fiction.

That is of necessity a much less thrilling *kind* of story than one in which the protagonist is a human being like ourselves; but, even so, it is surely more persuasive than a dogmatic statement of contemporary fact. There is magic in the formula, " Once upon a time . . .," with which the old fairy tales begin; and, because we live by action, our first instinct, when we read, is to want a tale of action.

This is why fiction is so good, and indeed so necessary, a means of propaganda.

GERALD GOULD

Can the Author Keep Out of It?
R.H. Mottram

from

The Author, vol. 44, no. 1, 1933.

CAN THE AUTHOR KEEP OUT OF IT?

By R. H. MOTTRAM

I N setting out to study the situation in which the author finds himself, owing to the present state of the nations, I ought, of course, to begin with a profession of impartiality. Alas! I cannot. I hate and detest the political experiments of the last ten years, and the only pretence of fairness I can make is that I hate them all alike. I could find excuse or indifference for some of them, in my capacity as a private citizen. As a writer, I consider it as plain as a pikestaff that they are all equally bad for literature.

It is the fault of the Author, of course. He never was any good at politics. His excursions into that arena have been notoriously unhappy. No exceptional penetration is necessary to ascertain so patent a fact. The first quality with which an author must be endowed is receptiveness. If he cannot perceive and transmute his perceptions, he is not worthy to be called a member of the trade. But that quality is the last thing a practical politician requires. If *he* is going to achieve any political result he must first fix on something so obvious that it cannot be mistaken, so primitive that it appeals to instincts that are common to the majority ; he must then shut ears and eyes and nose and shout his particular slogan until he deafens and drives the crowd. He need not, and commonly does not, bother about argument, and the most recent type, the Totalitarian, does not pretend to. It does not matter. Those who can or will listen are too few. Nor, in parentheses, does he bother about authors, although there must be in Great Britain at least three-quarters of a million people writing some sort of book, for 15,000 volumes are published annually, and experienced " readers " tell me that these represent but 2 per cent. of manuscripts submitted. Yet authors do not stick together or support their one professional society, as they might, to their own advantage.

But, as Count Smorltork said, " The word politics surprises himself." The word must have surprised his descendants several times since then. It has surprised me. I notice that, in trying to define the politician's qualities, I have incidentally stated the case of the newer exclusivist or Totalitarian politician against the older parliamentarianism, and here I come to the point at which the international politics of the nineteen-thirties hits the author, and hits him hard, and makes me inquire if he can afford not to take up some definite attitude towards the things that are being done in Europe to-day.

When, in 1919, it became apparent through the clearing atmosphere that the world was in the presence of a novel political experiment on a colossal scale, it did not seem to matter much to most authors who wrote in English. The sale of English books in Russia can never have been large, and must always have been highly specialised. No doubt individuals suffered, but in the welter of misery and death from which we were then emerging, individual suffering did not bulk very large. It is only now, looking back, that one sees the significance of the Russian Revolution to us. It seemed novel, but it was mediæval in its methods. I do not know how many authors tried to sort out facts from the welter of wild stories then current. To those who did, the antiquity of the Bolsheviks was obvious enough. Anyone who has studied the history of almost any English city will have come across the record of books burned, of authors forced to fly or perish for their opinions. It was one of the odd things that used to occur, right up to the seventeenth century, like witch-hunting and religious persecution. Moreover, we have still with us the clumsy English Police-Court literary censorship, the mediæval Examiner of Plays, and the Papal Index, little felt, it is true, incidental in their application, so that they have never invited organised opposition. But these were a sufficient reminder of such things, making the mediævalism of the Bolsheviks seem less of an innovation.

With the outburst of Fascism in Italy in 1924 the sinister control of opinion by pure violence seemed to come a step nearer. But its effect was modified by one reason similar and one dissimilar to those that seemed to obscure the literary importance of Bolshevism. For while Italy also was a very small literary market and only a few English books found their way into it; on the other hand, the Duce knew better than to offend England, and soon modified his deeds, if not his words. My only concern is with the fact that, shortly after 1924, it was possible for English books to be translated and to obtain a fair sale in Italy. And there was also the considerable stream of English editions which made their way there as part of the tourist traffic.

The events of this year in Germany, however, are on a different scale and offer a distinct challenge to the English-writing author, for three reasons: The Nazi regime is more violent, in proportion to the level of civilisation in Germany, than anything of the sort that has happened yet. The wholesale burning of books and maltreatment of authors for irrelevant political and racial, in fact, party reasons, shows that. Secondly, Germany was a very considerable customer for English books, which will now come under a purely party discrimination, for the greatest humbug about the Bolshy-Totalitarian propaganda is its claim to be non-party. It is not. It is one party trying to silence discussion. Thirdly, Germany is near to England, geographically and, to a degree in habit, nearer than Italy or Russia. The danger of infection is therefore greater. People still smile at the suggestion, but it is not impossible if the present faint signs of economic recovery should prove deceptive that we may see some wholesale attempt to suppress opinion.

And what is the answer? Violence in reply to violence? No good to the author. He has not the organisation and violence is fatal to him. People who are engaged in it do not stop to read. What then? Support for Parliamentary institutions? Was it much better under them? Well, a little. While "Parliamentary Government" will never be a slogan, the author might as well cease being funny about Parliament. It let him alone. No dictatorship will do that. The weak-minded will answer, "But the Totalitarians always get hold of the money and that's what we want." Very true, they do. They get hold of opinions, too. There are authors who may be able to keep every spark of feeling about the trend of human existence out of their writing, and they may do well under one of the more exclusive fancy-shirt movements. But even these movements, try as they do, cannot quite keep the human intelligence from working. They do succeed in preventing any literary renaissance in their respective countries. Nothing noteworthy has found its way those ten years into current European literature from Russia or Italy, and Germany is busy burning the very considerable Post-War contribution she has made. Nor could it fall out otherwise. Those who condone tyranny and obscurity have so little left to say, and are too frightened and insecure to look round for more.

This is merely negative "don'ting." Is there anything the author can do positively and directly against the present loutish trough into which half Europe has fallen? I think there is. I cannot, as I would, advise a Magenta - shirt conspiracy to bludgeon the bludgeoners. For I was one of those who, in utter innocence and good faith, helped to let loose the deluge of Force in 1914, of which contemporary exhibitions are but the aftermath or exhaust. Nor can I proudly boast of a belief in *laissez-faire*. To that all too easy creed we owe our newspapers.

What then ? Why, this. In the long run, and probably not until he is dead, the writer, even of fiction, influences opinion. His writing may be excluded from wide tracts of the earth's surface, but it is not possible—modern machinery, the cause of so many of our discontents, makes it impossible—to keep man for ever in little water-tight separatist compartments. So let every writer say and keep on saying that his is the right of individual expression and criticism, and that he will not cease to call Brute Force by its ugly name. He knows that is true. He knows that it is his business. He knows that the sword is not mightier than the pen, nor one head, be it ever so dictatorial, better than two. So he will keep his self-respect. So, incidentally, and only so, may he save himself from being superseded by some Totalitarian Loud-Speaker.

The Author and Politics
Charles King

from

The Author, vol. 44, no. 3, 1934.

THE AUTHOR AND POLITICS

By CHARLES KING

EVERY issue of the " Author " reports a number of legal cases involving principles of material interest to authors. Who made the laws on whose interpretation the issues rest ? Though authors may have been consulted in the drafting of Copyright Acts, etc., it was certainly not they who had any kind of decisive voice on the questions involved. The candle-stick-makers and brass-door-knob-polishers send to Parliament representatives who may vote on trade union law and matters of kindred interest. But the authors, where are they ? Never, in any number, in Parliament ; and in their daily lives squeezed out, very often, between the upper and the nether millstone, between big business and the organised claims of manual workers. Intellect is on the whole woefully underpaid, and if, as one must assume from all the evidence, Mr. R. H. Mottram's article in the Autumn " Author " is representative, authors in the mass are content with a policy of laissez faire. Now the manual workers are still very much on the war-path. The members of their political movement are energetically working for the attainment of power, against which day they have plans prepared for the " letting blood " of big business and yet a bigger place in the sun for manual work. Men of intellect often and rightly sympathise with these demands, but if they insist, to use the words of the heading of Mr. Mottram's article, on " keeping out of it," it is quite possible that their last state will be worse than their first : for in the movement as it at present exists there is still, in spite of paper statements, and a willingness to use brains as long as the owners thereof are kept in a subordinate position, an unholy jealousy of intellect which does not bode well for the future, in the event of the attainment by the movement of the power at which it aims. If one dismisses such a prospect as chimerical, and looks at the immediate situation, it may be true that some sections of the book trade have held their own, and that some have even made progress during the slump, but who can doubt that all the same authors are suffering in pocket from leaving the affairs of the nation to be conducted by persons who have rarely shown any competence for the tasks with which they are, at election-time, so clamorous to be entrusted. So far I have suggested reasons based on narrow grounds of self-interest why authors should abandon their traditional policy of laissez-faire and bestir themselves actively in politics. These reasons are relevant, but I admit that if the case is argued on them alone, the quietist may answer that he is asked to sacrifice substance to shadow, to neglect his own immediate interest without the certainty of achieving in the wider sphere of politics anything which will either benefit authors as a class or compensate himself personally for the diversion of his energy. So I admit that the main reason why authors should take part in politics is that of public duty.

Now I may be unduly optimistic, but I do not think that anyone, even the politicians, would deny that authors as a class are abler than politicians. But politicians, while admitting the intellectual superiority of authors take care at the same time to imply that *they* are the men of action. It is the function of authors to spread ideas : *theirs* to carry them out. What the politicians do not appear to realise, although the fact must be obvious to ninety per cent. of the electorate, is that even in the carrying out of ideas the politician fails. The vast lag of the present state of things behind that which would exist if the ideas of authors and thinkers were applied to the exploitation for the general benefit of the advantages of

▲ 13

modern science surely suggests that it is time to examine carefully the facile parrot-cry of vested interests that the best people to carry out ideas are those who can't think of them for themselves.

If it be suggested here that I am confusing the issue by identifying authors with political thinkers, I deny the impeachment. Not only have such writers as Bernard Shaw, H. G. Wells, G. K. Chesterton, Hilaire Belloc, Lord Russell, among others given a very great deal of their thought to politics, but there is a mass of social criticism, of which the logical outcome would be political action, in the works of authors not known for their political interests, e.g., to take a few names at random, Somerset Maugham, Aldous Huxley, Richard Aldington; and apart from what may or may not be expressed in published works the majority of authors do think carefully on political questions.

Mr. Mottram says that the excursions of authors into the arena of politics have been notoriously unhappy, and suggests that this is in the nature of the case. I can tell Mr. Mottram, from what is perhaps a closer first-hand acquaintance with politics, that the ordinary voter would be glad to be rid of the " slogan-shouting politician." Though the movement is slow, as such movements must be, there is in fact an increasing appreciation of the value of intellect in politics. This movement is particularly marked in the Labour Party, the improvement in the average quality of whose candidates was widely noticed at the 1929 election. As for the alleged ill-success of authors who have adventured into politics, there is so far too little evidence to justify general deductions. It is true that the majority of the few authors who have so far entered the political field have lost faith and surrendered to disillusionment, but this we must expect until authors are present in Parliament in sufficient numbers to give each other moral and active support. The strength which only numbers can provide is what is needed :

and it is numbers for which I am appealing, to the younger generation of authors.

It may be objected that to enter politics would hinder one's writing. Admittedly, to some extent : but the butcher and the baker carry on their avocations when Members of Parliament. After all there are plenty of literary masterpieces in the world, and anyone who devotes himself to nothing but literary self-expression all his life is apt to repeat himself.

It is the first hurdle that is the hardest. In spite of the slow spread of enlightenment which I have mentioned, the fervent partisans who constitute political committees are still apt to want sheep, yes-men, rather than men who think for themselves. But whatever may be the requirements of political committees, the country does want men of principle who can form their own judgment ; and the prejudices even of committees can be dealt with by tact and persistence.

It may be argued that a " concert of authors " can no more be achieved than a " concert of Europe " and that failing such concert there is nothing to be gained by summoning authors from their ivory castles. Mr. Chesterton, proposing, in jocular mood, that I should convene a council of literary men with a view to formulating an agreed policy as a basis for concerted action in politics, saying he would be glad to be there to see the fun, suggested also that I should find it difficult to get Lord Russell and Mr. Hilaire Belloc, for instance, to see eye to eye on the question of private property.

Such considerations do not seem to me fatal. Ordinary Cabinets are often at sixes and sevens, and though authors are not unanimous there is among them, as intelligent men, a natural homogeneity of political feeling. I am sure it is true to say that the majority of authors of standing (and I have little doubt that the same is true of all authors worthy of the name) are of Progressive political principles, of a broad Liberal-Labour outlook : by this description I mean that those who lean nominally to one or other of these parties admit in practice a good deal of value in the distinctive principles of the other. If a " political council of authors " were seriously thought desirable it would, I am sure, be possible for them to work out a policy for the integration of the in defeasible claims of individualism within the framework of national organisation which modern experience has shown to be desirable. But apart from the possibility of preliminary agreement on policy, the problems of the country demand the practical, no longer the merely theoretical, application of all the brains available. Mr. Somerset Maugham, tacitly admitting the main obstacle to the participation of authors in politics to be lethargy, said to me " You need a Mussolini to compel us to come in." Personally I hope that their social conscience, as well as a long view of their own interests, will " compel authors to come in."

The Writer's War
'Ajax'

from

Left Review, vol. 1, no. 2, 1934.

The Writer's War

by AJAX

Peace with Honour, by A. A. Milne (Methuen 5/-).
Journey to the End of the Night, by Louis-Ferdinand Celine, translated by John Marks
(Chatto & Windus 8/6).

PERHAPS it is not surprising to find the gentle Mr. Milne among the pacifist writers; not more surprising than to find a Beverley Nichols or (in his unproduced anti-war play) a Noel Coward joining the same company. Mr. Milne's main object is to persuade himself that if all Powers agreed to arbitration war could be abolished; alas that it all should end in an argument which as he says "just goes round in a circle."

Elder Statesman :	We want peace if we can get it. But how ?
Milne :	By accepting arbitration in every dispute that arises.
Elder Statesman :	That's all very well, but what's to prevent a country refusing to accept an adverse judgment and resorting to war ?
Milne :	But you said you wanted peace.
Elder Statesman :	If we can get it.
Milne :	You can get it by accepting arbitration in every dispute that arises.
Elder Statesman :	Yes, but what's to prevent a country refusing to accept an adverse judgment and resorting to war ?
Milne :	You said you wanted peace—and so on interminably.

It moves with the forcible feebleness of a *News-Chronicle* leaderette defending the Kellogg Pact. If Mr. Milne were to work on the assumption that his Elder Statesman (as he sometimes suspects) has no desire to keep the peace unless time serves, it might lead Christopher Robin to the place where small boys' hairs turn grey. Still, he has made his protest. That he should have felt under the necessity of making it is the interesting thing : that writers with greater pretensions should find similar occasion for asserting their refusal to protest is perhaps still more significant. " I am strongly in favour of all the Powers making the very deadliest preparation they can afford for the next war," wrote Bernard Shaw last month in his four-line contribution to the LEFT REVIEW. " However it does not matter a brass farthing whether I approve or not as they will do it in any case." I am not so much struck by the futility of his argument* as by his self-abnegation. " It doesn't

* The *New Statesman* quoting The Left Review made the rejoinder that Mr. Shaw replied to his own argument in 1905. " In *Major Barbara*, Undershaft, the cannon maker, is offered this ' usual excuse for his trade ' and replies that so far from its being true that ' the more destructive war becomes the sooner it will be abolished,' the fact is that ' the more destructive war becomes the more fascinating we find it.' "

matter a brass farthing whether I approve." And the answer seems to be " Evidently not." Believing this a writer gives up writing. Perhaps Mr. Shaw has ?

In a writer of duller intelligence such a sentence would not be noticed ; but G.B.S. knows his world. He may not believe now as he once did in his own power to persuade others. He no longer sees the writer naïvely as " unacknowledged legislator " ? Good. That is a stage. Then he must see the writer as the voice of influences and forces that persuade *him*. If G.B.S. is content to be the voice of Rothermere, Simon, Hitler, Mussolini, Roosevelt and the Emperor of Japan, it is good we should know. Maybe it is the conscience of this which brings his sense of helplessness : " it doesn't matter a brass farthing what I think." The same helplessness characterizes Mr. Milne. Mr. Priestley is another victim. Why else should he in the letter he wrote to the LEFT REVIEW choose " thickening nightmare " as the proper symbol for these times ? In thickening nightmare we can do nothing except hope to wake. But how can England wake up from the Black Country which an angry Mr. Priestley has himself been describing ? Here is something more solid than nightmare. That is why I hesitate at Mr. Priestley's debonair : " What we want in this business is more plain questions and plain answers, more common sense, more laughter, and the light of reason," and ask whether it rises to the height of the argument he has himself propounded ? Recently Mr. Priestley dramatist has gone a good deal farther than Mr. Priestley novelist did; and that because he remembered that plain questions nearly always get crooked answers, and that common sense and laughter can only survive as victors on a desperate battlefield. Indeed the theme of two of his plays is very like that. In the one, *Dangerous Corner*, he took a smug publisher's party and stripped the people of all their mental clothes. In another, *Laburnum Grove*, he amused himself with the contrast of this or that suburban householder, so quiet a tomato-grower in Laburnum Grove, so red in tooth and claw in Lothbury. His fable about " making money " poses a coiner and intends plain business man. You say, Mr. Priestley, that you hope we " will not encourage the nightmare by adding to the bogey-bogey talk ? " Bogey-bogey talk—what else are these two plays ? Or rather they are bogey-petrifying, as opposed to bogey-encouraging talk, and you, Mr. Priestley have been finding, as perhaps LEFT REVIEW will find, that this is the central theme, and the only progenitor of laughter, common sense and the light of reason.

Bogey-bogey. Of course it all depends on how you cry it, and here's the point. There has not been a greater crier of bogey even in our generation than M. Celine whose novel, having sold its scores of editions in France has now bearded the pooh-poohing English reviewers in translation. It is a novel written as if to symbolize the eternity of some physically alarming moment when the heart misses a beat and the tongue licks sour sweat off the upper lip. The novel is a prolonged dramatization of a sense of physical shrinking and deadly fear. It is helpless not as Mr. Shaw and Mr. Milne who moan quietly in their service flats, but really afraid. The fear communicates itself, and the sense of helplessness. Helplessness in the war which goes on in its own dynastic way till one side or the other of a madhouse wall—you can't tell the difference. Helplessness in Africa (tropical colonies swallow war-wrecks and neurotics so willingly but what do they do with them when they have swallowed them?) Escape; and then helplessness in America where the Ford factory induces a new sort of fear, not the fear of the irrational but the worse fear of the murderously lucid. In the last resort and the last phase of a novel which is big in more ways than one, fear which has lost the hope even of any great matter to be afraid of, finds its consummation in a cheaply class-conscious disgust: and the novelist who has made reason, morality, society, government, and all the generaliz- ations men believe in, nothing but the conductors of panic fear, finds that he can achieve a singularly pure disgust in hearing a slum mother express her affection for her child in words which appeared to him insufficiently refined.* M. Celine voyaging to this his illuminating dawn, is a portent. He and his book have become almost the contemporary symbols of the disgust modern society rouses in the sensitive middle- class man. Here's the real bogey, father of all bogies, whether war, famine or Hitler.

Professional writers—and Celine explicitly is not that—have been proud of that disgust almost since the beginnings of capitalism. There is a tradition, stronger in France than in England, reaching back at least to Baudelaire, that literature is almost by definition inimical to and exists in spite of all that is bourgeois. When the war broke out some of the younger French writers as well as our own Joyce moved into neutral countries with a cry of " A plague on both your houses ! " At a time when Barbusse was producing work which was an effective weapon against war, Joyce and a group of young Frenchmen began a masochistic flaying (what else is *Ulysses* ?) of the bourgeois civilization, masochistic because it is also self-torture. This has since become the background of what is sometimes called " highbrow " literature. The most advanced " Modernists," the dadaists, who afterwards became surrealists (these young French writers who when the war began retired to have literary conference in Zurich) once issued a famous manifesto : " Before ripping open your choleric belly and using your fattened tripes for manure . . . before extinguishing thus your appetite for beauty, sugar, philosophy, metaphysical cucumbers, mathematical and poetic sardines, before disinfecting you with vitriol . . . here's your warning. We're here, the assassins ! " It is unreal, highbrow, selfconscious and yet nearer by a long chalk to reality than the fatal complacence of, for example, Stefan Zweig's " Tower of Babel " in last month's LEFT REVIEW. Here is at least a recognition that there was no such thing as a fine togetherness of all intellectual workers building a spiritual Tower of Babel till war came like a thunderbolt from the blue : a recognition that on the contrary a violent struggle cleaves all human activity, intellectual and practical. Those blows at the self-satisfaction of contemporary society struck by Joyce, by the Dadaists, by the surrealists and the rest, were valuable. Hatred at least is a start.

But there have been moments even in the English literature of our own

---

* The passage is in conflict with English printers' conventions and I do not find it in the translation.

day when the struggling and straggling literature of protest has flared out in a forked flash. Do we still remember Siegfried Sassoon's *Counter Attack*? It has a poem called " Fight to a Finish " :

The boys came back. Bands played and flags were flying
The Yellow Pressmen thronged the sunlit street
To cheer the soldiers who'd refrained from dying
And hear the music of returning feet.
" Of all the thrills and ardours war has brought
This moment is the finest " (so they thought).

Snapping their bayonets to charge the mob
Grim fusiliers broke ranks with glint of steel.
At last the boys had found a cushy job.

I heard the Yellow Pressmen grunt and squeal
And with my trusty bombers turned and went
To clear those Junkers out of Parliament.

*   *   *   *

" We are on the eve of Armageddon *and we are not ready*." Mr. Milne quotes this, one of the recent sayings of Lord Rothermere with suitable consternation. Certainly we are on the eve, and the *Eleventh Hour Bulletin* which comes out now every week has at least got its title right. But how to combat this unreadiness ? How combat the unreadiness of all who wrote in the LEFT REVIEW symposium last month on writers and war ? How combat the unreadiness of the writers of the two books under review, the unreadiness of all anti-war fighters and anti-war writers ? I am not sure that it is quite so simply a question of " the substitution (among intellectuals) for vague idealism of an objective Marxist analysis " as those extracts last month from Charles Madge's Russian article seemed to say. If, for instance, the agreement to denounce war and its causes, does exist as it seems to, between Mr. Milne and, say, James Joyce, between Mr. Priestley and the surrealists, between Siegfried Sassoon and M. Céline ; then the question becomes, how shall we make this writers' war against war effective *now* ?

A writer's usefulness depends on his influence : that is to say on the size and enthusiasm of his public : or, in the case of writers' writers, on his ability to set scores of other pens writing. In either case any lasting influence depends on his power to express the inarticulate feelings and forces that make for change. Here is a world threatened with the mad destructiveness of Fascism and imperialist war. The opposing force is in fact the mass of mankind, more or less articulate, more or less organized, more or less awake. And the writer's job becomes, as I believe, that of gaining a first-hand knowledge of such opposition in terms of people : learning to talk " as a living man to living men." This process will develop very often, I believe, towards Marxist under-standing. Often it will halt short of clear analysis. But a book, a play, a poem, which expresses the stage we have reached, in England, at this moment, in the human opposition to the system's annihilating con-clusions, could be itself a blow struck against the plans for war.

Pens Dipped in Poison
Charles Madge

from

Left Review, vol. 1, no. 1, 1934.

Pens Dipped in Poison

In 1934 with a second world war oppressively near it is as well to look back over the words of the many writers who might have been thought of as men preferring life to death, and construction to chaos, and who failed us conspicuously when in 1914 -1918 the test came.   The article printed below is an abridgement of a fuller treatment written for translation into the Russian.   It is not intended as a close analysis—the subject must be returned to again and again in THE LEFT REVIEW —but it gives warning of the necessity of intensifying the combat against war preparations in the field of existence covered especially by THE LEFT REVIEW.

By CHARLES MADGE

THE object of this study is not to discuss the comparative literary merit of those authors and poets who were writing during the Great War, nor to determine the influence which the war had on English literature.   Its purpose is to show the wartime attitudes of the different writers of that time, both good and bad, and to point out how, from lack of any scientific explanation of what the war was about, they one and all were involved in various confusions of thought, which led to contradictory and ineffective action.

There were of course various degrees of confusion in what they said and did, and it is important to note how those whose theory of the causes of the war was nearest to the scientific point of view were also those were least inconsistent in their actions, while those who had a vague, idealist, liberal ideology committed the greatest excesses and lost their heads most completely when war broke out.   It is therefore all the more necessary that writers and intellectuals of the present in England and other capitalistic countries should have the clearest ideas on the subject of war, its causes and the possible means of preventing it.   The victories of Marxism in the European ideological field since the war are likely to have a decisive influence on the attitude of intellectuals to the next war.   The substitution for vague idealism of an objective Marxist analysis must mean that a greater proportion of intellectuals will present a determined and consistent front against imperialist war.

In 1914, when the shadow of war fell on the bourgeois intellectuals, they were taken completely unawares, and accepted quite uncritically the doctrines of a " righteous war " offered them by their Liberal leaders. Robert Bridges declared : " I hope that our people will see that it is primarily a holy war. It is manifestly a war declared between Christ and the Devil" (*September* 1, 1914). Chesterton wrote : " This war is at bottom a religious war. . . . Pacifism seems merely a sort of allotropic variation of the Atheism which is the foundation of the Prussian State " (*The Prussian Hath Said in his Heart*, 1914). Galsworthy asked : " What are we going to do for Belgium—for this most gallant of little countries, ground, because of sheer loyalty, under an iron heel?" (*Daily News, August* 31, 1914). Arnold Bennett wrote : " A lesson for Potsdam is imperatively needed. . . . Stupid bullies should be treated according to their mentality. . . . Nothing will impress the Potsdam mentality so much as a public humiliation. Many a savage brute has been permanently convinced of the advantages of civilization by the idiom of one knock down blow " (*Daily News, October* 1, 1914).

Henry James, on assuming British nationality, said in an interview to a " Daily News " reporter : " Personally I feel so strongly on everything that the war has brought into question for the Anglo-Saxon peoples that humorous detachment or any other thin-ness or tepidity of mind on the subject affects me as vulgar impiety, not to say as rank blasphemy ; our race question became for me a sublimely conscious thing from the moment Germany flung at us all her explanation of her pounce upon Belgium for massacre and ravage in the form of the most insolent ' Because I choose to damn you all ' recorded in history. . . . Never do cherished possessions, whether of the hand or of the spirit, become so dear to us as when overshadowed by vociferous aggression."

Such were the lengths to which bourgeois idealism carried the supposed intellectual leaders of England after a few weeks of war. As the war progressed, the same tendencies increased to the point of mania and incoherence. War for its own sake is upheld by Professor Ridgeway, speaking to the Classical Association, " In a world of perfect peace, humanity would perish from its own physical and moral corruption." Evelyn Underhill argues that because strife is necessary and a " mighty source of action," therefore war represents " something which is integral to the general process of creation. . . . War may yet be justified and the purpose of creative love made plain." Rejoicing that, " civil conflicts in England have been arrested," and that " the social danger which the late Lord Salisbury foresaw has been averted by the shock of war," she carelessly displays her own social standpoint.

Kipling deserves fame for the following : " There are only two divisions in the world to-day—human beings and Germans. And the German knows it. Human beings have long ago sickened of him and everything connected with him, of all he does, says, thinks, and believes " (*Speech at Southport, June* 22, 1915).

The belief in a just war led the more radical liberals into strange contortions of argument. Thus when in 1918 there was prospect of the war coming to an end, Gilbert Murray wrote : " If we make peace now, we make peace with militarism triumphant. . . . If we propose peace now we are offering terms to the very dragon we set out to destroy " (*Daily News, January* 1, 1918). Gerald Gould, in " The Way to Peace," points out the cause of war : " No ; we are not fighting for treaties or small nations ;

we are fighting for our own interests." But in looking for an alternative, he falls back on pure idealism : " We have built the British Empire with the sword : it is only with our dreams that we shall build the City of God."

The case of H. G. Wells is so revealing that it deserves a fuller treatment. In his pre-war days he was described as " the most obstreperous pacifist in Europe." His novel " The World Set Free " was a remarkable prophecy of 1914, and set out to prove the folly of war. In another novel he wrote : " There was not a man alive who could have told you of any real permanent benefit, or anything whatsoever to counterbalance the obvious waste and evil that would result from a war between England and Germany, whether England shattered Germany, or was smashed and overwhelmed, or whatever the end might be " (*In the Days of the Comet*). Yet in the second week of the war he wrote : " I find myself enthusiastic for this war against German militarism."

" Into this war we have gone with clean hands, to end the reign of brutal and artful internationalism (*sic*) for ever. Our hearts are heavy at the task before us, but our intention is grim. We mean to conquer. We are prepared for every disaster, for intolerable stresses, for bankruptcy, for hunger, for everything but defeat. Now that we have begun to fight, we will fight, if needful, until the children die of famine in our homes, until every ship we have is at the bottom of the sea. We mean to fight this war to its very finish, etc." (*Daily News, August* 14, 1914).

The key to this extraordinary attitude is to be found in a pamphlet written in the first few weeks of the war, and addressed to the Labour Movement. The first sentence gives away the secret. " All the realities of this war are things of the mind. This is a conflict of cultures, and nothing else in the world. All the world-wide pain and weariness, fear and anxieties, the bloodshed and destruction, the innumerable torn bodies of men and horses, the stench of putrefaction, the misery of hundreds of millions of human beings, the waste of mankind, are but the material consequences of a false philosophy and foolish thinking. . . . This monstrous conflict in Europe . . . it is all of it real only in the darkness of the mind. At the coming of understanding, it will vanish as dreams at awakening . . ." (*War and Socialism*).

Towards the end of the war, Mr. Wells wrote " Mr. Britling Sees it Through," in which he describes his gradual disillusionment with the conception of a righteous war ; " Was our cause all righteousness ? . . . There came drifting to Mr. Britling's ears a confusion of voices, voices that told of reaction, of the schemes of employers to best the trade unions, of greedy shippers and greedy house-landlords reaping their harvest. . . . It came with a shock to him, too, that Hugh should see so little else than madness in the war, and have so pitiless a realization of its essential futility. . . . The war, even by the standards of adventure and conquest, had long since become a monstrous absurdity."

In the pamphlet which Mr. Britling writes when his son's death has finally opened his eyes to the uselessness of war, he is made to say : " Fools and knaves, politicians, tricksters, and those who trade on the suspicions and thoughtless, generous angers of men, make wars ; the indolence and modesty of the mass of men permit them. Are you and I to suffer such things?" But to the end he continues to talk in the same idealist terms: "There's two sorts of liberalism" said Mr. Britling, "that pretend to be the same thing; there's the liberalism of great aims and the liberalism of defective moral energy."

Pacifism—many of its exponents became "conscientious objectors"—had found a very congenial doctrine in Norman Angell's "The Great Illusion" (1910). This work sets out to prove that "Military and political power give a nation no commercial advantage; that it is an economic impossibility for one nation to seize or destroy the wealth of another, or for one nation to enrich itself by subjugating another." The conclusion is that as there is no advantage in going to war, therefore it will be possible by the power of reason to dissuade nations from a warlike policy. Angell sets out to change men's ideas about war. He says: "The only permanent revolutions in the history of civilization are those that result from a revolution of ideas."

As evidence that this *ideal* revolution is taking place, he points to the growing internationalism *of all classes*, in the following significant passage, where after describing the international activities of trade unions, he goes on to say: "So much for the labour side. What for the side of capital? With reference to capital, it may almost that it is organized so naturally internationally that formal organization is not necessary. When the Bank of England is in danger, it is the Bank of France which comes automatically to its aid, even in a time of acute political hostility. It has been my good fortune in the last ten years to discuss these matters with financiers on one side and labour leaders on the other, and I have always been particularly struck by the fact that I have found in these two classes precisely the same attitude of internationalism. In no department of activity is internationalism so complete as in finance. The capitalist has no country, and he knows, if he be of the modern type, that arms and conquests and jugglery with frontiers serve no ends of his, and may very well defeat them."

Bertrand Russell and Lowes Dickinson were much persecuted on account of their opinions. Though their pacifism was of a very moderate and conciliatory kind, their names were known and abused throughout the country. Bertrand Russell was a leader in the movement for "conscientious objection"; he based his pacifism on idealist grounds, as is shown in his letter to Professor Sorly, published in the "Cambridge Magazine":

"So far from hating England, I care for England more than for anything else except truth. News of defeats or successes raises in me exactly the same feelings as in you. But I do not desire for England only, or chiefly, the outward success which is to be achieved through worldly advancement. . . . I do not believe that our material existence as a nation is at stake in this war: so long as our Navy remains invincible our material existence is safe. But I do believe that our spiritual existence, as a source of freedom and justice and humane dealing, is very gravely imperilled, and can only be preserved if we realize that we are not wholly and in all things above reproach. The spirit of the German Government is hateful to me, but I see much of the same spirit in many Englishmen, and in them,

I mind it more, because the honour of England is more important to me than that of Germany " (*October* 30, 1915).

Lowes Dickinson was a strong advocate of a " League of Nations," and he and his friends were largely inspired by Romain Rolland's pacifist declarations in " Above the Battle." A contemporary criticism of him in the " Socialist Review," organ of the I.L.P., points out his idealist way of thinking. " He regards the war as a conflict of 'ideals,' as a struggle between the ideal of liberty and the ideal of authority. To me, on the other hand, it seems that the war against war is a conflict of economic tendencies, a struggle between the tendency to exploit and the tendency to resist exploitation—a struggle to be waged to the uttermost, that in the end economic exploitation may vanish from the earth " (*January*, 1917).

Bernard Shaw declared in " Commonsense about the War " that it was " a Balance of Power war and nothing else " (*Daily News*, *August* 11, 1914), but a reviewer in the " Socialist Review " criticizes his as usual self-contradictory point of view : " After denouncing the patriots of all nations as stupid, and asking us what earthy or heavenly good is done when Tom Fool shoots Hans Narr, he goes on to insist upon the need for vigorous recruiting, and to declare that a German victory 'would literally shut the gates of mercy on mankind.' "

Some intellectuals fell back on a position of superior detachment. Clive Bell, whose pamphlet " Peace at Once," was suppressed by the Government, writes, " I take no further interest in schemes for social reconstruction " (*May* 12, 1917).

Of the younger poets, some like Rupert Brooke (a Fabian), wrote on the theme " Dulce et decorum est pro patria mori." Other poets, of whom Siegfried Sassoon is typical, described the horrors of war. Sassoon, after conversion to pacifism, was in the end induced by his friends to return to the front. Wilfred Owen, another poet in revolt, was killed.

Hardy, though deeply averse to war, tried to keep out of the controversy. His support was indeed claimed on both sides, but his chief feeling seems to have been of the complete futility of the whole proceeding. At the time of the South African War, he had condemned it in bitter terms, and his point of view is shown in the poem called " His Country " (1913).

" He travels southward, and looks around : and cannot discover the boundary of his native country ; or where his duties to his fellow-creatures end ; nor who are his enemies.

> I asked me : ' Whom have I to fight,
> And whom have I to dare,
> And whom to weaken, crush and blight ?
> My country seems to have kept in sight
> On my way everywhere.'

Some twenty of his poems were collected under the title " Poems of War and Patriotism " and include such titles as " A Call to National Service " and " An Appeal to America on Behalf of the Belgian Destitute." However, his own feelings are best shown in these lines :

'Would that I'd not drawn breath here!' someone said,
'To stalk upon this stage of evil deeds,
'Where purposely month by month proceeds
'A play so sorely shaped and blood-bespread.'

In Time of Wars and Tumults, 1915.

The revolt against war in the front line is well expressed in the plays of Miles Malleson, which were performed secretly during the war to working-class audiences. In "D Company" the hero is made to say: "I am not one of the many who are burning with an eagerness to get into the firing line. I think, if I aimed at a German officer, the obvious symbol of Prussian militarism, I should be sure to miss him and hit a private who would probably be a Social Democrat with many an idea in common with me."

Even more striking is the passage in "Black 'Ell" where the hero describes how at night he has lain within earshot of the German trenches. "It's all a bloody muddle!... If you'd heard them. There was a man there, a Socialist or something, I suppose, talking against the war ... and the way they all sat on him. They got furious with him. They talked just like you ... how they were afraid of Russia and France and England all against them, and how nobody wanted the war; and how, now it had come, they must all protect their wives and their children, and their homes and their country.... That man in their trenches—he'd had enough ... he said he was going to refuse to kill any more, and they called him traitor and pro-English and they've probably shot him by now.... Well you can shoot me ... because I'm not going back.... I'm going to stop at home and say it's all mad. I'm going to keep on saying it ... somebody's got to stop sometime ... somebody's got to get sane again. ... I won't go back ... and I won't, I won't ... I won't."

These feelings were re-echoed in the ranks of the armies of all nations.

Art and Propaganda
Harriet Monroe

from

Poetry, 44, 1934.

W E ARE confronted in these days with a new aspect of an old question, a re-statement, in terms sanctioned by an ardent revolutionary group, of the ancient discussion about the artist's — or more specifically the poet's — "message." The over-precise formula of the 'nineties — "art for art's sake"— is quite out of fashion with the earnest Russ-minded communists who are leading the charge against the entrenched forces of capitalism in the columns of *The New Masses* and other weeklies and monthlies, and on the plat-forms of the John Reed clubs in various cities. If the nation's millions of voters seem as indifferent to the political as to the esthetic aspects of their appeal, yet we may well pause and listen, and permit our complacency to be shaken by historic examples of speedy growth from a small seed.

On the esthetic side, I would go with these crusaders so far as to admit that not only such art as they sanction but all art of all the ages is propaganda. Every artist has some-thing he wishes to tell the world in his picture or statue or poem, if it is no more than the beauty of a flower or the grace of a human pose. The most abstract cubist was vigorously preaching a new gospel of art when he assembled his mys-terious design. The most cryptic poet hides a world's eye-opener in his elliptical unpunctuated lines. The artist must please himself — yes — but not himself alone; though he pretend to indifference, he is appealing to his peers of his own or later ages — he is sending out propaganda to promote his fame and his point of view.

So the subject of his propaganda, as well as the degree and amount of it, becomes merely a question of what he is most interested in. If an artist's chief interest is the turn of a phrase, a new color-scheme or rhythmic pattern, some delicate half-tone of beauty perceived by a sensitive ear or eye, his propaganda will float so high in the upper esthetic air that ordinary denizens of the common earth will be blind and deaf to its meaning, to the self-important message it would write upon the sky. On the other hand, if an artist's chief interest is a communistic or socialistic "revolution," he will be utterly unable to keep that interest suppressed in his art, and any effort to do so will give a half-hearted and half-realized aspect to both his art and his "message."

The trouble is, however, that the artist's message must be so profoundly at the center of his inmost being that it insinuates itself unconsciously into his art. It cannot be driven or hammered in by any effort of individual will or any collusion with mass sympathy or class prejudice. If all art is propaganda, a heroic effort to convert the world, its force comes from the artist's spirit and not from his will — that is, it is a force elusive, intangible and free, not to be directed or confined. Thus the deliberate propagandist rarely achieves art, and the artist, though possessed by a cause, can rarely become a successful propagandist. The combination is not impossible — Rivera has proved in our own time, at least in his Mexican frescoes, that great art may speak for a cause as long as the colors last; and history, from the *Sermon on the Mount* to the *Marseillaise,* furnishes a few examples of great art achieving such powerful propaganda as to change the whole structure and aspect of human society. It is not impossible that some communist poet may write an immortal poem more powerful than ten thousand speeches to promote the "Revolution" which has thus far been more vociferous in talk than in art. And if such an inspired masterpiece of genius should arrive at the POETRY office, we may hope that the editors would recognize its quality and print it.

But we cannot believe that it is our duty to accept and spread before our readers such half-baked efforts at class-conscious poetry as *The New Masses, The Anvil, Partisan Review, Dynamo, Blast,* and other enthusiastic organs of the Left groups, listed last month in M. D. Z.'s review of *Recent Magazines,* may perhaps legitimately use. Stanley Burnshaw, now poetry editor of *The New Masses,* has been giving a series of fiery talks before middle-western John Reed clubs in which POETRY is berated as a decadent in language almost unprintable, and the violent young poet-propagandists on his list are given extravagant adjectives. Although we have not studied his discoveries closely enough to speak with critical authority, we have observed as yet little evidence of artistic value to match their fiercely inflammatory eloquence. In our opinion, the best poetry inspired as yet by the sufferings of the underdogs is that bitter thousand-line epic of the depression, Robert Gessner's *Upsurge,* which was published as a book last year by Farrar & Rinehart.

Mr. Burnshaw would strike out of the modern picture not only POETRY but all the poets, living or dead, on our records who are not "aware of this changing world"— that is, who are not idealizing the Russian system and anathematizing our own. He has all the zeal of a new convert; only four years ago, when POETRY printed his *Eartha* sequence,

Instead of swords he clamored for a harp —

and no solitude was deep enough; he longed for

a place so still
That the darkened grasses wake to no sound at all,
Nor float their shadowy fingers in a wind.

But today he must be in the thick of the battle; since swords are unavailable, he must fight with words.

We missed his lecture in Chicago, but received soon after the following report of his talk in a neighboring city:

According to Mr. Burnshaw's vitriolic statements, Edna St. Vincent Millay, in spite of her original genius, can no longer make an appeal to the adult mind. Her rebellions against the conventions of sex, and her "ahing" and "ohing" about the wonderful male and the wonderful female are only interesting to high-school girls. She is "bourgeois," as also are Robert Frost and Edwin Arlington Robinson. The first is a decadent member of the Emerson-Thoreau school of introspective individual rebellion, one who clings like a leech to the past, and is hemmed in by walls — although "something there is that does not love a wall!" Edwin Arlington Robinson is an acrid ironical recorder of the various types of failure — but he is purely objective, supremely indifferent, and he offers no solution, nor does he probe beneath the concrete for causes. Elinor Wylie was a brilliant mind who sought refuge from this "brave new world that has so many people in it" in a seventeenth-century mysticism — so much so that the lines of her last book, *Angels and Earthly Creatures,* are paraphrased from Crashaw, Donne, and the others of that time. POETRY: A MAGAZINE OF VERSE likewise did not escape criticism. . . . Unfortunately, I cannot remember the names of the great poets Mr. Burnshaw mentioned. Also, I regret that I left before the last act, as sleep was about to overcome me — in spite of all the fire-works. To be sentimental, I still prefer the stars.

And in a second letter this listener offers a lament:

Poetry cannot be quiet any more, and talk about fields and streams and meadows, or gallant gentlemen and ladies, or the spots on a butterfly's wings. It must concern itself with Stalin and strikers; it must be very much like the blaring red posters of the Soviet. It must face the firing squad or go to prison for its beliefs or to the coal mines of Pit College. In my opinion all this is well and good, but I still think there is room in this changing world for Herrick and his mythical ladies, or for John Donne and his extremely individual passions, or for Elinor Wylie and her "jewelled brain"— all of which will last longer than the strikes, which have a way of being settled; or longer than the communists who, as Isadora Duncan discovered, were disgustingly bourgeois.

Malcolm Cowley, in *The New Republic*, and in his new book, *Exile's Return,* is less violent than Mr. Burnshaw, not quite so firm in his conviction that the poet should lead the world to the barricades. But Mr. Cowley, he of the "lost generation," has joined every group that came his way: the self-conscious adolescent yearners of his Pittsburgh high-school; the Harvard malcontents seeking "a key to unlock the world" and slipping lightly through the War, which taught them "to regard as vices the civilian virtues of thrift, caution and sobriety"; then the trek home to Greenwich Village and thence back to Montparnasse, where we find Mr. Cowley shouting for "furious unintelligibility" with the Dada-ists. Now, once more in his own country, he is shouting for the workers' millennium with the Soviet-instructed communists, and one can only wonder what cause will attract him next.

"What is the function of art?" he asks. "Should artists devote themselves to art or propaganda? Should they take part in the class struggle?" And he hopes and trusts that they "will take the workers' side" and thereby become "better artists."

We may let Mr. Yeats answer his queries, a poet whom these ardent theorists have doubtless dropped long since into the discard. Years ago, at the banquet POETRY gave in his honor a few months before the War came to make the world safe for tyrants, the distinguished Irish poet said:

The Victorians forgot the austerity of art and began to preach. . . . It is not the business of a poet to instruct his age — he should be too humble to instruct his age. His business is merely to express himself, whatever that self may be.

So the issue is drawn, with *The New Masses,* Mr. Burnshaw, Mr. Cowley, *et al.,* speaking up vociferously on one side, and POETRY, Mr. Yeats, Mr. MacLeish, Mr. Tate (these two in recent essays) holding their ground more quietly on the other. But since all poetry is propaganda, it is for the individual poet to choose the kind of propaganda he prefers. Will he be inspired to "instruct his age," or to celebrate the spots on the butterfly's wing? Whichever way he turns, may the muse go with him!   *H. M.*

The Purpose of a Left Review
Montagu Slater

from

Left Review, vol. 1, no. 9, 1935.

The Purpose of a Left Review

Montagu Slater

W hat is the purpose of a LEFT REVIEW ? It is a question which should be always in front of us, but especially at the present stage in the progress of this one. There are several good reasons for saying so. Some of them came out very clearly at the Conference of LEFT REVIEW contributors reported on page 366, a conference which itself marked the end of a phase. The calling of the Conference was due to a feeling shared by the editors, and those readers and contributors they consulted, that we ought to examine our purpose and the reasons for our existence as a means to the big new advance which must begin from now. The position is as clear in terms of the reports of the treasurer and circulation manager as in the criticisms expressed at the Conference. We have to acknowledge, first, that LEFT REVIEW has established itself. Beginning without capital it has in eight issues built up a circulation which is beaten by only one of the existing literary reviews. It has gathered an impressive list of contributors. It has grown a character of its own.

On the other side we have to emphasize that to pay its way LEFT REVIEW must at least double its circulation : and it is evident that its usefulness depends on its beginning to pay its way reasonably quickly. This is not only a matter of attention to the business part of circulation. To double circulation demands the strengthening of an already strong list of contributors. Nor will the objective be gained unless the character, function, purpose of LEFT REVIEW become clearer all the time. As part of the self-criticism which progress and widening influence make necessary it has been agreed to set aside part of the next few issues for a discussion of What is our job and How should it be carried out ? My own contribution to the discussion which follows, has been read but is not necessarily endorsed by the other editors, who will intervene with their own opinions as the discussion goes on.

For my own part, then, I regard the period covered by these first nine issues, rather as the first stage of mobilization than as the beginning of the attack. " There is no clear line " was a complaint against LEFT REVIEW of a good many speakers at the Conference. And they are partly right, though, to press my metaphor, they may do well to restrain impatience while mobilization is carried through. Once that period is over, then a different atmosphere prevails. I believe the mobilization period is rapidly merging in the next. Here is one practical sign : it now seems reasonable to make a far greater use than before of the international resources of revolutionary writing and criticism. To have filled the review at an earlier stage with international material would have been to run the risk of swamping our own identity, and never gaining an independent standing. We could not expect to share in the benefits of an International until we were able to bring our own contribution. At present the international trade of LEFT REVIEW shows a favourable balance. Our exports have exceeded our imports. Then we shall do well to increase our imports. The result should be—*will* be, if the Dimitrov speech printed in this issue is an index—that the standard of the REVIEW goes up, goes up, I hope, with a jerk. It will bring us a number of foreign writings which are effective for a revolutionary purpose : writings which will bring an example and an incentive to raise the pitch of our own performance.

It will thus help to correct that sense of " lack of position, direction, purpose,"[1] of which some of our critics have complained. But perhaps still more corrective is wanted: Some of those who felt the force of the criticism suggested to the Conference that we should provide ourselves with editorial notes. I believe the problem is more profound than this apparently simple solution suggests. But for the moment let us take it on the level. I think we shall find some pointers.

Now editorial notes, as they are known to other reviews fall into three categories. " No being is more godlike " runs somebody's wisecrack, " than the writer of editorial notes in the weekly reviews." The paragraphist who takes all the statesmen of the earth in the palm of his hand every week, and finds them very unintelligent, is a traditional figure in English journalism. I am not sure that some of the critics of LEFT REVIEW's necessarily different way of proceeding do not secretly hanker after his lucidities. His notes are the type of the first of my three categories. They are rooted in the conscious or unconscious belief in the intelligentsia as a separate class " which aspires to independent thinking." The function of each paragraph is to prove that to the " detached " judgment both sides are wrong. Nobody has won and only the judges will have prizes. (Look up the *New Statesman* of the week before September 9th last year : and there are stronger examples.) It goes without saying that notes of this kind are out of the question for a LEFT REVIEW. It is not only that we no longer believe in " detachment " : it is also that we take political analysis more seriously. We are not content with a few shrewd paragraphs at the beginning of a journal which devotes the rest of its space to " more intellectual " topics. Full political analysis is being done seriously and well elsewhere. It demands, and gets, not one, but four or five journals.

So much for the first category. In the second the editor takes another pose. He is the humble seeker after truth. Mr. T. S. Eliot in *The Criterion* fills the role to satisfaction, with his quarterly *Commentary*, the first of the articles in the smaller print. The print, the position, and the style of the commentary combine in humility. Quarter by quarter it describes the journey of an individual through a bewildering world. Often, whatever the starting point, its conclusion is to pose against the dilemma : Christianity or Communism? And again, although some of our readers have suggested this kind of partially disguised editorial as the style to adopt, I am not yet persuaded that the still small voice ought to be whispering its message in LEFT REVIEW.

The third category is most frequently recommended. It is the kind of editorial we used to associate with the *London Mercury*, a series of editorial

[1] *Daily Worker,* January 9th.

paragraphs commenting on the news of the month in the broadly cultural field, the opening of the Royal Academy, the latest purchase by the British Museum, the presentation of a tract of unspoiled countryside to the National Trust. And although there is nothing but advantage in having this kind of news collected and analysed, I cannot think that it quite " gives us our lead."

No. We are out for bigger game. LEFT REVIEW is here to develop a new conception of the function of a monthly review. The problem we are considering here—just how should its editorial lead be given—is only an aspect of the ruling problem of how to win and how present a new view of literature and of life : of how to change the world at the same time as we are changing our understanding of the world. LEFT REVIEW does not consider literature and the other arts as the domain of a cultivated intelligentsia who condescend occasionally to look down on vulgar politics. Nor does it discover with the *Criterion,* that literature is not enough (since all have sinned) and shudder into mysticism. Neither is it satisfied (like Sir John Squire) with a view that makes the enjoyment of intellectual activity a pleasant and comparatively unimportant sideline, an occupation which from the social aspect must be considered sparetime. LEFT REVIEW has its own standpoint and that is what we are coming to. It will not serve my turn at this point to escape with the pious platitude that the editorial lead for LEFT REVIEW must not be on any one page but implicitly everywhere. We must press on further.

II

First, I think it is worth restating what was, I believe still is, and certainly should be the driving force behind LEFT REVIEW. I imagine that it is generally accepted by readers of LEFT REVIEW that " literature is propaganda." But I am not sure that we emphasise often enough the converse that the most lasting and persuasive propaganda is literature. There are some ghosts still to exorcise before that consistent emphasis can be given. One of them is that literature is of minor importance in the revolutionary struggle. In the VOKS publication *Literature of the Peoples of the U.S.S.R.* there is a statement by a Chinese writer Emi Sayo which has, I believe, a fairly close application for many writers in England. " The environment of socialist construction," he said, " made me a ' professional ' man of letters . . . I never wanted to be or could have been, nor did I consider myself, a professional writer although literature greatly interested me at a very early age, and when I was thirteen or fourteen I wrote poetry and prose . . . The thousand-year-old traditions of Confucianism looked upon literature and art as worthless occupations. ' A gentleman cares for his dignity first of all and then . . . come literature and art.' This tradition even influenced some of my comrades. They considered (as some of them do even now) writers as people who were not ' serious,' and the title ' man of letters ' appeared to them in the light of a ridiculous and shameful defect in a revolutionary fighter.

" Living in the U.S.S.R. and taking part in its literary life I gradually came to the conclusion that I could no longer stand aloof from literature which, as Lenin said, ' is part of the proletarian cause.' I saw that literature can and must be the weapon of the education of the masses, and that writers are 'the engineers of the soul,' as Stalin said. I now seriously directed my attention to literature and began writing constantly, and not by fits and starts, as before."

There is a fairly long tradition of Confucian contempt in England. Voltaire was shocked when he found that Congreve thought it was better to be an English gentleman than—Congreve. The three-hundred-year-old tradition of capitalism looks upon literature and art as worthless occupations! By a fairly normal dialectical twist an unconscious underrating of literature is often disguised as an exaggerated respect. This, I think, is what happens when critics, as some did at the Conference, advised the publication of " only a small proportion of creative work to ensure that it shall be of the highest standard." This word " creative " is itself suspect in the usual contexts.[1]

It often implies an almost Pater-like sanctification of the work of true art. (And this very easily implies that monster, the work of pure art " unmixed," as Mr. Eliot has put it somewhere, " with irrelevant considerations.") Perhaps we need not avoid the word " creative " but we should be wary of its overtones. Our wariness must also be sharpened by a consistent iteration of the truism that it is the job of literature to influence readers, to work a change, and to record change both in reader and writer. Perhaps it is not necessary to stress at this point how very much more is implied in that than the story with a moral. " The revolutionary proletariat wants a Cervantes," says Dimitrov, " at any rate a little Cervantes to give it such a weapon [as the book *Don Quixote*] in the struggle." Wanted a Cervantes such as he who made a changing world laugh at its growing pains! It is this feeling of growing pains that we want—and haven't enough got—in our writing. We need more feeling for the way in which good writing by recording a changing world in fact changes it. Our imagination ought, I think, to resemble the chess player's. He *must* see several moves ahead. But he's no visionary. What that long-distance seeing gives him is *the next move*. To see things in their relation to one another is what we ask of the poet as well as of the scientist. I was pleased to see on the front page of to-day's issue of the *Daily Worker* (May 2nd) two examples of the effect of a comparatively unimportant bit of such seeing. In the course of his account of the May Day demonstrations to Hyde Park and the destruction by the police of anti-jubilee posters, the writer says : " Scotland Yard had a special job to-day. It was the job of holding together the busted myth of London's loyalty." Some LEFT REVIEW readers will get the echo of Connolly's phrase about " blowing the myth of Dublin's loyalty sky high " in the Ajax article on *Connolly and another Jubilee* in LEFT REVIEW Number 7. On the same page there is a more practical echo of this article. I read that the Bethnal Green Unemployed Association affiliated to the T.U.C. " has decided to hold a day of mourning in opposition to the Jubilee celebrations . . . The marchers will wear black crepe armbands and their war medals." I happen (by an unfair advantage) to have private information that makes

[1] But I recall that advertisement copy-writers understand " creative work " as the upper part of an advertisement in big print, " the sales talk," in contrast to the nether part in the small print which contains the specifications and the price.

it seem at any rate highly probable that the description of Connolly's funeral inspired the Bethnal Green day of mourning. It is true these are examples on a superficial level. A historical article gives a reporter a new phrase to describe the May Day demonstration in the particular circumstances of 1935, and gives Bethnal Green the idea of a new sort of protest demonstration. It is good so far as it goes. But suppose one day we were able to press farther. Suppose " the thing happened " and instead of the fairly obvious historical article we are able to publish the poem or the story with as much new vision in it, in its different way, as Palme Dutt's analysis of fascism as " the organization of social decay." And add such a work that would have the greater persuasiveness, the greater resistance to wear and tear that fable and rhythm give (a little Cervantes, only a very little Cervantes would be good enough)! The influence, the driving force would work through many a pamphlet, *many an action* afterwards. To read, not history, but the contemporary world by flashes of lightning, is a high aim and one that we have to achieve. Our Mayakowsky may be nearer than we suppose.

It becomes then the chief aim of LEFT REVIEW to help create the conditions in which such an event may take place. The great work is not as some of our art for art's sake purists think, something that occurs in a limited section of a magazine set aside for " creative work of the highest standard." It comes, like the Shakespeare play, in the midst of a crowd of inferiors, jostling its way among them, climbing their shoulders, swallowing them whole. It comes at a time of intellectual avidity, at a time of sustained advance in theory—every kind of theory. LEFT REVIEW has not done much in the theoretical line yet. It will have to. One of its functions is to begin to catch up the leeway of forty years stoppage of Marxist theory in England. There has been a good deal of talk at LEFT REVIEW conferences and elsewhere about the uselessness of intellectuals (a slogan less fitted to revolutionary thought than to fascist lack of thinking). What LEFT REVIEW should say to intellectuals is : Intellect is what we want more than most things ! To the intelligentsia : Be intelligent. We are still in the period in England where the last two volumes of *Capital* itself are available only in a poor (and expensive) American edition of what must be one of the world's worst translations. Engels's *Origin of the Family* is also available only in an American edition. Marx's essays, or some of them are available if you're lucky, in an inadequate edition bearing the imprint of a publisher who no longer exists. These are pointers only, but significant. I am not sure that it may not yet prove to be one of the functions of LEFT REVIEW to create demand by reprinting, says, Marx's *Essay on The Jewish Question*—that treatment of the problem of liberty which makes some of the welcome and unexceptionable expositions of Marxism recently published in England, read like the elementary simplifications they in fact are.

Theoretical advance is one of the conditions of literary advance. Another condition is knowledge of the ordinary world of people and of things, the world of work, the world of everyday economic struggle. A function which LEFT REVIEW must learn to perform has been exemplified and then only partially in one number—the issue in which nine workers described a shift at work. Descriptive reporting is something which the tabloid press has almost replaced by wisecracks, which the revolutionary press has often no room for, and which for one reason and another has a particularly revolutionary import. (We have even invented a jargon name for it, *reportage*.) Certainly to describe things as they are is a revolutionary act in itself. Look at Brien O'Neill's brilliant bit of reporting on p. 339! It is at once a cure for being blinded with indignation, a useless occupation which some pseudo-revolutionaries enjoy too much, and for being complacently short-sighted. Descriptive reporting can be a scientific and literary discipline of some value. It can also be one of the most effective means of changing an enemy's mind. I am quite sure that a good many catholics would be severely shaken, whether they admitted it or not, if they were to read Egon Kirsch's description of Lourdes.

Reportage for the old world, and—for now we can have the word—creative work to build the new world. " As engineers of souls in the epoch which began with the October revolution in Russia, writers are called to play an important part in this transition of man from society based on class to a classless society . . . and the work of the writers in this human transformation, like charity, begins at home." Thus Louis Aragon. It brings me to the other purpose of a LEFT REVIEW. The change that begins at home is something we are beginning to note in many writers who are far from being revolutionary. It is a change, gradual and sometimes very slow, which can be discerned in many writings, vague, inconclusive, unrevolutionary which have appeared and must continue to appear in these pages. The influence of juxtaposition (and also of listening to such open criticisms as were expressed at the last conference, and will doubtless be expressed in this discussion) the influence of writing whatever it may be in a review whose purpose will become sharper and clearer as crisis deepens and time goes on—this too is part of the necessary process of a changing world.

To whom are you appealing ? It is the question that comes oftenest to LEFT REVIEW. To which section, to which stratum ? In answer I would say that we are appealing to all who are looking for a vital expression of revolutionary work. If you want to get a notion of how men can change the world by understanding it and conquering their own past : come and look. If you want to see how men are changing themselves as part of the process of world change : read. If you want to take part in the creation of the literature of the classless future, and help prepare the ground for the masterpieces in which that future will live before it has come true: write. It took many a score of writers to make a Cervantes. It is a more crowded world now. We shall need thousands.

I began by asking whether LEFT REVIEW should have an editorial and if so what kind. In so far as I have answered it it seems to me that the answer is negative—unless I have just written an editorial. But then I should add that this kind of editorial might well be kept for every ninth number, and should then be considered the beginning of a collective editorial running for the next two or three numbers, with many readers and writers taking part.

Which anyway will do for the beginning of the discussion.

Writers and Manifestoes
Stephen Spender

from

Left Review, vol. 1, no. 5, 1935.

Writers and Manifestoes

Stephen Spender

" WE can no longer permit life to be shaped by a personified ideal, we must serve with all our faculties some actual thing," Mr. Yeats has written in a recent preface. This seems to me true. The " actual thing" is the true moral or widely political subject that must be realized by contemporary literature, if that literature is itself to be moral and serious. Any other art will tend to become a " personified ideal." The weakness of Lawrence is in this tendency. He wrote about a kind of life which was serious and real : but whereas he meant to write about people, about the life around him, he tended, as he went on, only to write about himself. For in his search for values he invented a way of life that did not betray those values : but, most unfortunately, it was only possible to himself. It was the outcome of a personal struggle : and the result dangerously bordered on the " personified ideal."

It seems then that the position of writers who are endeavouring to serve some " actual thing "—that is, who are endeavouring to write about it—is worth considering. Mr. Day Lewis has said :

> " Yet living here
> As one between two massing powers I live
> When neutrality cannot save
> Nor occupation cheer.

> " None such shall be left alive :
> The innocent wing is soon shot down,
> And private stars fade in the blood-red dawn
> Where two worlds strive.

> " The red advance of life
> Contracts pride, calls out the common blood,
> Beats song into a single blade,
> Makes a depth-charge of grief.

> " Move then with new desires ;
> For where we used to build and love
> Is no man's land, and only ghosts can live
> Between two fires."

This poem asserts that two worlds exist and are fighting : the striving worlds are obviously intended to represent the class war, or at all events the rivalry between revolution and reaction. This contest is so important that neutrality is impossible. " The innocent wing is soon shot down." The poet is evidently on the side of " The red advance of life " because he believes that " only ghosts can live Between two fires."

The poem then is not only about communism, it also has a propagandist element : it argues, and some of the argument is, to say the least, controversial. For example, the simplification of issues might seem to some people premature, if not grotesque. But this does not really affect the real claim of the poem to value. The implicit assertion of the poem is that it is about realities : that the struggle between two worlds is *real*— as real as the descriptions of environment in novels—that the material of the poem is life.

If I am right in saying that the struggle of communism or socialism against the anti-socialist forces of the whole world exists, I think that the reader, in judging left-wing literature, must not judge it in the same way as he argues against communism. It is not a question of whether he thinks the premises are false, but of whether the premises are about realities, in the sense that there are political and moral realities which are more enduring than the external world of literary realism. What he should ask is : Does this communist approach lead to a greater and more fundamental understanding of the struggle affecting our whole life to-day ?

Now one of the chief claims of communism as a political creed is that it is materialist. The materialist conception of history, the theory of surplus value, the idea of crystallized labour : all these are solids, they are material subject matter and yet move in the world of ideas. The writer who grasps anything of Marxist theory, feels that he is moving in a world of reality, and in a purposive world, not merely a world of obstructive and oppressive *things*.

Lastly, it is well to remember that perhaps the most fundamental of all ideas illustrated by drama and poetry, in all history, is the idea of justice. We live in an age when we have become conscious of great social injustice, of the oppression of one class by another, of nationalities by other nations. Communism, or socialism in its completed form, offers a just world. A world in which wealth is more equally distributed, and the grotesque accumulating of wealth by individuals is dispersed : in which nations have no interest in destroying each other in the manner of modern war, because the system of competitive trade controlled by internecine and opposed capitalist interests is abolished.

These aims are so broad and so just that no amount of abuse and sneering can affect the people who hold them. It is no use telling me that I am a bourgeois-intellectual. that I know nothing, or next to nothing of the proletariat, etc. All that and a lot more may be true. The point is that if I desire social justice I am not primarily concerned with myself, I am concerned with bringing into being a world quite external to my own interests ; in the same way as when one writes a poem, one is allowing the poem to have its own, impersonal, objective being, one is not shoving oneself into it.

The socialist artist is concerned with realizing in his work the ideas of a classless society : that is to say, applying those ideas to the life around him, and giving them their reality. He is concerned with a change of heart.

He is not primarily concerned with ways and means, and he is not paralysed by the argument that the economic system is rigid. The economic system was made for man, and not man for the economic system, so that if man changes, that is to say, if he has a new and strong conception of justice, the economic system will also change.

It also follows that the writer is primarily interested in man, and not in systems, not even in a good economic system. Systems are rigid, and they must always be forced externally, by external criticism, to change. In that sense art, because it insists on human values, is a criticism of life.

Good architecture is a criticism of slums. Good painting is a criticism of the pictures we have, the clothes we wear, all the appearances with which we surround ourselves. Good poetry is a criticism of language : of the way in which we express ourselves, the direction of our thoughts, the words we hand down to our children. Our industrial civilization has proved almost impervious to that criticism of life which we find in architecture, painting, music and poetry. Art has been resisted, and the artists have been driven to form cliques with a private language and private jokes. But no system can afford to be without the criticism of art. The whole point of artists adopting a revolutionary position, is that their interests may become social and not anti-social, and that their criticism may help to shape a new society.

When one considers the position of artists in a socialist state, it is well therefore to remember that the art which has " roots in the masses," must be free to tell the truth and to criticize life. Lenin said, " Art belongs to the people. It ought to extend with deep roots into the very thick of the broad toiling masses. It ought to be intelligible to these masses and loved by them. And it ought to unify the feeling, thought and will of these masses, elevate them. It ought to arouse and develop artists among them."

A democratic art has always been popular with certain writers, who have appealed in their work from a small set of fellow artists to the people (the classic example is the appeal to the taste of *das Volk* in *Meistersingers*). The point of such an appeal is that by widening his audience, the artist also widens and deepens his subject matter : he draws strength from deeper roots. The writer who is starving because he cannot reach any audience but a small clique, and who finds the whole literature, painting and music of his time a prey to the same cliqueiness, will suspect that there is something wrong with our sectarian literature. Now whatever may be the faults of Russian writers to-day, they do at least reach a wide audience, and they do succeed in writing about matters which passionately concern the people. In order to awaken this wide interest they do not play down to their audience, in the fashion of our popular modern writers, and the English press.

Nevertheless, Russian literature suffers, or has until recently suffered, from its own sectarianism. This consisted in the establishment of what amounted to a monopoly of publishing and criticism by a small group of writers who formed an organization called RAPP (Russian Association of Proletarian Writers). The business of this Union, and its various companion organizations, was to insist on the proletarization of art, and to persecute artists who were not correct in their party ideology. Mr. Max Eastman has written a book called *Artists in Uniform*, which is an extremely prejudiced account of the activities of RAPP : he is clearly carrying on a personal vendetta against the editors of the American Communist periodical, *New Masses*, which he finds to be subservient to Moscow. He is also a Trotskyist, and a violent critic of the Stalin dictatorship. He draws attention to RAPP's many blunders, but he does not admit that several writers have been exceptionally well treated.

For example, he ignores the case of Nekrassov, and he is so anxious to prove that RAPP has destroyed all literary talent in Russia that the name of Gladkov does not occur in his book. In spite, though, of defects of over-statement, the indictment he draws up is alarming, and, in some ways, almost overwhelming. There are many examples of persecution by RAPP. The suicides of Yessenin, Maiakovsky, and several other poets, may have been inevitable, since their faulty "individualism" perhaps made it, in any case, impossible for them to adapt themselves to the revolution. Far more serious is the case of Zamyatin, whose novel *We* was not published in the Soviet, but a copy of which was pirated in a Prague émigré magazine : this misfortune was used as a frame-up against Zamyatin, and he was compelled to live in exile. Romanov, who is well known in England for his novel, *Three Pairs of Silk Stockings*, was so unfortunate as to receive a favourable review in the London *New Statesman*, in which the reviewer remarked that it was a mystery that Romanov's books should be allowed to appear in Soviet Russia. The mystery did not cease, but Romanov was compelled to recant publicly. Another writer, Pilnyak, on being charged with counter-revolutionary tendencies, managed to make an art of humiliating himself and begging for Marxist instruction: he has become one of the most prosperous writers in the Soviet Union.

Since RAPP no longer exists, Mr. Eastman's remarks may now seem irrelevant, because I do not suppose that even the Soviet Government would now defend RAPP's actions. But he holds that matters are now little if at all better, and that RAPP was only liquidated because its destructive function was completely performed. The next few years will show whether or not this accusation is just : but meanwhile Mr. Eastman's charges should be read and considered. It is not enough to dismiss him as a counter-revolutionary, if what he says is true.

The following principles were dictated to the Kharkov Congress, a meeting of communist writers gathered from every part of the world, by Auerbach, a young representative of the political bureaucracy :—

" 1. *Art is a class weapon.*

" 2. Artists are to abandon ' individualism ' and the fear of strict discipline ' as petty bourgeois attitudes.

" 3. Artistic creation is to be systemized, organized, ' collectivized,' and carried out according to the plans of a central staff like any other soldierly work.

" 4. This is to be done under the ' careful and yet firm guidance of the Communist Party.'

" 5. Artists and writers of the rest of the world are to learn how to make proletarian art by studying the experience of the Soviet Union.

" 6. ' Every proletarian artist must be a dialectical materialist. The method of creative art is the method of dialectic materialism.'

" 7. ' Proletarian literature is not necessarily created by the proletariat it can also be created by writers from the petty bourgeoisie,' and one of the chief duties of the proletarian writer is to help these non-proletarian writers to ' overcome their petty bourgeois character and accept the viewpoint of the proletariat.' "

It is evident that the aim of this manifesto is to convert art into an instrument that can be used for party purposes. It is not the business of the artist to observe, but to conform. He must not be a two-edged instrument which might turn against the party. It is his business to go where he is sent, and to observe what he is told.

There is not the least doubt that a great many communists look on art purely as a party instrument. To take a small instance, I read in a proposed manifesto sent by Alec Brown to the third number of LEFT REVIEW, that " during the initial period of our magazine (it is) most important to carry on rigorous criticism of all highbrowism, intellectualism, abstract rationalism, and similar dilettanteism." And to whom do these abusive, ill-defined terms apply, one must ask ? The answer is only too simple : to everyone who is not one of US.

It may be argued that there is a severe censorship now in almost every country outside Russia, and that even in England there will soon be no great freedom of speech. But there is a great difference between even the most stupefying and severe censorship and the attempt to regard art as a mere instrument in the hands of a party. The difference is that censorship cuts or bans books which are already written : but the principles laid down in this manifesto order the manner in which they should be written ; what books should be about, and what attitude the writer should adopt to his material. No censorship has ever gone so far as this. This instrumentalization encourages, too, a school of critics whose business simply is to apply the canon. To attack writers because they are bourgeois, because their novels, if they are about life as they know it, are not proletarian; or, if they are about the working classes, because they are not militant. One need only read the American magazine *New Masses* to discover plenty of such criticism.

Against this, one must set some statements by Russian writers, which are published in *Literature of the Peoples of the U.S.S.R.*, vols. 7-8. Some of the declarations here seem admirable and honest. For instance, A. Selivenovsky, in an essay on " The Poetry of Socialism," says : " To become an artist of socialism means, if you come from the intelligentsia, that not only must you be convinced that the ideas of socialism are correct, but that you must alter your previously-formed poetic style. It means that you must overcome and discard many of your former ideas about life ; you must change your way of looking at the world. But this alteration does not imply, of course, that the subject-matter, imagery, and style of the poet of socialism is made to lose all individuality, is reduced to complete uniformity. That is far from the case. The fact is that it is socialism that ensures the all-round development and growth of the human individual."

This seems excellent. Good, too, is V. Kaverin's essay on literature and science, in which he pleads for a more scientific subject-matter in modern literature. C. Zelinsky is narrower : " Criticism acquires a function of a principally intellectual-educational order : to struggle against the heritage of capitalism in consciousness by exposing it in art." He has hard, almost sinister things to say of Voronsky, a figure of the recent past : " Voronsky based his conception of art on the work of Tolstoy and Proust, writers in whose work direct observation is most prominent. In such a system of views, however, the very core of the

Marxian conception of literature, its very heart, class activity, was lost.
It was not by chance, therefore, that Voronsky proved to be allied with
Trotskyism."

Even officially, the position of literature in communist society, seems
then to be extremely controversial. All I want to emphasize here is
that if one is on the side of the greatest possible degree of freedom, if
one insists that one should write as one chooses and about what one
wishes, one is not a traitor to the cause of world socialism. No system
is in itself a complete solution of world problems. If there is to be any
sort of freedom and improvement, one has go to push and even sometimes fight the systems of one's own choice. Unless artists insist on their
right to criticize, even to be " humanitarian " (a despised term), communism will become a frozen epoch, another ice age.

Lastly, the view of Lenin was not at all that of a bureaucrat. Polonsky
in his *Outline of the Literary Movement of the Revolutionary Epoch*[1] relates
how he pencilled comments on an article of Pletnev, *On the ideological
Front*, which was printed in *Pravda*, in the autumn of 1922. " ' The
creation of a new proletarian class front is the fundamental goal of the
Protecult,' wrote Pletnev. ' Ha, Ha ! ' " wrote Lenin in the margin.
There are many other comments such as " humm ! " and " What a
mess ! ", surviving in that margin. " In two places he writes ' Bunk.' "

[1] Polonsky's article forms an appendix to Max Eastman's book.

The Socialist Theatre
John Allen

from

Left Review, vol. 3, no. 7, 1937.

The Socialist
Theatre

JOHN ALLEN

THE ENGLISH THEATRE is springing to life in a way that a year ago would not have been thought possible. The Left Book Club Theatre Guild has made contact, during the first three months of its existence, with over 130 groups, from Aberdeen to Plymouth, from Swansea to Clacton. In the East-end of London alone there are eight Left Wing groups already formed or in the process of being formed. In South Wales, Yorkshire, and Lancashire, with centres at Cardiff, Sheffield, and Manchester, regional movements are being formed, and already existing groups are taking such plays as *Waiting for Lefty* and *Till the Day I Die* into Miners' villages, showing the miners the power and value of the theatre, and stimulating them to start groups themselves.

This should not be difficult in South Wales, for here there is already a strong theatrical tradition as a result of the social activities of the Miners' Federation, and in most of the mining towns there is a well-equipped hall. It should only be a matter of local organisation and finding suitable material to get some of these local movements well on their feet.

LOCAL ACTIVITY

In many other parts of England there is a fairly considerable amount of activity, especially where the National Council of Social Service has been at work. But it is depressing to find that the plays on which so many of these groups have been working are outworn West-end successes—*The Ghost Train* and the works of Ivor Novello, for instance. The trouble with the N.C.S.S. is its dependence on a government grant, for this must inevitably prevent its affiliated groups from expressing their social discontent with a freedom they might otherwise achieve. But the fact that the first two prizes in the recent British Drama League Festival were given to companies who did plays dealing with vital economic problems is an encouraging sign that there is a definite swing in favour of plays with subjects that matter.

History shows that no theatrical movement has had a literary source; and so the incubus that shrouds the contemporary theatre is the old one of absence of material. Many groups would have presented Left Wing plays long before this if such plays had been in existence. The proof of this is the great and immediate demand for the plays published and recommended by the Left Book Club Theatre Guild; and that when a frankly political play like *Waiting for Lefty* comes along, the Unity Theatre Club is able to give eighty performances of it in a little over a year, with every prospect of giving eighty more.

UNITY THEATRE'S *LEFTY*

The achievement of the U.T.C. is notable. Most pertinent to the future of the whole English theatre was the show it gave at the Phœnix Theatre, London, last May, a performance that compared in no way unfavourably, either in standard of acting or in general presentation with the work of an experienced and highly salaried professional company. I say that this performance was pertinent to the future of the theatre because it showed that the Socialist movement is capable of creating a theatre of its own that will in a short time surpass the bourgeois theatre in technical proficiency, as it already surpasses it in the vitality of its content.

Many people at the end of a performance of *Waiting for Lefty* explain the power of the acting, almost in a tone of dismissal, by saying, ' Oh, it's because they believe in what they are saying,' which implies that most of the actors they have ever seen do NOT believe in what they are saying, or only believe in their lines— which is actually the case—within the limits of what they are pleased to call ' their art.' Until quite recently most actors would as cheerfully have given a sympathetic portrayal of a Fascist general, as they would have acted the part of Lenin himself. Their only qualification would have been that the part should be a ' good acting part '—all of which shows a divorce between art and the world of which that art should be a product, which is patently ludicrous.

The situation to-day is definitely this: that although it is not possible to draw many actors together on a pro-Socialist basis, it is possible to get them on an anti-Fascist one. Most of them have wits enough to realise from example that Fascism is more an enemy than a friend of a vital theatre, but they have not wits enough to perceive, nor intellectual courage enough to admit, that a Socialist Britain would remove those conditions which make a career on the stage to-day absolutely untenable for anyone who really cares tuppence ha'penny about the business: conditions in which the actor, as Gordon Craig describes, is sucked like an orange until he is dry and then chucked aside, if he is lucky enough to be sucked at all—and if he is not, he starves. (Independent incomes are so essential for a ' professional actor ' that class distinction reaches a nauseating extreme.) This situation would be removed, and the actor would be given conditions, such as exist in the U.S.S.R., which would enable him to have a say in the sort of plays in which he acted, the way in which he should act them, and so on. The Capitalist Press is careful not to mention that one of the first things the popular front government did in France was to put the most active and enterprising directors at the head of the Comedie Francaise and the Opera Comique.

JUDGMENT DAY

Anti-Fascism brings us to the question of a play running in London that has unusual interest and importance—*Judgment Day*. To understand its implications it is necessary to go back a little.

The problem which faces the dramatist who wants to express Socialist ideas in his plays, is the form into which he should cast his plays to give them a popular basis. I do not mean this in a disparaging sense. On the contrary, a play that draws nobody into the theatre has no value as a play. One must, therefore, present one's ideas in a way that will make them enjoyable, understandable, and attractive to a considerable number of people. (I do not mean this in a sugary bourgeois sense; but I do mean that the theatre is no place to be eclectic. There will always be plays for which there will be a very limited public, and many of these have an important place in the development of the drama, but the theatre has a popular basis which makes the number of such plays far less than the number of poems of parallel limited appeal.) To combat this difficulty, Auden enlivens his plays with music-hall ditties; Herbert Hodge, the author of *Where's That Bomb ?* and *Cannibal Carnival*, gives his play a basis of broad English humour; Elmer Rice in *Judgment Day* uses the form of melodrama. Let's be clear: to use an obviously popular formula is not ideal. The greatest Left Wing play of them all, *Lefty*, has a technique of its own. Treated by a mind of real depth and integrity, the Reichstag Fire Trial could have been the subject of a tremendous play; but

H

it is probably the fact that Elmer Rice has sacrificed complete truth for melodrama that has given his play its immediate popular success. Thousands of people will come to see his melodrama, and will go away amazed at this great exposure of Fascist justice, who would never dream of going to a theatre that was known to have Left Wing sympathies.

IMPORTANCE OF GOOD PRODUCTION

One of the easiest and most dangerous things in the world is to underrate your opponents; and there is nothing easier for us to do than to mount our little horses and be thoroughly snobbish about the West-end theatre. But proletarian snobbery is even more to be condemned than intellectual snobbery, and that, God knows, is bad enough. And curse the bourgeois theatre though we may, it has got some points in its favour, and some points of which we should take careful note. Perhaps the most important of these is that the bourgeois theatre is ' aesthetically convincing.' The convention within which it works is a miserable one, but it is at least true to its own limitations. It does not upset anybody. It deals with unimportant matters in an unimportant way. Its staunchest supporters are those who say after a none-too-good performance of a Left Wing play, ' Oh, it's all right and very interesting, but you can't mix art and politics.' Now, I have already commented upon the folly of this point of view from another angle, but it is important to study what it is that drives people to make these dogmatic assertions. First of all, there is a deep-rooted middle-class prejudice that anything connected with the working class will be crude. Secondly, the play may be a bad one. Thirdly, the content of the play may have disturbed their complacency. Fourthly, and this is the point with which I am especially concerned, the content of the play might not be sufficiently at one with its form for the whole to be ' aesthetically convincing.' If, therefore, you are deliberately challenging old aesthetic canons, if you are saying, ' The bourgeois theatre is lousy—ours is the real thing,' you must not give the audience a loop-hole to distract them from the main issue. You must allow them to concentrate all their faculties on the points that are new to them; for if there are obvious faults in the production, if the actors are inaudible and the clothes which should be clean are dirty, and those points which a little trouble would put right are not cared for, the audience cannot possibly concentrate on the finer and more startling points of the performance.

It is a pretty vile phrase this ' aesthetically convincing,' but it really is brimful of meaning. The approach of a vast majority of people to a play is purely literary. Contemporary dramatic criticism is clear evidence of this. It is concerned wholly with the structure of the play. So when the critics are faced with the bad production of a classic whose qualities are theatrical rather than literary—as, for instance, much of the work of Ben Jonson—they are entirely bewildered. The production of a play is a process of bringing to life a flat-dead written text. It is not a matter of deciding who moves where on the stage, and at what moment; but a far deeper and more creative question of decision upon style. (I am only discussing scripts of merit. Most of the plays now written have no style at all.) It is the job of the various craftsmen involved in putting on the play to decide what sort of scenery, what style of acting, how much formalism, how much realism, what sort of music, and what kind of dancing the play demands. And if the play is a difficult one, this sometimes takes months of discussion. And since so many are actively involved, it is essential that they should have the completest unanimity of outlook; for bad choice of music, wrong-coloured decor, or one of a dozen small points, may be enough to distract the audience's attention from the real purpose of the play.

Cannibal Carnival, produced at the Unity Theatre Club in June, was a notable example of this. Economic pressure necessitated the Unity Theatre Club producing this play before the production was properly ' achieved '—before, that is, these problems had been solved. The whole style of this play was new; and because the production was not ' achieved,' many people who saw the play admired the acting and the decor, praised the production, and enormously enjoyed the writing, but, at the same time, were sincerely dissatisfied by the piece as a whole. Why, exactly, they could not say; and nor, as things were, could anybody else, not even the author or producer. What poet can say what his poem will be like when he has finished writing it? If he could write it as he wanted it to be first time, what need would there be for him to write a dozen drafts? The poet has an instinct for what is right and what is wrong, and that is the end of it. And the moral? Simply that enormously more care must be given to a Left Wing production than to an orthodox one.

I hope that what I have said will not alarm any member of some young or newly formed group with more enthusiasm than financial resources, who should happen to read this. One act plays can, and must be done by new groups simply and straight-forwardly—absolutely as well as possible, but not with elaborate scenery. The palaver I have described is one that faces a group only after it has reached a fairly advanced stage of development. But it is important that groups should realise the nature of the difficulties that lie ahead of them, and that ordinary theatre-goers should appreciate the problems that the advance-guard of the Socialist theatre is even now encountering. The future of the working-class theatre depends upon two major problems—its ability to get good plays written, and to organise the working classes to form a regular audience for the theatre. But especially it is a question of plays.

Writing in Revolt
Four articles by Storm Jameson, Stephen Spender,
John Allen and Arthur Calder-Marshall

from

Fact, 4 July 1937.

WRITING IN REVOLT

I. THEORY

Documents

by Storm Jameson

I BELIEVE we should do well to give up talking about proletarian literature and talk about socialist literature instead—and mean by it writing concerned with the lives of men and women in a world which is changing and being changed. A socialist must be intimately concerned with this change; he must be struggling continually to understand it. His writing must reflect his experience of it and his understanding of his experience. And since the change is worldwide, and is taking place on innumerable levels at once and all the time, the difficulty of attempting to write anything on the scale of *War and Peace* is so great as to make it unlikely that it will be written—yet. The difficulty excuses none of us for retreating into a world made artificially static by excluding from it all the factors of change and the rumour of the real world.

Literature concerned with change and the changing world is concerned with revolution, and with all the stages of revolutionary action. The type of socialist hero is a revolutionary (required reading is Ralph Fox's *The Novel and the People*), and here, if he is a novelist, the writer is not likely to be able to create a revolutionary hero under the eyes of the living Dimitroff. Even Tolstoi, writing fifty years after Waterloo, is not able to make a figure of Napoleon: Stendhal, a greater writer, and a contemporary, does not try. It is perhaps necessary (this is not the place to consider it) for a really great figure to become diminished in time before he can be re-created by the imagination, which can tackle lesser men (a Baldwin, for example) easily enough. Note that in Ralph Bates's very fine novels his heroes are least convincing when they are behaving as revolutionaries. In quarrelling, in gathering olives, in enduring, they appear as whole men. Compare the hero of Malraux's last book with the figure of Dimitroff; he is a shadow. Compare him with himself—he begins to be alive only when he leaves the prison and is talking to his wife.

The use of the term 'proletarian novel' suggests, quite falsely, that socialist literature ought to concern itself only or mainly with working-class life. In fact, a novel about Lord Invernairn, written from full insight into what this man actually is doing, a novel which exposed him, laid him open, need not bring on to the stage a single one of the people who do not exist for him as human beings. It would still be socialist literature. The process of change, of decay, of growth, is taking place everywhere all the time: it does not matter where you open up the social body if you know what you are looking for.

This misconception is not the worst of it. The worst is a dreadful self-consciousness which seizes the middle-class writer who hears the command to sell all he has and write a proletarian novel. He discovers that he does not even know what the wife of a man earning two pounds a week wears, where she buys her food, what her kitchen looks like to her when she comes into it at six or seven in the morning. It has never happened to him to stand with his hands in greasy water at the sink, with a nagging pain in his back, and his clothes sticking to him. He (or she) actually has to take a look into the kitchen to know what it smells and looks like: at that he does not know as much as the woman's forefinger knows when it scrapes the black out of a crack in the table or the corner of a shelf.

The impulse that made him want to know is decent and defensible. If he happens to have been born and brought up in Kensington the chances are that he has never lifted the blind of his own kitchen at six in the morning, with thoughts in his mind of tumbled bed-clothes, dirty grates, and the ring of rust on the stove. But there is something very wrong when he has to contort himself into knots in order to get to know a worker, man or woman. What is wrong is in him, and he cannot blame on to his upbringing what is really a failure of his own will; it is still clenched on his idea of himself, given to him by that upbringing but now to be cast off as the first condition of growth. Too much of his energy runs away in an intense interest in and curiosity about his feelings. 'What things I am seeing for the first time! What smells I am enduring! There is the woman raking ashes with her hands and here I am watching her!' This self-centred habit is not peculiar to the middle-class writer (see R. M. Fox's *Smoky Crusade*), but it is natural to him. If, as a child, he had escaped from the nursery and been found in some Hoxton backyard he would have been bathed and disinfected and made conscious of having run an awful danger, much as though he had been visiting savages. The mental attitude persists. Breeding will out!

The first thing a socialist writer has to realize is that there is no value in the emotions, the spiritual writhings, started in him by the sight, smell, and touch of poverty. The emotions are no doubt unavoidable. There is no need to record them. Let him go and pour them down the drain.

The writer living in one moment of time and in one

society, and perpetually conscious of another trying to break through, has been set a task which calls for special discipline and effort. He must enquire into a revolution, but he cannot create a revolutionary hero as impressive as the still living Dimitroff. If he could he would be mentally of the size of Dimitroff and, at the present instant, that would lay on him the compulsion to work in other ways than as a writer. He must not, he ought not to indulge himself in self-analysis, since that is to nail himself inside his own small ego at a moment when what is individual to each man is less real, less actual, than that which he shares with every other man—insecurity, the need to become a rebel for the sake of human dignity. What then should he do?

A task of the greatest value, urgent and not easy, is waiting to be done. George Orwell has begun on it in the first half of *The Road to Wigan Pier*. The instinct which drives a writer to go and see for himself may be sound. If a writer does not know, if his senses and imagination have not told him, what poverty smells like, he had better find out. Even if in the end he prefers to write about Invernairn or Krupp. But if he goes for his own sake, for some fancied spiritual advantage to be got from the experience, he had better stay at home: his presence in Wigan or Hoxton is either irrelevant or impudent. He must go for the sake of *the fact*, as a medical student carries out a dissection, and to equip himself, not to satisfy his conscience or to see what effect it has on him. His mind must remain cool; he must be able to give an objective report, neither superficial nor slickly dramatic. And, for pity's sake, don't let us have any 'slices of life' in the manner of the Naturalists of the 'eighties. In their determination to show life up they became as sentimental, as emotionally dishonest, as Miss

So-and-so 'embosoming freely' with her readers in the fiction columns of the woman's magazines. For their own purposes they fictionalized reality as obtusely as she does.

The conditions for the growth of a socialist literature scarcely exist. We have to create them. We need documents, not, as the Naturalists needed them, to make their drab tuppeny-ha'penny dramas, but as charts, as timber for the fire some writer will light to-morrow morning. The detailed and accurate presentment, rather than the representation, of this moment, and this society. A new *Comédie Humaine*—offered to us without the unnecessary and distorting gloss of the writer's emotions and self-questionings. Writers should be willing to go and live for a long enough time at one of the points of departure of the new society. To go, if you like, into exile. Without feeling heroic, or even adventurous, or curious about their own spiritual reactions. Willing to sink themselves for the time, so that they become conduits for a feeling which is not personal, nor static.

They might, for instance, tell us what is stirring, if anything, in one of those Durham mining villages about which a staid report in *The Times* says that 'no hope exists for thousands of men and boys ever to lead a normal working life again'. A report made by two women doctors to the Council of Action on *Motherhood in the Special Areas of Durham and Tyneside* remarks, 'It was amazing that in this century people should be living in such dens, that mothers should go through their pregnancies there and infants be born.' I don't know who reads these reports with their ghastly 'cases'. They are not documents in the proper sense of the word; they are not full enough; they do not give the essentials of speech and action. They could not: the observation, however acute, is made from outside, too briefly, and as a stranger would report upon strangers after an hour's visit. We do not *see* the woman stripping the filthy, bug-ridden wallpaper from the thin wall of her attic; nor the pregnant woman waiting her turn for the lavatory which serves eight families (forty people); nor the gesture of the woman setting on the table the little pie she has bought for her consumptive child; nor the workless man looking at the soles of his shoes when he comes home. It is necessary that a writer should have lived with these things for him to record them as simply and coldly, even brutally, as if he chooses he can describe what has been familiar to him from his infancy. Something can be discovered in an hour's visit, but not the quick. Not the seed, if it exists here, of a different growth.

It is not necessary—in a great many instances it would be impossible or undesirable—for a writer to work alone. He might work with other writers, if it were decided to report on a district or a town (see the American classic in this sort, *Middletown*). He can enlist the help of social workers to supplement his own experience of such specifically modern horrors as the effects on girls and young women of 'rationalization' in the factory. (When Charlie Chaplin goes mad, in a recent film, unable to stop himself jerking at anything that looks like the top of a screw, he is caricaturing a horrid reality: the girls from one of these rationalized factories cannot keep their hands still; they walk round the club room nipping off the heads of flowers, turning off the heating; they jerk and twitch and scream.)

A writer living in a Nottinghamshire mining village could not possibly do his job properly without the help of confidential reports from the workers themselves, which he would have to wait for and deserve by his behaviour. He could not expect the wife of a miner living in one of the new 'compounds' to tell him at sight how she likes shopping in an employer-owned store. Why, he might be in the pay of the Economic League. (The connections and activities of this organization deserve a document to themselves—more than one.)

A well-placed novelist might bring out a double-sided record: one day or one week in the life of a family of five living in one of the wealthier residential districts of the West End (if he or she can find one which has so far forgotten itself as to breed), set down opposite the life during the same length of time of a similar (in ages, size, etc.), of a Paddington, Hoxton, Lambeth family. Again, this might be team work.

The number of documents to be got is infinite. How are they to be presented? This is the crux. A journalist can observe and report. No writer is satisfied to write journalism, nor is this what is wanted—visits to the distressed areas in a motor-car. Nor must the experience, the knowledge waited for and lived through, be fictionalized, in the sense of making up a story or a novel on the basis of facts collected (e.g., *The Stars Look Down*, by Cronin). Perhaps the nearest equivalent of what is wanted exists already in another form in the documentary film. As the photographer does, so must the writer keep himself out of the picture while working ceaselessly to present the *fact* from a striking (poignant, ironic, penetrating, significant) angle. The narrative must be sharp, compressed, concrete. Dialogue must be short—a seizing of the significant, the revealing word. The emotion should spring directly from the fact. It must not be squeezed from it by the writer, running forward with a, 'When I saw this, I felt, I suffered, I rejoiced . . .' His job is not to tell us what he felt, but to be coldly and industriously presenting, arranging, selecting, discarding from the mass of his material to get the significant detail, which leaves no more to be said, and implies everything.

And for goodness' sake let us get some fun out of it. Nothing is less to our taste, and less realist, than the inspissated gloom of Naturalism. A novel by Ignazio Silone, *Fontamara*, offers itself as a model—this tragic, bitter story of a village is extremely funny, and sticks faster in the memory by it. Let us write decent straight English, too; not American telegraphese. Social documents are familiar in our literature. The sermons of preaching friars are still alive wherever the preacher threw in a scene that was under his eyes as he walked about—often a savage indictment of poverty created by greedy merchants and landlords.

For the sake of compression—the field to be covered is, after all, enormous—and for the sake of sharpness, much must be left out that a writer will be tempted to put in. 'Atmosphere', for one thing. It has been overdone, too—all those novels in which infinite pains have gone to the evocation of rain and moonlight, novels 'set' in Cumberland, in Sussex, in Paris and Patagonia. For another thing, the static analysis of feeling, and thought. No more peeling of the onion to strew the page with layer after layer. No stream of consciousness—that famous stream which we pretend to see flowing, as in the theatre we agree to pretend that the stream on the backcloth flows. No commentary—the document is a comment. No æsthetic, moral, or philosophic enquiry—that is, none which is not implicit. To say this is not to say that a novel such as *The Root and The Flower* is of no value. It is of the greatest value and it is concerned with those human values we are trying to save. It offers—in a form entirely unsuitable to our present purpose—a criticism of social values which is just and suggestive. Its method is useless to us—for a good reason. We must be field workers in a field no smaller than England, our criticism of values implied in the angle from which we take our pictures. By choosing this detail, this word, rather than another from the mass offered to us, we make our criticism, our moral judgments.

Writers write to be read. If they are not read, by as many people as will do to keep them vigorously alive, they have failed *as writers*. People will listen even to what is disagreeable to them if the speaker's tone takes them by the ear. The Naturalists flung tear-sodden lumps of raw life in the public's face and complained because the public went home to amuse itself in its own way. There is a technical job to be done. It can't be done until the instruments have been made and improved, as astronomy had to wait on a lens. How to make people listen to what they don't want to hear. How not to bore the people who do want to hear. If they want to hear, you say, they'll take anything. But why the devil should they? Why should they be bored by what is nothing more or less than incompetence or amateurishness? It is not a question of setting out to be a best-seller—if that is what you want there are shorter and easier ways—but of learning a craft. Again the relevant comparison is with the documentary film. It takes a sharpened and disciplined mind to handle a mass of material in such a way that only the significant details emerge. We're confronted by the extreme difficulty of finding phrases which are at once compressed and highly suggestive. It's hardly a job for an amateur unless he happens to be a genius. When a genius arrives he can and will look after himself.

The isolation of writers from each other is almost as deadly as their isolation from the life of farmers, labourers, miners and the other men on whom the life of the nation depends. If something of this unnatural apartness can be broken down, by writers working together, by their coming into relation with their fellow-men and women, they may, between them, provide the conditions, the warmth, for a new literature. We have been attending the death-bed of an old one for some time; a birth is about due. It may actually be the birth of a great writer, and the documents we have collected, the activity we have stirred up, will form the conditions into which he is born. They will shape him and he will use them. A great writer has more than one father and mother, as well as more than one nurse.

One technical difficulty remains to be solved. The solution may turn up any day, in the course of the experiments going on all the time. This is the frightful difficulty of expressing, in such a way that they are at once seen to be intimately connected, the relations between things (men, acts) widely separated in space or in the social complex. It has been done in poetry. At certain levels of the mind we see and feel connections which we know rationally in another way. In dreams things apparently distinct are seen to be related (but Surrealism is not the solution). We may stumble on the solution in the effort of trying to create the literary equivalent of the documentary film.

Poetry

by Stephen Spender

THE best of the contemporary poets who write of political themes have been led from poetry to politics not from politics to poetry. The poet is essentially sensitive to the life of his time. We happen to be living in a political age: that is to say, an age in which the future not only of individuals but also of our whole civilization is being fought out by political parties both in parliaments, and now on the battlefield in Spain. The starting-off point of the political theme in contemporary poetry is the realization of the historic situation in which we are living:—

'Seekers after happiness, all who follow
The convolutions of your simple wish,
It is later than you think; nearer that day
Far other than that distant afternoon
Amid rustle of frocks and stamping feet
They gave the prizes to the ruined boys.'
(W. H. AUDEN.)

Why should poetry be concerned with public affairs rather than with the private interests of the individual? The answer is that it is precisely within the consciousness of many separate individuals that the political struggle is taking place. So far is this true that the critics of the modern school of poetry own it themselves when they say that poetry should be beautiful in the sense that beauty, like gardens, provides a quiet escape from the noise and traffic of our time. But poetry claims the right to go to the very centre of the problems with which the mind of man is most passionately concerned. It is not that the themes of love, landscape and the beautiful have no place in contemporary life, but that they are not the central drama of our time, which is the historic struggle as it effects the mind of the individual.

Why should the writer take sides? Why should so many of the modern poets be Left Wing?

I believe the answer to be firstly that the socialist movement has a far profounder grasp of the political and

B

economic problems of our time, and a programme that is more concerned with the morals of political justice, than any other political movement. Socialism concerns itself materially with the equal distribution of wealth, an international world order, social revolution; culturally with freedom, justice and equality. Vague as these generalities may sound, the problem of translating them into actuality is the political problem of our time, and that of defining in imaginative terms their moral and cultural significance, indeed their significance as the form of life which is the centre of a better civilization, is a problem which several poets feel impelled to attempt.

Secondly, the poet is a human individual living amongst other individuals in a world of social injustices, threatened by tyranny and war. Of all evils, tyranny is the most destructive to his freedom of expression as a writer, his livelihood and even his life. Therefore his practical interests as an artist make him side with a world which is not threatened by war nor split in two by class differences.

But the poet is still primarily poet and not politician. The fact that poets happen to choose political subjects for their poems to-day is a comment on the life of our time, in which political issues have become so important, rather than on a change in the attitude of the poets themselves, who are certainly more inclined to be the critics of reality than the hidden legislators of mankind. It is true that occasionally a poet may decide that 'writing is no use to-day, what we want is action' etc. This attitude is, of course to misunderstand the nature of poetry altogether, and he who adopts it is more likely to be a politician for whom poetry is only the growing pains of a protracted adolescence, than a true poet. For poetry is concerned not with action but with the vital sources from which the necessity of action springs. When I say that modern poetry is political, I am not thinking of John Cornford giving up poetry in order to fight the fascists in Spain, but of the fact that the best poetry of our time, the outstanding poems of Thomas Hardy, the war poems of Wilfrid Owen, Eliot's *Waste Land*, much of Auden's poetry, is concerned with the individual faced by an unprecedented crisis in the history of civilization, and with far-reaching public calamities such as the Great War, the prospect of a greater war, and the crisis in the capitalist system.

Poetry which is not written in order to advance any particular set of political opinions may yet be profoundly political. Thus although Marxists would not agree with the consciously expressed beliefs of some of the poets whom I have mentioned, yet they would accept their interpretation in imaginative terms of the crisis taking place in the mind and soul of man. Only the poets, the Marxists and some psychologists have acted or written in a way which reveals a realistic understanding of the significance of the period of history through which we are living.

However much we admire the actions of a John Cornford or a Rupert Brooke, poetry is not the same as action and a poem is not the same as a political thesis. Political action is a short-cut by which the individual conforms to the particular shape which the political will assumes at a given moment—a strike, a war to save democracy. To be a poet is not to give out the propagandist word of order, nor even to re-state in an imaginitive idiom the materialist philosophy from which actions, seeming at times contradictory and opportunist, spring; it is to understand and interpret the need for justice and civilized values, from which the materialist philosophy and all the actions resulting from it are themselves a projection.

The political thesis translated into terms of poetry is, like the life of action, also a short cut if it enables the poet to accept at second hand what he can only know by his understanding and experience of life. By 'experience' I do not mean only action and participation I mean the ability of the artist to imagine and recreate life in an idiom which is unique to him and for that very reason entirely convincing to the audience which enters into his mind.

A great deal of Marxist poetry suffers from the fact that the poet has not been led on from Marxism to a profound imaginative understanding of the conditions in our actual environment which led Marx to write *Das Kapital*. Poetry, like science, does not dogmatically restate accepted theories, it always goes back to the evidence. Poetry differs from science not in its accuracy or the search for truth, but in the kind of truth with which it is concerned. Poetry states the conditions within which an emotion is valid. It is an account not of absolute truth nor of isolated truth, but of symptoms. The whole purpose of the poems is to create an environment, a mood within which that which is stated is true. Given the artifice, the prettiness, the falsity established by metre, imagery and language, the sentiments contained in 'Drink to me Only with Thine Eyes' are true—because they are so palpably artificial and even false. True poetry provides a moral measure of the emotions: in poetry the little is little, the great great, the sentimental sentimental, the passionate passionate in exactly the measure and degree to which we recognize these emotions to be valid: and the truth of the poem consists in the objectivity with which the poet—however deeply he may seem to be involved—is able to stand outside his own emotions and relate them to a larger view of life.

The opposite to poetic truth is not poetic untruth but bad poetry in which that which is stated—however true may be its prose meaning—is not conditioned by the poet in a mood which we can accept as valid. Marxist poets are particularly liable to this mistake because they have so much faith in the truth of Marxist doctrine that they tend simply to translate dialectics into a poetic idiom, convinced that in doing so they cannot stray from poetic truth. Unfortunately correctness or uncorrectness of opinions do not make a poem true or false: a theory of life in poetry only has value in so far as it intensifies or enlarges the vision of life contained within the poem. Marxism is supremely qualified to do this, but to imagine that the dialectic is the same as the view of life is like imagining that a lens is the same as that which one sees through it.

I take an example of what I suppose to be bad Marxist poetry from a poem in a recently published book by Rex Warner; (*Poems*, Boriswood, 5s., which also contains the excellent Marxist poem 'Nile Fishermen'). In the first two stanzas we get Warner's particular vision:

> 'What I watch most is moss
> or leaves in alleys of air,
> the rasping blade of grass.
> tiny berries on a huge moor;
>
> the sparkling black bill
> of stonechat on a spine,
> water tumbling from a pool,
> or a hawk in the sky alone.'

In the third stanza he turns away from his private vision and puts on his Marxist spectacles:

'But what most moves my mind
is torture of man by man;
how hearts in every land
are stamped upon like stone.'

Now this is a true statement firstly of much that is happening in the world, and secondly of Mr. Warner's own sincere feelings. Yet, as poetry, it is so inadequate that it immediately takes a lower place than the first two stanzas, in the world of poetic truth created by the writer. We feel that a way of looking at things, a theory, a habit of mind, have been translated into an idiom and substituted for the poet's unique and authentic experience.

'Sermons in stones' says Shakespeare. The trouble with most Left Wing poets is that they hear the sermons before seeing the stones, and then try to deduce the stones and their feelings about them, from what has been said. But what we want is a vision of the stones themselves; the stones, realized more deeply than our own mental habits, and re-created as a unique and individual experience.

In Marxist politics there are always two processes which become one process, the process of dialectics and the process of action. The part played by words in the revolution would seem to be on the one hand the extension of Marxist theory with its application to altering circumstances, on the other hand propaganda which is simply the verbal counterpart of mass action at any given moment. Recognizing this, some Marxist poets have assumed that poetry is merely a branch of propaganda, and we get notorious examples of it being put to this use, such as the poem by the Soviet poet laureate denouncing as sons of bitches the generals sentenced to death in a famous trial.

I do not agree that the right function of poetry in the revolution is propaganda, least of all popaganda of so crude a nature. The function of a political poetry is vividly to bring into our consciousness the origins in life from which political theory and action spring, and at the same time to face, on another plane of reality, the significance and implications of that which is being done. Now although propaganda may spring from a real necessity, that does not mean that it is realistic, any more than a lie becomes true because it is necessary.

It may be argued that the Marxist poet who had a complete grasp of all the issues involved would always be able to follow the 'party line', and even interpret party propaganda from day to day, because his valuable function would be to relate the necessity of the day and moment to the fundamental purpose of the political movement. Now even supposing that the party line of action were in fact always consistent with that Marxist interpretation of life which is indeed of great value to the poet, this still would not be true. For the poet is bound to condition what he feels, relating it to a whole view of life, he is not bound to feel all the implications of a whole view of life at any given moment. I repeat that he is not dealing with absolute truth or a dialectic, he is dealing with reality and establishing the significance of his emotional reactions to reality, by stating what are the conditions within which he experiences these emotions.

It is best to illustrate my argument with concrete examples of the poet's attitude towards reality, and no example could be better than war, where one sees political action in its most expressive form.

Now the poet may believe, as Wilfrid Owen and Siegfried Sassoon believed during the Great War, that his side is in the right, so far in the right even that he feels bound to fight for it. The attitude of the propagandist to the war which the poet supports is, of course, that everything should be done—by heroic propaganda for Our side, atrocity propaganda against the Other side, even by the pretence of 'not shirking realities'—to make war seem, in the last analysis, desirable: and perhaps necessity does indeed justify the lying propagandist, since he is entitled to feel that, by whatever means, the war must be won. The poet, however, is under an entirely different obligation to truth: he is bound to condition his direct responses towards his experience of war.

Wilfrid Owen was the greatest English war poet and he wrote some poems creating with great intensity the horror of war, and attacking all the lies of war propaganda. This does not mean that Owen stated the final truth about the Great War. He did not even pretend to see the War as a whole or from the viewpoint of a future historian. He had certain experiences and he did not lie about them. He stated the mood and mental environment within which they will go down to future ages as true. One of the lies which he opposed most resolutely was propaganda about War heroes. This does not mean that he denied there was heroism in war: on the contrary he writes in the Preface of his Poems that his book is 'not about heroes. English poetry is not yet fit to speak about them.' He adds 'All a poet can do to-day is to warn. That is why the true poets must be truthful.' Truthful to their own experience.

What Owen did oppose is the propagandist lie which makes the dead into heroes in order that others may imagine that death is really quite pleasant. If there is a heroism in war, it is not beautiful. It is too terrible for the propagandists to describe. And the poet who would attain the paradiso of the War heroes, must first of all pass through an inferno far worse even than that of Owen's fragmentary poems.

What Owen meant when he said that English poetry is not yet fit to speak of heroes becomes doubly clear if one considers the kind of poetry which endeavours to serve the purposes of heroic war propaganda.

> 'I rose from the bed of my wife's young body
> at the call of liberty.
> O feed with my blood our flag's red flame,
> Comrades, remember me.'

So sings Jack Lindsay, putting the sentiments into the mouth of a young militia lad in Barcelona.

Writing such as this may be effective recruiting propaganda but it is supremely untruthful as poetry. These lines are not bad because there are no conceivable conditions in which one man might experience the sensations they record, but because this man's case is represented as typical, so that the lines have the air of a generalization. Such writing is simply a record of hysteria which the poet shares with his audience and himself and does not see at all from the outside.

Such sentiments as Jack Lindsay expresses in these lines provoke the brutal comment: 'If that's what you think dying at the barricades is like, why not try it?'

War poetry which is an echo of war propaganda—for however just a cause; and none could be more just than that of the Valencia government to-day—has as much relation to the reality of war as the scraps of paper left on Hampstead Heath after Whit Monday have to the holiday itself. For most of those who participate in it, a war is simply a short way to a beastly death. Any heroic poetry which fails to take into account this elementary truth is simply an insult to the dead and a trap for the living.

Auden's poem *Spain* (Faber and Faber) falls into a very

different category. It succeeds because Auden limits himself to an almost theoretical, certainly a bird's eye view of the war, rigidly excluding the element of personal experience:

'On that arid square, that fragment nipped off from hot
Africa, soldered so crudely to inventive Europe;
      On that tableland scored by rivers,
Our thoughts have bodies; the menacing shapes of our fever

Are precise and alive. For the fears which made us respond
To the medicine ad. and the brochure of winter cruises
      Have become invading battalions;
And our faces, the institute face, the chain-store, the ruin

Are projecting their greed as the firing squad and the bomb.
Madrid is the heart. Our moments of tenderness blossom
      As the ambulance and the sandbag;
Our hours of friendship into a people's army.

Auden limits himself to this wide, objective view, with no comment on the struggle itself but only an account of what it is about.

If Auden deals only with that which is theoretical and not experienced, I in my poems on the Spanish war deal exclusively with that which is experienced:

'I have an appointment with a bullet
At seventeen hours less a split second
—And I shall not be late.

Where the sun strikes the rock and
The rock plants its shadowed foot
And the breeze distracts the grass and fern frond,

There, in the frond, the instant lurks
With its metal fang planned for my heart
When the finger tugs and the clock strikes.

I am that numeral which the sun regards,
The flat and severed second on which time looks,
My corpse a photograph taken by fate;

Where inch and instant cross, I shall remain
As faithful to the vanished moment's violence
As love fixed to one day in vain.

Only the world changes and time its tense
Against the creeping inches of whose moon
I launch my wooden continual present.

The grass will grow its summer beard and beams
Of light melt down the waxen slumber
Where soldiers lie dead in an iron dream;

My corpse be covered with the snow's December
And roots push through skin's silent drum
When the years and fields forget, but the whitened bones
        remember.'

A greater poetry of the Spanish war would be a synthesis of the theoretic approach, concerned with the ideas
for which men were fighting, with the approach of
experience, exploring the tragic and terrible results of
these ideas, the agony of individuals in the face of death,
the unreasoning brutality of a war. Heroism lies indeed
in this synthesis: and the heroes are those who without
forgetting the horrible reality, fulfil in their lives the idea
for which they are willing to die.

I have said earlier in this essay that poetry is the conditioning of emotional truth, a way of relating the poet's
feelings to objective reality. In the single poem the poet
explores the limitations of a single subject: in his life-
work he explores the limitations of his own soul. 'Greatness' in poetry is universality: the conditioning of that
which is true in the widest possible context and which

contains the greatest possible amount of what Henry James called 'felt life.'

Universality in poetry cannot be attained by a 'correct' attitude of mind. A comprehensive philosophy of life cannot be translated into poetry. The poet's greatness must spring from that which he has felt in life: knowledge is only an implement with which he approaches life, it is no substitute for life itself.

Indeed any set philosophy with which the poet approaches life presents many dangers: for it may be more comprehensive in its conclusions than the amount of life which he is capable of feeling: then he will import hunks of crudely transcribed philosophy into his poetry. Christianity inspired some of the greatest works of art in the world: but one has only to look at the hymnal to see how many writers were incapable of an imaginative grasp of the material of Christianity, although they imported hunks of Christian doctrine and legend into their work.

Marxism, because it presents the most comprehensive view of contemporary life, also sets the writer the most gigantic tasks for his imagination. It is possible that Communism will produce a St. John of the Cross. His task will be to experience imaginatively and to re-create the vast tracts of life documented with great genius and patient research by Marx in *Das Kapital*.

Theatre
by John Allen

THE Editors of FACT have asked me to write some notes on the relation of the theatre to politics. If, therefore, I write at what might seem disproportionate length on such subjects as the Unity Theatre Club and the Left Book Club Theatre Guild, it is not because I want to take this opportunity to advertise organizations with which I am in sympathy, but because we have theorized long enough upon the theatre. To-day we can do what a year ago would not have been possible—discuss this subject in concrete terms.

It is not necessary in such a paper as this to spend much space confuting the notion that you can't mix art and politics—though people still bleat out this fantastic piece of dogmatism at the end of a performance of *Waiting for Lefty* which defiantly and extremely successfully does mix art and politics. The idea that a play which is not constructed according to the canons of Aristotle is not a play, is a notion that dies hard. And the still common dogma that to show the working of economic laws in a play is to prostitute the art of the theatre is intolerable. The fact that the theatrical masterpieces of the past exist for us to-day as something hallowed called 'works of art', a phrase which is usually taken to mean the spectacle of the human soul in various crises, makes us forget that the plays of Aeschylus were once as topical and actual as a modern newspaper. Even the tragedies of Racine were dramatic versions of the love affairs of Louis XIV. The Third Symphony was an expression of Beethoven's ideas on democracy and Napoleon. Sheridan was a vigorous Hogarthian social satirist—see contemporary prints—and not a writer of pommaded comedies as he is represented to-day. The reason why any play even remotely connected with contemporary problems and events is labelled 'political' or 'propaganda' is because the capitalist theatre has become so removed from actuality that any sort of topical reference comes as a disturbing blow to the complacency of the middle classes who go to the theatre to be doped.

This domination of vague æsthetic hypotheses must be clearly realized so that it can be openly fought. It means that the socialist theatre must be as æsthetically convincing as the theatre it is trying to supplant; for nothing is more dangerous than to under-rate the power of one's opponents. There are many prejudices, difficulties and misconceptions binding the socialist theatre, but one of them is not that you must avoid plays that make people think. Socialists are aware of the great movements of their times, and they want to see those movements expressed in their theatre. Entertainment is not for them confined to drivelling comedies about fornication. They are entertained not by being side-tracked and doped, but by being instructed and enlightened.

The demand that exists for plays with definite political content is clearly shown in the rapid growth of the Unity Theatre Club. In January 1936 there was almost no theatrical activity among the British working classes at all, nothing that could be considered as a contribution to the political theatre beyond the sporadic and not very efficient efforts of a number of isolated groups. In May 1937, a working-class amateur group, the Unity Theatre Club, put on a show at one of the biggest West-end theatres, packed the house to capacity, and raised £125 for the cause (Spanish democracy) for which the show was presented.

The Unity Theatre Club has risen within a single year from an organization with no assets except a few actors with stout hearts and a vigorous but undeveloped talent, to one that has its own theatre and equipment and two well-trained companies. It has a membership of fifteen hundred, and seventy performances of *Waiting for Lefty* and thirty-five of *Where's that Bomb?* to its credit. The policy of the club has been uncompromising: vigorously to present plays which expose capitalism without attempting to disguise their purpose, and to take those plays to as wide an audience as possible. The fact that the Club has insisted on its plays being as rich in entertainment as it was possible to make them brings us to the first of the many difficulties the socialist theatre has to face.

Many people think that the humour of such a play as *Where's that Bomb?* is so broad and vigorous that it blunts the edge of its purpose, distracting attention from the fierce attack on capitalist misconceptions which is the play's real subject. Others do not agree: for whether you like it or not, it is the humour of *The Bomb* that draws people in such numbers to see it, and unless you succeed in getting people into your theatre, you thunder against capitalism in vain.

The position and function of the theatre as contrasted with that of a political meeting has been brilliantly expressed by Randall Swingler. He says: 'The validity of a play depends upon its ability to convince, not upon its purely intellectual argument, but upon its ability to be felt as true. . . . Anything said on or from the stage is only an expression of opinion with which it is always possible to disagree. . . . The force of drama lies in the fact that it must compel the spectator to undergo a process of experience whether he likes it or not. . . . All experience changes a man. . . . He may go away violently hating or disagreeing with the play, but if it was true, it has changed him, because he was emotionally implicated with the development of events on the stage.'

The political theatre, therefore, has to cater for two

kinds of audiences, the 'unconverted', for whose benefit the political message must be not sugared but humanized; and the already converted, the politically conscious, who require entertainment in their plays so long as it is not at the expense of a clear political line. The Unity Theatre Club, therefore, pursues a double policy: the presentation of full length plays with a broad, almost liberal content, in its theatre in King's Cross; and that of short plays, sketches, burlesques, and mass recitations, with a more definitely left-wing content at political meetings, socials, rallies, etc. Such performances serve the fourfold purpose of training the actors, spreading socialist ideas and opinions, taking plays to people who would never dream of buying a ticket for a theatre, and enlivening political meetings. The Unity Theatre Club has done an enormous amount of this kind of work, and the twofold activity I have described is being followed by groups all over England.

The formation of the Left Book Club Theatre Guild came just in time, and enabled a number of more or less isolated groups to be organized into a movement which is likely to gain, within the next few months, a national rather than a purely local importance. The situation in the theatre is ripe for a national organization of this kind, and the reason is interesting.

I have already spoken about the necessity of the left wing theatre being aesthetically convincing. The presentation of its plays must imperatively be of a very high artistic standard. This means big production expenses. But because such a theatre is appealing to a working class audience, the price of its seats must be as low as possible. This means the margin of profit will always be extremely small, and three successes will not be enough to make up for one failure. This is the situation that defeated Piscator and Brecht in Germany, and is now defeating some fine theatrical movements in America. Fortunately, the situation has been realized by the Unity Theatre Club early in its career, together with its solution. This is simply to get the organized support of the whole working class movement through already existing organizations, Trade Unions, Co-ops, and so on.

And even then the movement is liable to be frustrated by lack of plays. It is very difficult to find a formula for a play which will stimulate the left and convert the right. The magazine story treatment of a social theme is impossible. The melodramatic treatment Elmer Rice uses in *Judgment Day* is a fine experiment. The naturalistic treatment of such plays as *Peace on Earth*, *Tobacco Road*, and *Waiting for Lefty* is the least dangerous and the most direct of all possible methods.

A new formula has been used for Herbert Hodge, the London taxi-driver, in his two plays written specially for the Unity Theatre Club. Of these the first, *Where's that Bomb?* is a broad, pantomimic satire on capitalist propaganda. The hero, a worker-poet, is sacked because of a poem which has been printed in a socialist paper. He is at his wits end for money. One after another, the tallymen come round for their payments: and he is only saved by the representative of the British Patriots Union, who makes the proposal that he should write a romance to be printed on toilet paper, the lavatory being the only sanctum into which capitalist propaganda has not penetrated. Need drives him to accept and he sits down at his typewriter to earn his fifty pounds fee. In the second act, he has just finished and lies down on his bed and has a nightmare, in which Money Power appears and enacts his ghastly magazine story before his eyes. But even these pasteboard characters cannot bear the

c

lies put into their mouths. They revolt against Money Power and when morning comes with its tallymen and British Patriot, the hero tears up his story. 'I'm not the person to write novels for the lavatory,' he says. 'Get the journalists to. That's what they've been doing for years.'

Cannibal Carnival is a satire on capitalist imperialist exploitation, the adventures of a bishop, a bobby and a boss wrecked on a south sea island and bringing to the natives the blessing of European culture and business methods. These plays are political cartoons. They are drawn in strong, clean, simple lines. With one exception vice is painted very black and virtue very white. The exception is the character of Joe Dexter in *Where's that Bomb?* who has the most natural existence of any character in these two plays. In him, even Conservative-minded members of the audience can find sympathy, and from him they get an orientation on the attack on capitalism that follows. *Cannibal Carnival* presents more difficult problems, for there is no central character with which the audience can make contact, and characters drawn in flat, with the swift but passing existence of a cartoon, can be sustained for an act or even two, but in order to hold the stage for two and a half hours, must be given a realler and deeper existence. *Cannibal Carnival*, therefore, needs a more careful production than it is likely to have in any theatre except those under socialist control. For an exact degree of formalism and caricature must be achieved, *after* the play has been brought to life, and the actors have found the truth in the characters. The movement to-day among directors reacting against the slovenliness of the contemporary theatre, is to formalize everything, and we are given, time after time, degutted, castrated, formalized productions of Shakespeare's plays—the greatest *human* creations in literature. Guthrie's productions, for instance especially of the comedies, depend for their fun entirely on stage business; for he does not take his actors deeply enough into the lines to find there the deep humour of which Shakespeare is a master. So people look at *Cannibal Carnival* and say the production must be formalized. That is an easy escape. Anyone with half an ounce of sense of pattern can arrange a few stage pictures, but it is a very difficult thing to live deeply enough in a play, to make the form in which it is eventually cast so right that it cannot be viewed apart from the content of the play. And it is even more difficult to explain the need for this depth of understanding, even if the characters are caricatures, to other people.

The various forms of isolation from which most of the middle-class writers are suffering to-day leads them to join left-wing political parties and identify their work with institutions that have some sort of roots in the life of the people. Composers veer between jazz and folk music, dramatists plump, like Auden has done, for the music hall. But whereas to my mind Auden has almost no connection whatsoever with this marvellous product of English theatrical genius, the work of Herbert Hodge has a close affinity. And I can think of no two writers whose work is more dissimilar than these two. Auden's is introvert and twisted, Hodge's extrovert and robust, Auden's exclusive, a thing of a class, Hodge's popular, a thing of the people. I have asked a great many members of the Unity Theatre Club, who are all working class, what they think of Auden, and the answer has nearly always been a sort of pale praise. The majority prefer *The Dance of Death* to *The Dog beneath the Skin*, and most of those who went at all took the trouble to go twice. Rightly, I think, they do not attack Auden's exclusiveness, his eternal adolescence, his boy-scout-mother-love complexes, his irritating neuroses, his lack of anything positive or forthright, judging that if that's the way he feels about things, that's the way he should write. The feeling is simply that he is speaking another language, writing for another class. He is the author of the dissatisfied bourgeoisie. His perceptive pen clarifies their bewilderment and prejudices; and these sentiments have little interest for the positive fighting spirit of the militant working classes. *The Dog beneath the Skin* would mean nothing at all to the sort of audiences who go to the Islington Town Hall where *Waiting for Lefty* has an electrifying effect. And yet it would be wrong to give the impression that working-class actors and audiences require to be spoon-fed. One of the biggest successes and most popular pieces of the Unity Theatre Club is their production of Jack Lindsay's *On Guard for Spain,* a poem whose language is far from easy and which lasts nearly half an hour.

The future of the Socialist Theatre, therefore, depends upon its ability to solve two straightforward, but immensely difficult problems—how to get plays and how to organize an audience.

Fiction
by Arthur Calder-Marshall

IN the last two or three years, bourgeois critics have been reiterating the two following ideas. ' The English language, both spoken and written, is flat and insipid, compared with American.' 'The English scene is less exciting and less colourful than the American.' From this they deduce that England cannot compete with

America in everyday realistic literature: and they console themselves that English writers are still masters of the 'reflective' novel.

This attitude, conspicuously adopted by Cyril Connolly, and less conspicuously by others, becomes more remarkable the more it is examined. The writer is exonerated. Blame is distributed between the writer's material, the English scene, and his tools, the English language. 'Admittedly *Two Men about a Dog* by Neil Brogue is flat, flabby and incompetent,' the critic is saying. 'But what can Mr. Brogue do? He's only got English to write in, and England to write about.'

Absurd as these critical explanations are, an element of truth lies behind them. The American novel and short story is direct, self-certain and vigorous. Modern English fiction is uncertain and equivocal. What brilliance it has is that of stinking fish. Why is this?

It is not because the English spoken language is dead. The verbal deposition of John Edward Samuel, reprinted in this issue from the Report on the Gresford Colliery disaster, shows a command of language and vividness of description, similar to Hemingway or Dos Passos. This deposition is printed as it appeared in the report. If the reader will break it up into the short paragraphs necessary for clarity, the resemblance to American fiction will be even greater.

John Edward Samuel is not unique. The same qualities appear in verbal statements made to the police and in everyday conversation of workers.

This faculty has largely, but not entirely, disappeared from the middle class. Modern education and newspapers have made the middle classes articulate in the sense that they have set phrases coined ready for the set situations and thoughts that occur to them: but this very glibness has at the same time destroyed the originality that less articulate workers strike in the labour of thought. The worker takes his imagery from experience, the semi-articulate bourgeois from the phrase book.

Consequently, when literary critics lay blame on the English language, they should in fact be laying blame on the use to which the English middle classes put their language, the abstract and Latinised substitutes for plain speech—which are governed of course by innumerable social factors, such as the desire for euphemism, false social dignity and class conformity. And his conclusion should be not that there is no hope for English fiction, but that the hope lies in the alliance of writers with the working class and the recruitment of writers from that class.

The second proposition is equally untrue. It is not the English scene that is dull, it is the English bourgeois domestic scene that is overworked. The life of the middle class has been written up over and over again for the delectation of the middle class public which subscribes to lending libraries. And as if the life of the bourgeoisie were not in itself narrow enough, the middle class novelists usually confine themselves to the domestic and emotional scene: the bourgeosie in bed. The complex structure of our class society, its changing forms, its conflicts, its triumphs and inefficiencies, its struggle for justice against self-interest, its apparent chaos and illogical order are neglected, in order to pose the question Should Brenda bed with Harry or with Herbert?

Just as the middle class writer's use of language is governed by his isolation within his class: so his material is limited to his own experience within that narrow limit: and so the subject matter of his working hours springs from the preoccupations of his play.

The emphasis of bourgeois literature is on the individual, the judgements made are moral, that is from the point of view of the individual's good. Consequently the writer who is in a transition stage from capitalism to socialism may change his subject matter, without realizing that he must also change his judgments. A great deal that is written about the working class to-day is written in the bourgeois tradition. The writer is sincere, but he has not broken from the tradition that views sorrow, suffering and striving as individual. James Hanley, for example, whose story *Episode* is printed below, considers that the 'insult' is the true subject of his work. The 'insult' is also the subject of Leslie Halward's *On the Road*. This fixing on the 'insult' is very interesting. Though both Halward and Hanley are of working class origin, this attitude is taken over from the middle class tradition. The first, and least useful reaction that the bourgeois feels, when he sees the treatment of the working class by the governing class is a righteous indignation at the insulting attitude to the workers as human beings, the indignity alike of employment and unemployment relief. 'My God!' he thinks. 'I'd never stand for that.' And the appeal of his story, centred on the insult, will be to other members of the middle class. 'Are you going to stand by and see men and women, oppressed and humiliated in this way?'

Now this may galvanize the middle class into action— or it may not. But it's no sort of comfort to the oppressed and humiliated. 'You can cut that stuff out,' they say. 'We know how things are a sight better than you do. We don't want to be told we're exploited: we want to know how not to be exploited.'

For the bourgeois writer of fiction, this is a smack in the eye. The tragic tradition of the literature he knows and admires is pessimistic. It expresses dissatisfaction with things as they are, the moral and perhaps economic ruin of individuals under capitalism. To have a soul above material things, a spirit invincible by adversity, is about the only way out offered. And now the writer is called on to break this aesthetic tradition in order to give the hope that material evils can be cured by material remedies, to scrap the Christian virtue of resignation in favour of constructive discontent. He has to realize that neither he himself nor any of his characters is the centre of the universe: that the significant struggle is not that of the individual against an unfriendly world, but between the many, individually weak, and the few, individually strong. He has something new to say and the old forms devised for the acute analysis of individual character are not suitable for his purpose.

I have suggested elsewhere that the form that the novel concerned with society rather than individuals will take is likely to be the composite method, employed variously by Jules Romains in *Men of Good Will,* by Dos Passos in his trilogy or by Cantwell in his *Land of Plenty* (now reissued by Bell in a cheap edition at 2s. 6d). The difficulty which every novelist outside the U.S.S.R. encounters in this time of transition is that there is in truth no end to his novel, because the political situation has reached no climax.

But my present concern is not with the novel, but with the short story. The technical problems which the socialist short story writer must face are in some respects greater than those of the novelist. The short story has become concerned almost entirely with incidents in the lives of individuals or the study of single moods. Its brevity is difficult to adapt to social purposes and used injudiciously is very liable to become defeatist. Readers will recollect, for example, the high death rate of revolutionary leaders in socialist short stories.

In the present collection of short stories, *The Cobbler and the Machine* by Mulk Raj Anand shows one solution of the problem. Anand has taken a very simple story and made a fable, which is capable of being applied to a much wider context. The cobbler and his sewing machine is in small the story of all Indian workers drawn into contact with capitalist industrialism. Because it is concrete and particular, it is easier to understand than abstract generalization: and it is more convincing, because it deals in terms of human beings.

My own story, *I want my suitcase back*, is more reportage than fable. It provides a good example of the three methods of treatment I outlined above, the bourgeois, the would-be proletarian but still bourgeois, and the socialist.

Treated by a bourgeois short story writer, the climax of the story would be the death of Brodzki. His hopes, his fears, his ambitions and his first success would be built up and then smashed by the suitcase incident. Moral, the futility of life etc. Treated by a transitional 'realist,' the story would be taken as far as the funeral procession. Moral, life's tough and even when you get together, the authorities beat you up. Taken in its wider context, it becomes an incident in the political education of a group, not the end of protest, but the beginning of militancy.

No doubt there are other ways in which the form of short story can be adapted to the social subject. But at the present moment, the fable and the reportage form seem to be most favourable. The sketch will be found ineffective, because it is too fragmentary.

It is needless to say, that however correct a socialist

writer may be politically, his stories or his novels will be useless, unless he is a good writer. Socialist fiction is not jam to hide a propagandist pill. If story and propaganda are separable, a socialist story is as bad propaganda as it is literature. Just as Spender emphasises that the poet, I emphasize that the novelist and short story writer, must write not just from what he has learnt but from what he has experienced. Unless his work is the product of his full self, it will be as unsatisfying to others as it is to him. And he must know his craft, not only as well as the bourgeois writer knows his, but better, because he has new ground to break.

In writing of the problems of socialist fiction, I have confined myself to those which confront the author in a transitional society. The English society is so split, so various in tradition and circumstance, that questions arise which would never need to be posed in a post-revolutionary state. The very conditions favourable to a lasting literature, security and a common culture, are lacking. We have not yet achieved the certainty that is implicit in the humour of Zoschenko (*The Dictaphone comes to Soviet Russia*) or the comedy of *The Little Golden Calf*. English writers have been slow to abandon the liberal attitude of their predecessors. But the last few years have shown an ever quickening responsibility. The threat of Fascism has been more persuasive than the traditional poverty, with which capitalist society has always rewarded the artist. The ivory towers are draughty nowadays. It's warmer in the street.

Should Writers Keep to Their Art?
John Lehmann

from

Left Review, vol. 2, no. 16, 1937.

Reprinted by permission of the author and Lawrence and Wishart Limited.

Statement by John Lehmann July 1977
I would like readers of this article to know that I now disagree with many
of the arguments and sentiments expressed in this article.

Should Writers keep to their Art?

by JOHN LEHMANN

WHEN I was in Moscow in late October, the one theme that was talked about, thought about, and written about, eclipsing all others, was—Spain. This seemed to me effectively to dispose of the theory, recently so popular in articles and books about the Soviet Union, that the Russian Communists and the Russian masses were now only interested in their own internal affairs. An illogical theory, anyway, that a Socialist State could fail to show a vital concern in the strength of Socialism and the popular, democratic movement in other countries ; but here, at any rate, was a solid proof that it didn't apply to the U.S.S.R.

But what was more interesting to me, as a writer, was the part that Soviet writers were playing in this movement of opinion. Already, not only in Moscow, but all over the Union, as I was able later to verify in other Soviet towns, particularly Tiflis, meetings had been held by the writers, and with extraordinary rapidity anthologies about Spain and for the benefit of the Spanish funds had been published. I was luckily able to be present at the biggest public meeting held by the Union of Soviet Writers, on October 21st, in the Hall of Columns in Moscow. It was an imposing affair, with nearly all the well-known figures in the Moscow literary and artistic world present, as well as many other outstanding people, politicians and generals and scientists, in a packed hall. And, finally, there was the new Spanish Ambassador. Popular Soviet poets such as Bezimenski, Kirsanov, Nikulin, read, to the accompaniment of vigorous applause, poems they had written themselves on the Spanish struggle (where it was interesting to note again the very strong rhetorical trend of modern Soviet Russian poetry), or Russian translations of such Spanish revolutionary poets as Rafael Alberti. A company from the Vachtangov Theatre gave a reading of Ramon Sender's famous one-act play about the two revolutionary prisoners, and at the end the excellent newsreels of the fighting, which have been taken by special Soviet cameramen sent out to the Spanish Front, were shown. But the climax of the evening was when the little Spanish Ambassador, insecurely balancing himself on a couple of chairs, rose to speak : everyone jumped from their seats and rushed forward, and his first words were drowned in the tumult of cheering.

This meeting set me thinking more closely than before about the problem : how can writers use their particular prestige and gifts to the best advantage for the furthering of the anti-fascist cause, of the cause of peace? Writers can, it is true, abandon their trade and sacrifice themselves for their ideals, as Lauro de Bosis so heroically showed in Italy, or as Ludwig Renn is proving to-day in Spain. But how can they help through their own trade?

There is no doubt that the holding of such meetings and demonstrations as that arranged by the Union of Soviet Writers is one excellent way of helping, though it seems to me unlikely that the moral effect would be as great in this country as in the Soviet Union, where the relations between writers and the masses are remarkably close. But they can also do a great deal of useful work in other—literary—ways. They can, for instance, turn their energies for a while into public speaking and journalism, as Shelley and William Morris did at various points in their careers, and Barbusse and Romain Rolland in modern France ; they can become journalists, describing what they themselves have seen and heard, using all their powers to bring before the public, say, the sufferings and heroism on a particular revolutionary front ; they can also become journalists of theory and polemic—Maxim Gorki and André Malraux provide excellent examples of writers who have used their authority in this direction.

The value of such work should not be underestimated, and one can only admire writers who, in spite of established reputation and success, take up work that may well be uncongenial and will certainly be exacting and full of strain. But it seems to me—and it is a point that was left almost entirely untouched in the peace discussion of the Writers' Congress in London in June—they can do, as writers, something even more significant, and can help without going outside their own province of creative, imaginative work, without spending energies on work that perhaps others who can't write their poems or plays or novels can do as well. And this without even necessarily having had experience in special places and on special occasions. They need not, I believe, have been through the War, as Barbusse before he wrote *Le Feu*, or through the crisis of the Chinese Revolution, as Malraux before he wrote *La Condition Humaine*, to produce work which can have a powerful anti-war, anti-fascist effect.

It is true, I think, in the last instance, that the very greatest literature, the work of the profoundest and most sensitive artists, however politically indifferent they may be, will implicitly contain a condemnation of the system whose extreme sadistic symbols at the present moment are imperialist external war and Fascist internal war. This is a point, to take only two examples, which was admirably made in connection with Marcel Proust's work by Edmund Wilson, and in connection with the best of Henry James's work by Stephen Spender in his recent book *The Destructive Element*. The ' pattern in the carpet ' is, in such works of art, on the side of the struggle for a healthy society, on the side of humanity's advance, the more

clearly so the profounder they are ; and the artist may apprehend relationships whose scientific and philosophical exposition, say in the works of
Marx and Engels, he may dismiss or deny. If one is convinced of this
one must admit the soundness, even from a political point of view, of the
Soviet Union's present emphasis on the classics, not only its own, in
Pushkin and Tolstoi and Chekhov and Ostrovski, but in the whole of
world literature, and the absurdity of mutilating or completely censoring
them, as was attempted in the past, in the alleged interest of the revolution.

But at the same time, though there may be unknown authors writing
now who in their personal lives do not come anywhere near the popular
movement, and whose works may nevertheless in time to come be very
highly prized by a peaceful and non-capitalist society, those imaginative
writers who have reached a clear decision that they should assist this
popular, anti-fascist movement (the reasons for which have recently
been persuasively developed in the LEFT REVIEW by Cecil Day Lewis
and Stephen Spender) can, as I see it, without any harm to their art, both
more consciously direct it in theme and detail, and also more clearly
inform themselves, and therefore eventually their work, of the whole
complex of facts and theories that make up the problem of Fascism, war,
and the social revolution. I do not by this mean that I think they should
become expert Marxists before attempting to write any more, but I do
think that the more they study the analysis of history and society made by
Marxist thinkers, the firmer the thought structure of their work is likely to
be. In the *Border Line*, to take a contemporary example, it is clear that
Edward Upward is a very close student of Marxism, though people
knowing little of Marxism might never notice it while thoroughly enjoying
the story ; the whole episode (published in No. 1 of *New Writing*) must,
to my mind, be considered as a kind of Marxian metaphor. Here Marxism
is implicit and assimilated, though conscious ; in Auden's *The Dance of
Death*, a poetic Marxian allegory, it is explicit. But it seems to me that
without being so explicitly Marxist as Auden, and without following
Marxian analysis as closely as Upward, a novel or play that is informed
by a general comprehension of the Marxist's map of the world (it is
superfluous to say that this can only happen when the artist accepts it as
convincing) is bound to have a propaganda effect, against Fascism and
against imperialist war, on the minds of its readers. There are many
examples of such stories and novels in contemporary literature ; I would
suggest as one that I personally find amazingly successful, Christopher
Isherwood's *The Nowaks*. And this example brings me back to the
question of theme. It is clear that to write *The Nowaks* it was necessary to
have a special knowledge of Berlin proletarian life, just as to write *The
Olive Field* it was necessary for Ralph Bates to know Spain and its people
intimately. Such experience can provide an author with great imaginative
stimulus as well as providing a rich storehouse of material ; but an author

with a far more limited field of experience can nevertheless direct his imagination, at times when the struggle is as acute as it is at the moment, to whatever within the orbit of his experience is most clearly connected with it. And a good author, with only this minimum restriction of subject, will be showing wherever he touches society or individual psychology how the present system leads to war and Fascism, just as Shakespeare shows how Macbeth, by an ineluctable train of circumstances once his first step is taken, turns from an ambitious and imaginative, but essentially good man, into a ruthless, massacring tyrant.

The case of the lyric poem is clearly a little different from the case of the novel, play or story, because a lyric is far more often a direct expression of opinion in the writer's person than the novel, and is expected to be so ; the test has always been whether the opinion is felt imaginatively as well as thought. But a poet can write as ' objectively ' as Keats in his *Ode to Autumn* and yet be making profound propaganda for his own view of life. It is, in fact, because I believe that if a writer's imaginative and artistic powers are really first class the propaganda he thus makes will in the end be far more valuable than any other kind of propaganda he could make as a journalist or ' committee-man,' that I also believe he should never engage in any other activity, for the cause of peace and liberty he is supporting, to the extent of abandoning, or seriously curtailing for any length of time, his activity as an imaginative creator.

Poetry and Politics
C.H. Salter

from

Poetry Review, 30, 1939.

Reprinted by permission of the National Poetry Centre.

POETRY AND POLITICS[1]

" O qu'heureux sont ceux qui avec une liberté entière et une pente invincible de leur volonté aiment parfaitement et librement ce qu'ils sont obligés d'aimer nécessairement." (PASCAL.)
" This class struggle plays hell with your poetry."
(JOHN REED.)

MOST people have the wrong idea of poetry. Addicted as they are to that kind which is called classical, they still contrive to forget the revolutionary passion of Swinburne, the avowedly didactic intentions of Vergil ; and in reading Vergil or Swinburne their critical spirit sleeps, and they bring to the operation a friendliness they deny to their own contemporaries. Yet they are partly right. Not all post-war revolutionaries have sufficiently perceived the dangers of a too close alliance between the metrical expression of their thought and the new creeds which have coloured all the background of that thought. The red of revolution can be as offensive as the very red-tape it sets out to destroy. Somewhere between the two extremist views a decision must be taken, for unless we continually realize what sort of poetry theory allows we cannot condemn what we dislike. Without this *prejudice* it is impossible to be fair.

There appear to be two senses in which a poet can deliver himself over to politics. He can in a crisis allow his knowledge of effective rhythm to be used for the formation of slogans and the writing of political satire, and in other ways suspend his activity as a " pure " poet on the plea of emergency, a doubtful plea since there will always be found persons to deny that a state of emergency exists, and in any case it is not by losing his own ideals that a poet will salvage a ship wrecked by the general neglect of ideals. Or he can write " pure " poetry susceptible of political interpretation. The alternatives correspond in their own sphere to the difference between politics itself and political causes : the former is partly contained in the latter. The latter is on the right lines, the former is not.

[1] The Chancellor's Prize Essay at Oxford, 1939.

Of the former kind of poetry plenty is being written in Germany to-day, too external indeed to be anything but the rhetoric of indignation, but seemingly imbibed straight from the feeding-bottle of the new Nazi Great Mother— mother or midwife, it makes no odds. Listen to this :

> Wir Narren sind wie einsam angetreten :
> Grell schwirrte Hohn auf, gellte Schimf und Scherz,
> Wir aber glaubten. Denn da half kein Beten.
> Wir wussten nur : in uns schlug Deutschlands Herz.[1]

Narren indeed ! and this of Friedrich Ekkehard, in all the nakedness of translation :

> You who died on the ninth of November,
> You dead, we swear it to you
> That there are still many thousand fighters,
> For the third, the United German Reich.

or this charming fable of Hitler and the Little Mice who disturbed his rest :

> Fortan vergisst er sicher keinen Abend
> Der Mäuslein und bedenkt mit Brot sie labend . . .
> Und Adolf Hitler blickt herzfröhlich nieder
> Auf seine Gäste und lernt lächeln wieder.
> Jetzt braucht er mehr als nur ein Häuschen,
> Denn wir sind alle seine Mäuschen.[2]

The attitude to art in the Fascist countries is certainly incorrect. But, thank God ! it is also ridiculous, not a serious menace.

> . . . Die Kunst ist lang,
> Und kurz ist unser Leben . . .

When Hitler and Mussolini are dead, when d'Annunzio and Binding have benefited from the kindly shortness of the memory of man, all those nameless refugees, from whom is mercifully withheld a celebrity which would only single them out for destruction, will attain the praise they deserve. They will not have been without suffering. Uncertainty of publication, the absence of an audience, misrepresentation, often bodily fear are conditions which at once wither their own sympathies and by their very difference from the normal conditions of existence divide them from the understanding even of those who wish to understand them. But they will at least have no doubts of themselves. A more complicated position obtains in Russia, demonstrating this fact above all, that we cannot consider as separate (though they are distinct) the questions of the political content permissible in a poem and of the manner of reaction of poets to the different political systems. The duty of a poet to his community is conditioned by the attitude of the community to its poet. But the present uneasy alliance between them in Russia envisages wrong definitions of both, and in so far as it has spread to this country, where artistic fashions are comparatively unbridled, will soon be dissolved.

In itself poetry is not subject to human conditions. The essence of it is preoccupied with itself, like the phoenix. But the poetic gift being situated in man suffers, even leaving out of account the destinations intended for particular poems, if it is divorced from the materials in which it resides. These materials are the stuff of human life. Thus *prima facie* politically didactic poetry appears unobjectionable. Difficulties only arise in determining the degree to which poetry may be or must be political. Little help is to be had from modern criticasters and poet-critics : they are for the most part incoherent theorisers, and as ignorant of opposition as they are incapable of discussion. All that they are able to say is that

> propaganda verse is to be condemned when the didactic is achieved at the expense of the poetic.[3]

But there is much more to be said ; as for instance that although the limitation implied by the practical subjection of art to human conditions is a source of strength, the strength does not accrue through the obedient acceptance of the limitation so much as by overcoming it. It was the difficulty of overcoming the limitation caused by the curious shape of their pediments and of composing sculptural groups to lie inside them which forced the ancient Greeks in the earliest period of classical culture to meet the whole problem of composition in sculpture and to solve it finally. Remove the actual pediments of Aegina or of the Parthenon, you condemn the sculptures to a wholly undesirable liberty. But to reason from this that the frame is the mistress of the picture is like saying that because the steel girders of the Bodleian extension will never be taken away, the building should never have proceeded beyond their erection.

In the wider sense of politics synonymous with human life as a whole, and consequently an admirable element in poetry, Aeschylus, Euripides and Shakespeare were all political poets. But the discipline they therefore underwent (especially the two Greek poets) did not mean so much as it necessarily does in modern England. Since the speed with which successive sections of the English community received the vote began to outstrip their own leisurely attempts to fit themselves for voting, politics has ceased to be anything more than an ignorant superstition to the majority of them. Their conception of Neville Chamberlain is of a man with an umbrella, exactly as their idea of Lord Baldwin used to be limited to his pipe. This pigeon-holeing of politics could not but have its effect on the poets. But in Greece politics really did mean what went on in the city. Hence such (to us) highly controversial utterances as

$$\text{ἀλλ' ὃν πόλις στήσειε, τοῦδε χρὴ κλύειν}$$
$$\text{καὶ σμικρὰ καὶ δίκαια καὶ τἀνάντια }[4]$$

assumed for the Greeks the character of something much nearer the personal than political theory, partly because such remarks had all the weight of the established religion behind them. Greek Tragedy is concerned to generalize : Shakespeare on the other hand is mainly interested in the effect of anything, even public movements, on the individual sufferer ; and for politics he at least always uses a kind of symbolism. (Lear is the exception which proves both these rules.) The argument for the general view finds perfect expression in Cassandra's line καὶ τοῦτ' ἐκείνων μᾶλλον οἰκτείρω πόλυ [5] but this view is neither in itself necessarily greater nor necessarily precluded from co-existing with its opposite. In *Richard II*, if we choose to seek a solution for our troubles respecting the theory of the divine right of kings, we shall find one. But it is there worked out in the guise of a personal conflict, and may be neglected if the characters themselves are correctly apprehended. No exception need be made for the occasional direct pronouncements on political matters found in Shakespeare and Greek Tragedy alike : on the contrary, it is only in the light of this theory that they can be understood. The truistic character of such utterances in Aeschylus, Sophocles and Euripides has long been criticized, as has also the banality of those speeches in Shakespeare which defend loyalty, good government, integrity and similar obviously excellent things. The reason is, no part of the audience must be antagonised. The reader of Shakespeare never feels himself cut off from the enjoyment of a phrase because his political colour is not that of the poet. The most hardened aristocracy must be moved by the condition of the mob in *Coriolanus*. The greatness of Julius Caesar does not escape even the most excitable proletarian. Yet it is well to remember that only five years ago a production of *Coriolanus* in Paris was stopped by the government because it was too " actual," just as Shakespeare's own company were prevented from reviving *Richard II*. To go outside our own literature, for ten years La Fontaine was kept out of the French Academy by rivals who drew attention to his supposedly progressive views : whatever their sincerity, the temporary success of their action points clearly to a tendency, even in an age when the majority of mankind was not politically conscious (indeed there has never been an age when it was), to assign to each individual, poet or no, his party pigeon-hole. The misunderstanding must have been there, or the argument based on it would have failed. Aristophanes used the same argument, based on the same misunderstanding, against Euripides ; and in this respect he misrepresents the poet exactly as he misrepresents the philosopher Socrates. It is a dangerous method, and not even usually accurate. After all Euripides, who regarded his rôle of poet quite definitely as a public office like that of the Priest of Dionysus, came nevertheless at last to the conclusion that politics were not his *métier*.

The misunderstanding would never have arisen if people did not generally exaggerate the intellectual content of poetry. They do not for the most part realize that this is what they are doing, and would probably deny it if so accused, but the fact comes to light incessantly, in the very-nice-but-what-does-it-mean school of criticism, the prosaic objections to poetic figures of speech, and a thousand chance remarks. By virtue of this superstition, though the statesman, it is acknowledged, has rarely been anything but a very lame poet (dear Gladstone, alas! was no exception), the poet is commonly and erroneously imagined as a sort of super-glamorous statesman. The error is repeated in Browning's poem " I only know one poet in my life," where he says of this symbolical personage " He was the town's true master, if the town but knew."

> We had among us not so much a spy
> As a recording chief inquisitor.

Yet if, as will be seen later, the poetic method is above much of the dirty work of practical life, it is equally at once insufficient for and, in its apparent sufficiency, prejudicial to the proper statement of any problem of the mind.

> Disguised as an angel of counsel it will lead the human soul astray on false mythical paths.[6]

To what end did prose come into existence, if not for man's moments of idealism? Even Milton, who wrote of

> . . . hogs
> Who bawl for freedom in their senseless mood
> And still revolt when truth would set them free,

descended to prose for his polemics proper, and made his verse simply a comment on them, not a statement of them. But prose is not popular in the twentieth century. I believe this is the first age, and I hope it is the last, when the proverbial poverty of poets has even denied them the luxury of a prose style. Poetry puts a man into a passive state where he is no longer able to make the clear judgments which theorizing demands. Indeed, the poet himself, recollecting his emotion in order to compose it, is seldom tranquil enough to avoid the pitfalls of this same state of passivity. Yeats did not avoid them, and they produced in him both the irritating strain of political dogma which invalidates so much of his work, and an entirely uneducated emphasis on the importance of race, which is curiously praised by at least one of his chief mourners.[7] Euripides did not avoid them, when he concentrated on showing that the humble characters in his dramas were as honest and human as the kings and princes ; not realizing that play-wrights choose princes and kings rather than simple shepherds for their protagonists merely because they bring with them an heightened sense of reality which οἱ βάναυσοι would not bring.

If the poet is not a clear thinker, he cannot be a leader of thought. " Ideas," wrote Mr. Day Lewis, " are not material for the poetic mind till they have become com-monplaces for the practical mind." Without understand-ing this we cannot understand the function of political satire. Satire as a *genre* can only criticize vices already known and hated. It is indeed utterly impotent of pointing the way to any kind of reform, because its statements are enforced by a kind of joke, and a joke must always depend on recognizable attributes. Satire attains its effect through a narrow circle of prejudices among its audience—worth-less, conservative, nationalist prejudices. Also, it must always be very appropriate, making the obvious criticism. Thus a rich man must be made out to be miserly, a poor man extravagant ; a humpback fancies himself as a lady-killer, a duchess marries a dustman. The absence of any quantity of modern satire in the sense in which Dryden and Pope were satirists is remarkable in view of post-war conditions, and has been variously explained. Perhaps the truth is that satire as I have described it demands a measure of contentment, a measure of communion between the satirist and the spirit of his age. After the war there was simply nothing to which he could give his allegiance or approval : no possible standpoint or angle of vision was supplied to him naturally from the situation itself. Every satirist is by a nature a *laudator temporis acti* : here past time was as unattractive as present, or in so far as it did contain elements deserving praise, irrevocable, possessing no reme-dies for present discontent. Between them the two founders of satire, Persius and Juvenal, exemplify all its rules : Persius, the failure, because he was too immersed in the beauty of a very dead past ; and Juvenal, the success, because while looking back to the past (in his case an imaginary past) he did not expect too much from his contemporaries. The habit of retrospection is not confined to satirists. *A propos* of *Coriolanus* M. André Suarès wrote :

Tous les grands poètes, sans aucune exception, si ce n'est au dix-neuvième siècle, ont été réactionnaires, comme on dit, également ennemis des tribuns et des pédants. C'est un fait, et on n'y peut rien. Les textes sont là, d'Homère à Baudelaire, de la Genèse à Goethe, d'Aristophane à Cervantes et d'Eschyle à Shakespeare.[8]

Where satire was written it was utterly unhelpful, like Mr. Roy Campbell's *Georgiad*. There have also been isolated attempts at purely political satire the failure of which is mostly due to the prosaic manner of their approach. Whatever is doubtful, there must be general agreement that the word " Czechoslovakia " does not fit well into a poem. The most extensive abolition of poetic diction, the most consistent application of the principle that nothing is absolutely beautiful or ugly, cannot overcome the sense or sound discords which certain words contain in themselves. Also, connotations are inescapable, and in the case of political words these are often unmanageably large and vague. Sagittarius in the *New Statesman and Nation* writes plenty of this kind of verse. In so far as he can be said to have thought out his intentions at all he is moving in the direction of satire, almost of satire in the Roman sense ; a conception implemented by his freer use of other metres beside the heroic couplet, which enable him to produce occasionally what can only be called an uneasy parody of serious patriotic verse. The best of Sagittarius comes out in such lines as :

> Democracy need not despond
> While Britain's word is still as good
> As Hitler's bond.

This spirit of parody was part of the stock in trade of Juvenal. The satiric method was in any case too leisurely for Messrs. Auden and Spender and their school. Accordingly they took the violent step of a complete break with tradition, and they did it with a curiously fierce joy. It cannot be too strongly emphasized that their action was deliberate, conscious and artificial. They disregarded the wise warning of Mr. T. S. Eliot,[9] and made in the twinkling of an eye a voluntary sacrifice of all human experience, denying themselves the numerous advantages of an audience prepared in a certain tradition by the literature of the past, and preferring to begin again from the very beginning. I do not mean that they are without influences : on the contrary, the borrowing is often crude, even in the Latin sense of undigested. But they desire to do what has never been done before. They use the word Revolution, with ecstasy, about their own trade, and seem totally unaware of the grim and barbarous connotations of the metaphor. If it were possible it would clearly be valuable to make such a statement of their position as would turn back into the main stream of poetic tradition these who have robbed, as well as burst, its banks. It should be possible, for they are already beginning to come back of their own accord, and we, who have no vomit to return to, may carry the process further. But what are we to think of the fact that they did not turn to Russia until the European slump ; or of their subsequent disposition, since the revival (through no fault of theirs) of comparatively comfortable economic conditions, to acquiesce in the very system they before desired so violently to change ; returning like Alpheus, as soon as the dread voice was past ? Equally, what are we to think of their noisy criticisms of the present order, which still sound in our ears ? Have they not degraded poetry in a way that makes the degradation of it laid at the door of Euripides seem positively ennobling ; inasmuch as they gladly labelled themselves writers of propaganda, branded themselves voluntarily with the stigma of escapism, which is indelible ? Yet their single error was the common one of poets, that they jumped to conclusions.

If we ask, whether post-war conditions, which are claimed to have invalidated the neutral poets, are really so specially urgent, most people's answer would be either a categorical Yes or a categorical No. There are but two alternative cure-all theories on the subject, and both deny the possibility

B

of a third existing. It must be difficult to decide between two such intransigeant beliefs as hold the field, beliefs which earn the name not so much because they have faith in the past as because they blindly trust the future (credulous beliefs, to be sure !) ; and, in the case of that one which answers Yes to our question, an analogous easier examination is provided by the formal aspects of its poetry. There was some excuse for the ridiculous caperings of those Georgian poets who abolished form altogether and wrote in *vers libre*. They were at least consistent. But the socialists do not disapprove of formalism, so long apparently as it is not too formal. They will rhyme " heart " and " coat," but not " heart " and " art " : one may be forgiven for asking which in fact rhyme : they are quite content to retain five stresses in a line, provided the unstressed syllables number more than five. All this is, or should be, to make them more intelligible to the masses, because the classical syllabically quantitive verse has become divorced from the common rhythm of speech. It certainly has not had that effect of increasing intelligibility. This is not of course to doubt the value of this kind of socialist poetry : it is indeed a sort of poetry which gives the well educated man a new respect for his education, without which he could never have traced the connection of it as far as he does. But it certainly does not cause him to lose confidence in himself, as it theoretically should. It is certainly not a poetry which is sung upon the housetops by the hungry proletariat. It is not the poetry of the Internationale. On the contrary, when it is understood, its effect is to provide a sufficient outlet for discontent in itself :

> And enterprises of great pitch and moment
> By this regard their currents turn awry
> And lose the name of action.

Once more, *La Révolution est fichue*. This could not happen if the real culture of England were not still that of its most cultivated age, the Victorian age, if Auden and not Tennyson were its spiritual dictator. It is true that the Victorian age did not feel certain social problems as acutely as we do, but this is not to say they are unprecedented. The age of

Shelley knew them : yet Shelley did not find conventional metre unsuited to his romantic and revolutionary verse. I mention this to refute the notion that to be romantic and revolutionary it is necessary to be incomprehensible ; which might seem to some people an argument against revolution and romance.

As with form, so with content.   The socialist poets are very ready to speak to the programme of Marxian ortho-doxy, claiming they need no longer feel a situation in all its details before composing it, or produce something which will be valuable when the ephemeral struggle is over. What right have they to feel exempted from the general laws of poetry ?   Was there no oppression before 1918 (or to be more precise 1931, when they decided to recognize it) ?   No economic disorder, Zeitgeist, discontent ?   On the contrary, they may if they wish call to their defence all the authority of the name of Wordsworth, the weighty authority of such lines as " Clarkson ! it was an obstinate hill to climb " (the hill was the traffic in slaves), or " Call not the royal Swede unfortunate " (the royal Swede is King Gustave of Sweden), or again " Ah ! where is Palafox?" (where indeed ?), or lastly, to take a more significant example still :

> Here pause : the poet claims at least this praise
> That virtuous liberty hath been the scope
> Of his pure song.

This shows Wordsworth already on the defensive, assailed by Doubts as to the Value of his Poems Dedicated to National Independence and Liberty, and making the excuse that his standpoint is outside and above all party feeling. It also shows in what direction the socialist poets are leading us—to " pure song " of which " virtuous liberty " is to be the scope.

If then there is no novelty in oppression (though of course the proletarian poet puts Wordsworth, after Wool-worth, on his roll of Enemies of the Revolution) is it perhaps nevertheless more comforting to the sad commun-ist to have his sorrows treated as merely part of the general *Weltschmerz*, and not even be paid the compliment of

personal consideration ? That is one of the many alternative theories that have sprung up to explain the unnecessary
phenomenon : there are others, as varied and as disingenuous
as the official justifications for the rape of Czechoslovakia :
as for instance, that the muddle is only temporary, and business will soon be as usual (then why ever shut up shop ?) ;
or that in a socialist poet the man is responsible for the
political preaching, the poet for the poetry (in which case it
seems unfortunate the poet and the man are on speaking
terms) ; or even that any poet would be well advised to
dress up his poems in such a way that they may appeal to
the politically-conscious (the exact opposite of the classical
method, taking public symbols for the personal instead of
personal for the public), because the politically-conscious
are the only confessedly intellectual class in existence to-day :
surely this last is plain prostitution. Besides, politics
does not bulk so large in anybody's thoughts as is thus made
out. Interest in it has certainly grown, but most intelligent poets will continue to save their intelligence for a
better purpose than trying to give rhythmical expression
to things which are not in themselves rhythmical ; or, if
they are, it is with the rhythm of the dynamo, not with that
of returning seasons and the rotation of crops. The liberation from tyranny of a million nameless serfs is less to us
than the judicial acquittal of one friend. The fine ideas
of Socialism are the common stuff of patriotism and life in
general, and were before Marx was born. What is new
is all details ; and could anything be more wrong-headed
and insincere than to choose to be concerned with formal
justice, rather than with the actual justice to which it is a
prosaic approximation ; or to call a slag-heap our Parnassus,
our Pierian stream the sweat which drips from the forehead
of the unsuccessful Bolshevik artisan ? It is difficult to
avoid the conclusion that the poets who skip with such
alacrity to fresh woods and pastures new have broken with
the past simply in order to avoid unequal comparison with
the past. In any case they would not have earned the
approval of the divine Lenin himself; who, so far from
despising *bourgeois* art testified repeatedly to the emotion

aroused in him by the music of Beethoven and the acting of Sarah Bernhardt.

This worship of things Russian, the *Drang nach Osten* of poetry, is as curious a phenomenon as the poetry it produces. Art is surely the weak point of socialism, as it certainly is of most socialists. They leave it outside their comfortable cosmology, as something merely embarrassing. They give artists the status of artisans, and this is supposed to solve the great question of their isolation in *bourgeois* communities. But the articles they produce cannot be brought down to the same status. Every garment woven on the same factory-loom is identical in all respects, but the august creations of the human mind cannot be mass-made. It is not sufficient in Russian for all poems to be as like as two peas, for every pea is unique : they must be as like as two pins. Yet, supposing the discipline of communism were benevolent, even with the orthodox the value of the individual decision to accept it and unite voluntarily with the will of the majority is lost if the individual is aware that his work will not be published unless it exhibits this unity of will. Christ, it will be remembered, did not make the mistake of converting by miracles. The heretics (that is, all bad socialists, and all good socialists who are also good poets but not good socialist poets) are of course in worse case. After all, it is the least objectionable feature of totalitarian states that they suppress complete liberty, which is licence ; or even that they suppress intellectual liberty—indeed the antithesis is unreal. Each recognition of joy and sorrow supplies an inner compulsion. We may even admit that an inspiring idea has been put before us by those states. What is objectionable, especially to the heretic, is that the idea has become an ideal, and is thus on its own level both too narrow for and inappropriate to anything so real (in jargon, so realist) as poetry. Yessenin wrote

> I accept all—just as it is I take it,
> I am ready to travel the newly broken road.
> I give my whole soul to October and May.
> Only my loved lyre will I not give.[10]

which to the ordinary Marxist must be simply incomprehensible, for dialectic materialism allows nothing to be more real than a *risorgimento*. The dilemma of Yessenin arises most acutely in poetry which unlike music and painting must always be in a certain degree explicit. Even in music and painting it is felt. True, Richard Strauss continues popular in Germany although the lesson of his music, properly understood, would be ceaselessly undermining the foundations of the Third Reich. But Shostakovitch was disgraced in Russia for writing *bourgeois* music. But in poetry the difficulty of holding the balance between the state and the individual has far more serious consequences. Yessenin hanged himself, with boxcord, and Kutznetzov died by his own hand in the midst of joyfully celebrating his country's factories. Even Maiakovsky committed suicide, though his final theory of poetry was as Marxist as it was unsound, if we may believe the following passage :

The poet is not he who goes around like a curly lamb and bleats on lyric love themes, but the poet is he who in our ruthless class struggle turns over his pen into the arsenal of weapons of the proletariat, who is not afraid of any dirty work, any theme about revolution, about the building of a people's industry, and will write agitation pieces on any economic question.

Maiakovsky, Kutznetzov, Yessenin : these three at least cannot be accused of indifference to the revolution. But indeed we are none of us indifferent, and the communist has no right to call us so because we do not choose to play his game. We have all grown up in the same atmosphere of tension, with wars and the rumours of war moving nearer like Tarquin in the dark. What wonder if we feel a greater attraction than ever to the " lyric love themes " which also with less cause pleased our serener ancestors ?

Maiakovsky's death is especially interesting. He had not always been an orthodox communist, but tried at first to follow his own brand of communism, with his poetry as his election agent. He thus committed the great sin of letting his personality interfere with his poetry, and in revenge the poet interfered with the man ; for had he not been a poet, he would not have felt it impossible to go on living. He does not deserve the extravagant sympathy which has been heaped upon him.   Yet in a sense the man always must interfere with the poet, for the poet transmits what the man receives.   But the very effect of this process depends on the extent to which the two are dissociated. Paradoxically, Maiakovsky erred in the same sort of way as the Auden-Spender school : he misunderstood the meaning of the theory that " the artist's whole personality must co-operate," which really demands the acceptance of discipline and a quality almost as ascetism.   He never accepted this discipline, the discipline of fidelity which it is necessary to accept, and his acceptance, finally, of the discipline of Marxism, to which the same awful authority does not attach, was what killed him.   There are, I suppose, three component forces in the poet : human, personal, and poetic. It is the human force which is influenced by the " maelstrom of the modern panorama," the " current of contemporary consciousness " or what you will.   It is the personal force which is bound up with the poetic, not disastrously as in the vanity of Maiakovsky but by a quite humble use of its own uniqueness, to which the poetic force supplies a counterpoint, or rather descant, of conformity.

The socialist experiment is one of many since Aristophanes to make the poet a good citizen : they have all failed.   When Aristophanes spoke with approval of the idea that children should be instructed by poets, he chose poets because they of all classes of men would, he knew, be able to see furthest beyond the narrow ideal of citizenship, not because they would best be able to interpret it.   Just for this reason Plato would lead all poets outside his ideal city and leave them to live at its gates.   It is not easy to envisage a closer relationship than this Platonic one : one cannot worship what the world generally neglects without a little neglecting what the world worships.   This is not to advocate a new kind of civil justice for artists, a sort of absolution from the normal law by which one has only to have had a picture hung in the Royal Academy to claim exemption from income-tax ; or as though it were to be permissible to cut the throat of one's mistress so soon as one had written an ode to her eyebrows.   Artists frequently do demand a similar exemption in case of bigamy, neglect of children or breach of contract; and the common opinion allows the "artistic temperament" excesses in less irrevocable misdemeanours, such as drinking and smoking, which it would not grant to the "respectable" man. But the more excellent artist does not make these demands.

If, however, we were to consider his feelings, would not the condition of society called an educated plutocracy (which is more or less what we live in) suit him as well as any, providing him at least with the necessary peace of mind, a measure of appreciation, and even bread? Those who object to the system of patronage because it "clips the wings of buoyant Pegasus" forget that this also occurs (and they probably glory in it) under other forms of government. If patron there must be, it is probably better to serve a personal patron, who has some intention of remembering the *sportula* of his client. Or if the contrary imputation be made, that an educated plutocracy takes too little account of its artists, it is difficult to see how official recognition can be more than farce. The poet's relation to the state may be very negative; but his feeling for his patron need not be insincere. It was, when Chaucer dedicated a poem to Richard II; and Wordsworth's dedication to George IV was in the circumstances still more absurd. But Tennyson at least did genuinely believe in a great deal that Queen Victoria believed in. In *Timon of Athens* a philosopher taxes a poet with deceit in his professions of admiration for his patron: the reply is in effect, that there is no deceit, the poet really does admire his patron. Even with the state the poet can have other relations than that of communism. In the past, even in England, especially in the eighteenth century, there was a very definite co-operation between art and government. It really did seem to be relevant when Canning rose in the House of Commons and belittled Napoleon's proverbial good fortune with the words

> . . . nos te
> nos facimus, Fortuna, deam, caeloque locamus.

If only this condition of society had not been destroyed!

The communist argument is certainly not answered by saying that art grows greater in a position of servitude, and will usually flourish under bad government. It grows greater only by struggling against the servitude ; and to make this defence of the *status quo* is like throwing a cat into the water in order to discover whether it has enough power and skill to swim to the bank. We may grant further, without giving in to Marxist aesthetics, that in a perfect state of society there would be no place for art, and perhaps that we spend on the perfection of art the energy we might spend on the perfection of life itself. But this is no solution of what to do with art, for it only maligns art. It also takes far too charitable a view of life. To answer that there is and can be no perfect earthly state, that entire liberty is unattainable outside the divine polity which supervenes on and sanctions human institutions, sounds like, but is far more than, a mere paradox of the popular preacher. We should strive towards a natural essential conformity with the divine where the laws of divine and human justice seem no longer restricting in their effect but rather amplifying. Meanwhile the spirit of the struggle has found and will continue to find propagation in the voice of the poets. Thus there need be no revolution.

CHARLES HENRY SALTER.

NOTES

[1] This and the following example are taken from an article in the *London Mercury* for June 1938.

[2] From the *National-Zeitung*, February 11th-12th, 1939. By J. M. v. Koenneritz.

[3] From *A New Hope for Poetry*, by Mr. Day-Lewis.

[4] Sophocles, *Antigone*, ll. 666–7.

[5] Aeschylus, *Agamemnon*, l. 1301.

[6] From an article on Poetry and Religion in the *Criterion* for January and May 1927, by M. Jacques Maritain, translated by Mr. F. S. Flint.

[7] Mr. Hone, in the *London Mercury* for February 1939.

[8] Quoted in *Have you anything to Declare* by Mr. Maurice Baring.

[9] I refer to the well-known essay on *Tradition and the Individual Talent*.

[10] This and the next quotation are from *Artists in Uniform*, by Max Eastman, and translated by him from the Russian.

I have been much impressed by some of the verse in THE POETRY REVIEW—particularly " Finis " by Winifred Coleridge. My mood was receptive I suppose, " How sad, but how brave," I thought.— JESSICA G. MONEY, Winnipeg.

Literature and Ideology
by
James T. Farrell

from

The League of Frightened Philistines by James T. Farrell.

Literature and Ideology

WHAT is the relationship between literature and politics? What should that relationship be? Such questions have produced major literary controversies in this country for more than a decade. About ten years ago these questions were central in the discussion of so-called proletarian literature. Today, these same issues are being discussed in connection with literature and democracy and literature and the war. In current discussions the language is different from what it was ten years ago, but both those who were the apostles of proletarian literature and those who to-day demand that literature be politicalized in the name of democracy have something in common: in both instances the aim is to compel the writer to abort his work in the name of *formal* political ends and to impose critical and political legislation on him.

The advocates of proletarian literature, who wrote principally in *The New Masses*, used to argue that literature is a weapon in the class struggle. If the writer is not on one side, he is either an open defender of the enemy or else he is giving aid and comfort to that enemy. At times it was even claimed that literature itself was on the barricades. These views were advocated in a formal and sectarian spirit, and behind them was the *real aim* of bureaucratizing literature so that it would become merely the docile handmaiden of politics, of ideology, even of a specific party line.[1] The writer who accepted

[1] I have discussed in detail my own views on some of these questions in *A Note on Literary Criticism*. Views directly counter to my own are to be found in *The Great Tradition*, by Granville Hicks. There are a number of books which relate to this question and in various ways. I cite a few of them: *Literature and Revolution*, by Leon Trotsky; *Voices of October*, Joseph Freeman, Joshua Kunitz, and Louis Lozowick, editors; *American Writers' Congress*, Henry Hart, editor; *The Destructive Element*, by Stephen Spender; *The Triple Thinkers*, by Edmund Wilson; *Problems of Soviet Literature*, by A. Zhdanov, Maxim Gorky, N. Bukharin, K. Radek, and A. Stetsky; *The Liberation of American Literature*, by V. F. Calverton; *Illusion and Reality*, by Christopher Caudwell; *Artists in Uniform* and *Art and the Life of Action*, by Max Eastman; *Forces in American Criticism*, by Bernard Smith, *La Littérature et l'Art, choisis, traduits et présentés par* Karl Marx *et* F. Engels; *Art and Society*, by George V. Plekhanov (introduction by Granville Hicks). In Ireland, during the, period of national revolutionary ferment, prior to the Easter Rebellion of 1916 the same question was discussed in literary controversies, but there it was an issue concerning literature and the aspirations of the nationalist movement. One who defended the writer against the criticisms of the nationalists—those who demanded that Anglo-Irish literature serve as a direct political instrument of the national movement—was the Lord Mayor of Cork, the late Terence MacSwiney (cf. *Principles of Freedom*). MacSwiney stated: "It is because we need the truth that

this conception and attempted to make it operative in the actual construction of novels would have to see politics first and then life, and he would have to deduce life from political programmes. To the theoreticians of proletarian literature the theme of a book was considered its most important, its most essential, element: the total pattern of a novel, its unfoldment of characters and events, its insights, which help to clarify for us the mysteries of man and his world, and its very style—these were all relegated to a secondary place. A true re-creation of social relationships and of human beings was considered to be less important than the merely formal ideology that was implanted into a novel and openly affirmed in the last chapter. The ending was stressed as against the entire story and its legitimate meanings and implications. Most of the great writers of the present and of the past were attacked, often severely, as bourgeois defeatists; and in their place novelists such as Jack Conroy, Arnold Armstrong, William Rollins, and others were hailed as the inheritors not only of the literary traditions of America but also of those of the whole world.

we object to the propagandist playwright.'' It is important to stress that these bureaucratically politicalized views on literature were presented in a formal and abstract manner, with utter heedlessness of conditions, of class relationships, of states of consciousness in America during the 1930's, when these opinions were more strongly and widely presented. It was generally impossible for a writer to make the bridge between these formal claims for literature and the character and quality of his own experience. By and large, life in America did not seem at all like the insistences as to what life should be like according to these formally asserted views on proletarian literature, and the claims that literature itself was on the barricades. The tactics (it was tactics, not strategy) of politics were applied to the practices of literature, which deals with the consciousness of men. This can be seen clearly if we consider that frequently—and especially in poetry and verse during the early thirties—slogans were used in poetry. One of these slogans was that which Lenin used in the period between the February and October Revolutions in Russia: "All Power to the Soviets.'' This slogan did not at all correspond to the general state of consciousness of the American workers during the early 1930's, and, in addition, if at that time this slogan had been made a central slogan politically, it would have led to disastrous adventurism, to *putschism*, to the most terrible defeat of the American working class. This slogan, politically untimed, was bad when used in many poems and verses. At that time scarcely one per cent. of the entire population of America understood, even in the most elementary sense, what the Soviets really were, theoretically or practically. Many critics of Marxism have never taken the trouble to study the problems involved in the study of literature in its relationships with politics, and in terms of its functions in society. Hence they cite the efforts of the Marxist and of the so-called Marxist critics of the early 1930's as proof that Marxism is harmful to literature. They accept formal, abstract, even utterly lifeless, expositions, and even caricatures of Marxian thought, as fair statements; and they then refute, or try to refute, these formal statements. If one writes to emphasize the veritable truism that you cannot seriously judge literature if you make it the simple handmaiden of ideology, of political tactics, of economics formally and abstractly considered, such critics often assume that you are thereby abandoning Marxism. The grievous mistakes of critics who call themselves Marxists do not excuse the ignorance of their adversaries. The errors of the former do not establish the validity of the arguments of the latter. In general, in the early 1930's, the proponents of pro-

In this article it is not necessary for me to go into historical detail or to discuss this point of view at length. Those who sponsored it have themselves abandoned all their claims. They have themselves forgotten most of the authors they lauded as proletarian writers, and they now praise the writers whom they then attacked—for instance, Thomas Mann. And most of the young writers who adopted this view of literature have themselves stopped writing. If a conception of literature produces no books, then it is obvious that that conception is defective. It remains sterile and formal. If the most rigid supporters of a conception abandon it, regardless of the reason, it is not necessary for me to refute here what they themselves have already refuted in the most positive manner.

It is ironical to observe that some of the writers who defended the complete freedom of the writer from politics in the early 1930's are now included in the vanguard of the newest group of politico-critical legislators; they now demand that the creative artist adopt the same type of approach that they themselves once attacked, even heatedly. The popular writers whose work appears in the slick magazines and who receive large sums from Hollywood are also included in this vanguard.[2]

letarian literature wrote with almost total irrelevance to the real situation in America, to the real states of consciousness of writers, and their readers, and to the types of characters depicted in the novels and stories then written. Mistaken, bureaucratically imposed, politically motivated applications of hypotheses do not furnish a necessary and sufficient refutation of these hypotheses. Finally, when critics and others demand that literature—art—be politicalized, there is a reason, a motive for this. Such demands imply or even explicitly reveal political aims and intentions, and the successful implementation of such demands produces consequences. In discussing such demands one needs to remember these truisms, and to consider them most carefully. In the case of the demand for proletarian literature, it should be remembered that most of those who made such demands were incapable of practising what they preached, either critically or creatively, and, furthermore that the political achievements claimed as possible on the basis of the political strategy and tactics that motivated this literary approach were never realized. Before one can, with real grounds, refute Marxism in general on the basis of the claims of the so-called Marxist critics of the early thirties, one must consider and evaluate both the political and the literary "lines" then in vogue. This is not usually done by critics. The real consequence of this line was that it prepared the road for a later politicalization or attempted politicalization of art, that which is in vogue to-day. The tendencies revealed in the recent writings of Van Wyck Brooks, Archibald MacLeish and others have a political character, and can, if successful, only end in an official art. And these tendencies are intimately related to the present war; in fact, they are involved as part of a general metaphysics of the war. A primary basis for a metaphysics of the war is the creation of what amounts to a metaphysics of the cause of the war. The present efforts to politicalize literature, to officialize it, are part of this effort: this is their *real politics*.

[2] *Pitfalls for Readers of Fiction*, by Hazel Sample, a pamphlet published by the National Council of Teachers of English, contains an able analysis of certain types of popular fiction and of the assumptions on which these are based. The most vulgar of those who would force literature to become official have even gone to the extent of hailing motion pictures—similar in content, basic assumptions, and in emphasis on escape values, to the novels studied by Miss Sample—

POSITIONS OF MACLEISH AND BROOKS

A leading exponent of this tendency is Archibald MacLeish (*Cf.* Archibald MacLeish, *The Irresponsibles.*) During the height of the bitter polemical controversy concerning proletarian literature, Mr. MacLeish was moved to write in defence of complete freedom of the poet. In those days he believed the poet should merely sing. And some of *The New Masses* critics did not stop at describing Mr. Mac-Leish as irresponsible—they called him a fascist. Today Mr. Mac-Leish has reversed himself, and he sharply criticizes almost all modern writers as irresponsibles. His major charge is that, during a period of growing danger to the entire human race, they merely tried to see life truly and to create honest pictures of life. They did not defend ways of thinking, ideas and beliefs that should have been defended. They did not use the word as a weapon with which to storm the barricades of belief; and consequently, they contributed to the demoralization of democratic forces, with the result that this demoralization left democracy in a weakened state at a time when it must defend itself against a sinister enemy. It is interesting to note in passing that the one writer whom MacLeish excepts from his blanket condemnation is Thomas Mann—and it is on record that many of the writers implicitly or openly attacked by MacLeish took a stand on the question of fascism before Thomas Mann would openly condemn the Hitler regime. Further, there is a stream of pessimism in the books of Thomas Mann that makes the assertions of MacLeish appear somewhat ridiculous.

Another person who has now adopted a position analogous to that of MacLeish is the critic Van Wyck Brooks (*Cf.* Van Wyck Brooks, *On Contemporary Literature* and *The Opinions of Oliver Allston.*) Mr. Brooks believes that modern writers are cynics and that they write out of hatred and a drive-toward-death. They have, he asserts, lost the idea of greatness, and inasmuch as they themselves are not great men, they cannot write great books. Excepted from this charge are Robert Frost, Lewis Mumford, Waldo Frank, Archibald MacLeish, and Thomas Mann. Modern writers—and

as greater contributions to American culture and the fight for a free world than serious works of American realism that try to describe conditions and characters truly. For instance, Mr. Strunsky, who writes the "Topics of the Times" column for the *New York Times*, has declared that serious American realists give us nothing to fight for, but that the escape movies of Hollywood do give us something we can fight and die for. In other words, the simple, tragic, spiritually impoverished people described in American realistic novels are not worth fighting for; but it is proper to die for Tyrone Power and his world.

Mr. Brooks makes no distinctions between various modern literary tendencies, including that of realism and that of radical experimentalism stemming from the French symbolists—have lost their connection with the soil. They have no roots in the region, in the country, or in its soil. In passing, it may be observed that this conception is, in essence, Spenglerian. Consequently, it is startling to see that Mr. Brooks, in his little book, *On Contemporary Literature*, charges that modern writers have been influenced by Spengler including those—such as the author of this article—who have for years been anti-Spenglerian. Furthermore, one of the European novelists of the soil, with roots in the soil, is Knut Hamsun, who was one of the first world-famous literary figures to become a fascist.

Mr. Brooks claims that modern writers write demoralizing books because they have no attachment to the family and because they do not take an interest in public life. On both of these points he is unspecific. He does not demonstrate in a concrete manner precisely how a writer will become a better artist by transplanting himself to the country and living close to the soil, by declaring an attachment to the family (most writers are attached to their families, love them, and try to support them), and by taking an open interest in public life. In addition, he is not specific concerning the manner in which a writer should become interested in and attached to public life. Should he take a political stand on issues? Should he run for an elective office? Should he abandon literature and dedicate himself to political theory or to political polemics? Should he ghost-write speeches for political leaders? And, incidentally, some of the writers whom Brooks accuses of lacking an interest in public life have been far more politically active on many issues than he has. In essence, Brooks is adopting the same general attitude toward literature as did his recent forebears, the apostles of proletarian literature, even though he clothes his views in a concealing dress of moralism. Like them, he and Archibald MacLeish and others are seeking to legislate for writing, to tell the writer what to do, what to write, what ideology to inculcate through his works, what conclusions to come to in a novel, and what to think.

ITS RELATION TO POLITICS

Those who adopt such an approach toward literature do not clearly focus the problems of literature, the nature of writing, the functions and purposes that literature can perform. When Karl Marx was a young man, editing a democratic newspaper in the

Rhineland and working toward the point of view which he finally adopted and developed, he wrote a letter to a friend which contains some remarks that are today a pertinent and decisive answer to the claims of those who would *sneak* politics and ideology into literature. At that time Marx had not yet been converted to socialism. He resisted the pressure of philosophical and literary friends who took a frivolous attitude toward serious questions, and he explained why he rejected the articles of these people. He wrote:

"I demanded less vague arguments, fewer fine-sounding phrases, less self-adulation and rather more concreteness, a more detailed treatment of actual conditions and a display of greater practical knowledge of the subjects dealt with. I told them that in my opinion it was not right, that it was even immoral, to smuggle communist and socialist dogmas, that is, an entirely new way of looking at the world, into a casual dramatic criticism, etc., and that if communism were to be discussed at all then it must be done in quite a different fashion and thoroughly."

Today, as then, literary men are trying to smuggle ideology into literature. "Smuggle" is an excellent word here. They seek to consider, to discuss, and to educate people in an indirect, oblique, yes, even casual, manner concerning the most serious problems confronting the human race. Instead of discussing questions such as socialism and communism, democracy and fascism, in terms of the relevant problems raised by those issues, they want to smuggle a discussion of such issues into novels, poetry, dramatic criticisms, book reviews, motion picture scenarios, cheap swing songs, soap operas, banquet speeches, and books labelled as literary criticism. I do not hesitate to characterize such conduct as frivolous; often it is positively immoral. Politics is serious. It is the arena in which the fundamental bread-and-butter struggles of men, of groups, of nations, of social classes are conducted. He who is frivolous about politics is guilty of a grave disservice to his fellow men, especially in times of deep social crisis. The problems of politics are basically concerned with action and with power. Literary men have the habit of rushing into the periphery of politics and they contribute to political struggles—not knowledge, not practical experience, not theoretical analyses, but rhetoric. Rhetoric is the one commodity in politics of which there has never been a scarcity.

My subject, however, is not the political conduct of literary men in politics. I do not criticize this *per se*. I merely suggest that the requisites of all responsible action are that one be serious and that one accept the obligations and duties which that endeavour imposes

D*

on one. My concern here is with the efforts to politicalize literature. The final result of the politicalization of literature can only be an official, or state, literature. The extreme example of a state, or official, literature in our times is that of the totalitarian countries. It need not be commented upon in this article. We know what it is and what it leads to and how it destroys genuine literature in the most brutal and ruthless fashion. It is possible to silence writers by force; a state power can put writers into jail and treat them as common criminals; it can prevent publication of their books; it can execute them. However, it cannot, either by open force or by offering prizes, praise, awards, or academic and institutional honours, make them write good books. Modern authoritarian rulers are not the first ones who have been taught this elementary lesson. But literary men often fail to learn it. During the period of the Second Empire, even the great critic Sainte-Beuve was ready to play along with the idea of an official literature. The attempt to create an official literature in that period failed. Two of the greatest French writers of the times, Flaubert and Baudelaire (both friends of Sainte-Beuve), were haled to court on censorship charges.[3] The poetry of Baudelaire was suppressed. Today we read Flaubert and Baudelaire but not the official writers of Louis Bonaparte.

Napoleon Bonaparte still remains the greatest of modern dictators. Himself a gifted writer and a man who developed literary taste through the course of his lifetime, he tried to impose an official art and literature on France when he was its ruler. In the year 1805 he wrote to Fouché, who was then Minister of Police:

"I read in a paper that a tragedy on Henry IV is to be played. The epoch is recent enough to excite political passions. The theatre must dip more into antiquity. Why not commission Raynouard to write a tragedy on the transition from primitive to less primitive man? A tyrant would be followed by the saviour of his country. The oratorio *Saul* is on precisely that text—a great man succeeding a degenerate king."

In the same year he wrote: "My intention is to turn Art specially in the direction of subjects that would tend to perpetuate the memory of the events of the last fifteen years." He justified expenditures for opera on the ground that it flattered the national vanity. A year later he confessed that his official opera had only degraded literature and the arts, and he demanded that something be done to halt the degradation caused by his own official policies and his

---

[3] The history of literature for decades now teaches us that it is not unlikely for serious writers to win the merit of having gained the solicitude of the police power.

control of the opera. Then he declared: "Literature needs encouragement." Something had to be proposed to "shake up the various branches of literature that have so long distinguished our country." But literature did not distinguish France during the period of *la gloire*. The writer was told to behave—and generally he obeyed orders. The chief of police and the ministers of the cabinet gave him instructions as to what to write, and they honoured him for obeying instructions. But Napoleon himself was forced—after all he was a man of some taste—to show contempt for his own official littérateurs. In exile at Saint Helena, he did not read them. He did not speak of them. He remembered Racine, and he remembered Homer, but he remembered no literature that could distinguish his own period of rule. And neither do we today remember any of it. Is more eloquent demonstration of the failure of this attitude toward literature needed?

WHAT IS GREATNESS IN LITERATURE?

It is a truism to state that the test of a work of literature is not to be found solely in its formal ideology. The most cursory examination of a few great works of literature will prove the validity of this truism.

Many of us recognize Tolstoy as a great writer, a genius, and a thinker of the first order. Is this because of the formal attitudes—the ideology—in his major works? In *Anna Karenina*, during the course of the novel, the character Levin develops the conception of political non-resistance which had become part of the gospel of Tolstoyism. Levin found reasons for refusing to take an interest in public affairs, and these reasons were Tolstoy's own for formulating this doctrine. Because we disagree with Tolstoy's views represented in his characterization of Levin, will we therefore deny the greatness of *Anna Karenina*? In *War and Peace* Tolstoy presents a view of history that succeeds in atomizing history to the degree that makes it impossible to distinguish between factors essential and of weight in the influencing of events and those incidental or secondary. According to this conception of history, every human being of a specific period influences the history of that period. History is the result of all the actions and all the thoughts of every human being. In a sense, this is correct. The history of man is everything that happens to man. But can we seek to explain and to understand man if we apply this conception concretely? If we do, we have no means of truly determining which factors are essential and important in a given historic study and which ones are non-essential. Not fully accepting this theory of history, which is embedded in the very warp and woof of *War and Peace*, and which is also presented in the novel in essay form, do we therefore deny the value of this work?

Balzac was antidemocratic, and his formal attitudes were those prevailing at the time of the Restoration, which followed the fall of Napoleon. The formal view of Theodore Dreiser concerning man's place in the universe includes crude materialism and social Darwinism. Are his books, therefore, to be dismissed? Examples to demonstrate this point are endless. If we literally adopt such a view of literature, we thereby deny ourselves an appreciation of many of the greatest works of the past. We cannot then appreciate the literature and the art that preceded democracy, because it is not democratic. If we are socialists, we cannot appreciate the great literature of the modern age and, even more important, we will be incapable of explaining literature. If we demand that literature reflect in a direct, obvious, and mechanical fashion, the major struggles of the period from which it springs or with which it deals, what are we to say of such a novel as *Wuthering Heights*? This work —in my opinion one of the greatest of all English novels—describes characters who lived during the period when Bonaparte was at the height of his power. Withal, it has nothing to say of the danger of old "Bony" invading England. Is it therefore invalidated as a novel?

Literature is one of the arts which re-create the consciousness and the conscience of a period. It tells us what has happened to man, what could have happened to him, what man has imagined might happen to him. It presents the environments, the patterns of destiny, the joys and the sorrows, the tribulations, the dreams, the fantasies, the aspirations, the cruelties, the shames, the dreams, of men and women. Life is full of mysteries, and one of the major mysteries of life is man himself. Literature probes that mystery. Just as science helps man to understand nature, literature helps man to understand himself. Just as science makes human the forces of nature in the sense that it makes possible the construction of instruments for controlling these forces, so does literature aid in making man human to himself. Literature, by its very nature, cannot, in and of itself, solve social and political problems. Any solution of a social or political problem in a work of literature is a purely intellectual solution. These problems are problems of action. Every problem delimits the kind of means which can, and those which cannot, be of use in its solution. This statement applies in logic, in mathematics, in the physical sciences, in the solution of social and political problems, and in the problems that any artist must face in his own work. It is just as absurd to assume that you can solve political and social problems with a poem as it is to expect a painter, by painting a picture, to save from death a man stricken with appendicitis.

HOW MUCH LITERATURE CAN DO

Literature generally reflects life. It often limps, even crawls, behind events. This is especially so in periods of great social crisis and of historic convulsion. What is the great literary work of the Napoleonic period—one which parallels our own age? It is Stendhal's *The Red and the Black*. But Stendhal did not write this novel when he was with the French army in Moscow. He wrote it some time after the Battle of Waterloo.

Some of those who take a view of literature contrary to the one I am presenting here demand that the writer be a prophet. His duty is to foresee what is to come, not merely to reflect what has already come—including what man has already dreamed, imagined, constructed in his own head—as well as what has happened in the sense of actual objective events. Let us examine this view concretely. What is prophecy? It is prediction. Whether one makes a prophecy, or prediction, on the basis of an inner vision or as the result of a close scientific investigation, that prophecy, or prediction, proves nothing. It is merely a statement of probability. It must be validated by the occurrence of the events predicted. Besides, it is obvious that when one makes a prediction one should base that prediction on relevant evidence. Therefore I ask: Is a lyric poem the proper form in which to predict historic events? If so, why do we not elect lyric poets as our political leaders? It is the exercise of simple intelligence not to confuse problems. We do not ask our doctors, our dentists, our scientists, our politicians, or our mechanics to confuse problems; we ask only our poets and our novelists to do this.[4]

Furthermore, those who want to officialize literature—those who

[4] I have here discussed prophecy in literature in terms of the prediction of events. Those who demand that the poet play the role of prophet from a regressively cultural point of view base their contention on the traditional philosophical conception of cognition as the sole factor in the process of knowledge. They then assume that the insights and "intuitions "of the poet constitute a form of knowing superior to that embodied in scientific method. They want to substitute the poet for the political theorist and analyst and for the scientist. There is, however, a sense in which the poet—Shelley, for instance—plays a role that can be considered analogous to that of the prophet. When a poet or novelist emphasizes the need for a change in values and attitudes required by the demands of social evolution, his role then is more or less analogous to that of the prophet. However, to perform this role he must have more than an alleged superior form of knowing—which is assumed to be poetic insight.

insist that the artist wear the uniform of an ideology—persist in calling writers who refuse to comply with their demand sceptics and cynics. Often they use the words "sceptic" and "cynic" as if they were synonymous. These words do not necessarily have the same meaning. A sceptic doubts. A cynic is without faith. It is possible to doubt, to be critical, and still to have faith. Moreover, there is no necessary opposition between scepticism and faith. Without a scepticism sufficient to enable us to be critical of evidence, we should have a faith that is unwarranted. We would then believe something without knowing why we believe it. Also, to say that a writer is sceptical or cynical does not necessarily constitute a valid ground for criticism. Was there no scepticism, no cynicism, in Shakespeare? Is there no scepticism in the Bible? Tolstoy was more than sceptical of modern capitalism and of the efficacy of political action; in addition, he was a pacifist. A pacifist is obviously sceptical of the social value of war. Generally speaking, it is the realistic writers who are called sceptical and cynical. Those who make this charge against realists do not, however, examine what the realistic writer has to say. They don't examine the conditions that he describes. In many instances the realist describes injustice, misery, spiritual poverty, and material poverty. The world described by modern realists is not free from the conditions producing these results. No less a person than the President of the United States, President Roosevelt, has spoken of "one third of a nation" submerged in poverty, suffering from all the physical and mental ills bred by poverty. But if the realistic novelist deals with existing conditions, if he dares to re-create a true and revealing picture of these conditions, of the patterns of destiny of the characters who are educated and live under such conditions, he is a sceptic and a cynic. The attempt to tell the truth in a precise, concrete, and uncompromising manner is demoralizing. And what is the proposed alternative to this type of literature? It is: The advice to write about justice, about morality, about heroism, and about greatness in general—that is, in the abstract. Just to state many of these arguments is sufficient. It even becomes embarrassing to be forced to answer them in detail.

THE ROLE OF THE WRITER

He who would put literature in uniform is afraid of literature, and his fear of literature reveals a more fundamental fear—that of social change. The demand that literature conform comes from fear, not from confidence and not from faith. Literature in the modern world could not thrive under official control. The result of official control would be silencing, crushing, destroying, the really talented among our writers and so enable those who are not serious, those who are not truly talented, those who have nothing to say, to come to the front. The notion that the serious literary artist is a major element in demoralizing a society is absurd on its face. No society can be demoralized with a few books. If a society is demoralized, the reasons for that condition go much deeper than the circulation of a few books. The actual spy, the actual saboteur, the actual agent of enemy governments, and so on, do not have the time—nor do they usually have the sensibility, the imagination, the intelligence, the culture, or the background—to create a work of literature. He who makes such charges against the artist makes them because he dare not look conditions in the face. And to look conditions in the face is precisely what the serious writer tries to do. In some instances these conditions exist in society at large; in other instances these conditions are in the mind, in the emotions, in the dreams, and in the consciousness of the artist himself. In all serious literature there is truth—truth of insight, of observation, truth about the social relationships of the world, as well as truth about the consciousness of men. And the truth will make men free, although it may disturb the critical legislator and the ideological smuggler.

It is inept, absurd, downright silly, to argue that in a world torn by the greatest convulsions of the modern period, literature can hide away in a hothouse. I make no such claims. I am not demanding here that literature exist in any ivory tower. What I do stress, however, is that literature must solve its own problems and that it cannot be turned into the mere handmaiden of politics and into a mere looking-glass of ideologies. The justification of literature must be made in terms of the functions it performs and not by seeking to make it perform functions for which it is unfitted. When Ralph Waldo Emerson died, William James, who as a boy had known Emerson, wrote that although Emerson was a monist—James himself defended a conception of an open, pluralistic universe—Emerson did not suppress facts in order to substantiate his monism. This statement provides us with the formula for understanding and tolerance, in both the world of ideas and the world of art. If the writer has not suppressed the facts, we can seek to understand him; and if we find value in his work, we can justify that work despite agreement or disagreement with his formal ideas. And it is to be remembered that in art the facts are not statistical; the facts are perceptions, observations, insights, revelations of certain aspects of those mysteries of life which surround us on every side and which exist even in our own consciousness.

It is now almost three centuries to the year since John Milton wrote his *Areopagitica*, one of the most eloquent defences of freedom of inquiry and freedom for the artist that has ever been written. Milton wrote: "As good almost . . . kill a man as kill a good book: who kills a man kills a reasonable creature . . . but he who destroys a good book kills reason itself." What Milton said is in the spirit of the eloquent apology of Socrates when he stood on trial for his life—charged with having demoralized the youth of Athens—and when he declared to his judges: " . . . the unexamined life is not worth living. . . ." And, to conclude, serious literature is one of the most powerful means contrived by the human spirit for examining life. This in itself is the basic justification of literature in any period. This is the answer that the artist can confidently hurl back at all Philistines who fear to permit the examination of life.

1942

From Engagement to Indifference: Politics and the Writer
W. Esty and D. Stanford

from

Commonweal, 67, 1958.

From Engagement to Indifference:

Politics and the Writer

Does our literature reflect our social thought? The political withdrawal of the younger writer, a much-remarked phenomenon of our times, is explored by a British and an American critic.

In Britain, Cautious Coexistence

by DEREK STANFORD

WHAT SORT of interest does the younger British writer feel for contemporary politics? On the whole, we may answer, a sketchy, tepid one. There is no love-relationship, as in the thirties; and when some sort of interest does exist, it reveals itself—with qualifications—in a guarded and critical approach, a kind of cautious coexistence.

Violence, whether national or individual, has a way of bringing opinion to a head, of precipitating in clearer terms what we have previously been more dimly feeling. Yet those in touch with literary opinion at the time of the Suez Crisis could not but contrast the multiple reactions with the comparatively uniform response made by an earlier generation in the face of the Spanish Civil War.

This incoherent climate of response was made manifest for me in the behavior of two of my friends on the occasion of the Suez landing. The reactions of both these people were unpredictable, cutting at their natural affiliations and at the *en bloc* nature of their thought. The first—a young literary editor, working on a right-wing weekly—resigned his job because his paper supported the Conservative policy. His own approach to politics, up to that time, had been an enthusiastic analytical right-wing sympathy. He was on the side of the younger Tories who did not consider that party loyalty precluded them from critical comment. He was also, by birth, a Jew. The other was a B.B.C. producer, who had long described

himself as a staunch republican, and had frequently proclaimed his dislike of "Public School imperialism." Suez, however, had worked upon his feelings to the point where he had been within an ace of volunteering for the Army—for the French or Jewish forces if the British declined him.

These examples illustrate the apparent incoherence or confusion of response with which the younger British writer meets the issue of political decision. Of course, I might have chosen a more representative case. During the most critical phase of the Suez expedition, I remember spending a whole evening with four other writers, all under forty, with not a single word heard or spoken all night about events then in hand. I might add, too, that a fifth author-friend, learning of our conversational omission, branded our talk as irresponsible. In turn, some of us might have inclined to pronounce his own sincere reiteration of party watch-words a *trahison des clercs*. We might have urged that the writer's first duty is to pick his words carefully, scan their meaning, and subject the words of others to a like examination.

Perhaps these few examples furnish some general notion of the literary-political picture. Mr. Kingsley Amis, who sketches his self-portrait as "an elderly young intellectual . . . with connections in the educational and literary worlds and with left-wing sympathies," sums up the position in the following sentence. "The decline in political activity," he writes, "among intellectuals as a whole must, I think, be taken as a fact in the perspective of the last twenty years, and it is particularly noticeable among our younger

Mr. Stanford, a well-known British writer, is the author of critical studies on Christopher Fry, Emily Bronte, and Dylan Thomas.

novelists and poets." This, I believe, would be taken as a commonly accepted account of the position.

THERE ARE a great many factors to explain this condition. The first are political, and they have all been mooted before. The second are cultural, and these have not previously, I think, been drawn out.

As for political causes behind the declining interest which the younger writer gives to politics, there is, initially, the new liaison between politics and science (humane literature's old rival). This makes any prospect of war and warfare a terrifying one for the imagination. There is the lack of enthusiasm, or downright disapproval, felt for the Welfare State. Those who do not condemn it on economic grounds believe that its advent has somehow taken the glory out of the Socialist Cause. It is all bread, margarine and jam. No aspiration, no adventure. There is the equal failure of the Conservative Party to provide an inspiriting program or to get down to rock-bottom planning. Its inability to control or halt inflation is particularly annoying to the younger writer, whose financial resources are usually precarious enough. To this must be added the refusal of the Party—despite Sir Anthony Eden's protestation that "the Conservative tradition is also a tradition of good writing"— to assist or encourage the arts. Indeed, one of its first economies, on entering into office after the Labor Government, was to cut down the grants allowed to the British Council for furthering national culture at home and abroad. And the general discrediting of Russia and Marxism left the idealistic left-wing mind without a country or an ideology about which its thoughts and emotions might cohere.

These are the factors operative in politics which make the younger writer diffident or unwilling with regard to a closer relationship between literature and the political life. But there are likewise a number of factors inhering in the cultural situation which incline to impede any *rapprochement* between politics and letters.

Literature and art tend to cohere around certain systems of thought and conduct, of which the two most socially important are politics and religion. The new spirit of academicism in younger British writing furthers the isolation of letters from political, civic or religious opinion. This esoteric specialization, as we find it, for example, in fashionable textual criticism of the poem-(or novel-) in-vacuum school, separates politics and letters and works against a joint study of them.

In addition, the declining fortunes of neo-romanticism, widespread and active in the forties, has meant the loss of Anarchism (with which the movement was associated) as a possible political choice for the writer. With its less dogmatic ideology, the diverse interpretation of its aims, its individual, de-centralized tradition, Anarchism held many attractions for the artist and man of letters. These attractions were heightened by the fact that three of its recent leading exponents—Sir Herbert Read, Alex Comfort, and George Woodcock—were, besides being men of theory, possessed of critical poetic sensibility. Kropotkin, the greatest figure of the movement in the nineteenth century, had likewise a liberal taste in the arts, and his book on *Ideals in Russian Literature* reveals a breadth of taste and intuition rare in the political thinker. Kropotkin was also a considerable ethical thinker (see his *Mutual Aid* and *Ethics*).

Anarchism was thus able to offer a more humane body of thought than is to be found in most political groups. It was idealistic, revolutionary, philosophic, and individualistic. These four qualities often commend themselves to men-of-letters, the more so when they themselves are young.

CONVERSELY, the absence of a sustaining emotion, by which political matters are colored, and by which they retain their imaginative appeal, may owe much to the neo-classicism now very much in vogue. The feeling-tone of this movement is low and chill. It lacks emotional expansiveness, free play for sentiment and imagination. Neo-classicism helps to keep down the temperature of man's instinctive responses, and does not look with approval on any variety of Gide's "*l'acte gratuit.*"

One of its spokesmen, Kingsley Amis, has defined romanticism, in a political context, as "an irrational capacity to become inflamed by interests and causes that are not one's own, that are outside oneself." This looks like a definition of quixoticism or of disinterestedness. Amis disapproves of such an attitude, finding it inflammable and unrealistic; and he seems to argue, by implication, that good politics derive from enlightened self-love.

Logical or critical positivism is probably another factor helping to keep the political circulation of the young writer from becoming overheated. The language of political parties is notoriously an idiom of platitude and jargon, a repository of unreflective statements. With their celebrated verbal analysis and their use of the Verification Principle, the critical positivists could not ask for less resistant subject-matter than political rhetoric. It is not to be expected that its disciples will display a large measure of political fervor.

Further, the shift in cultural attention from a

revolutionary to a traditional sensibility, as discoverable in the literature of the past, is most likely having its repercussion on the younger writer's interest in politics. The present waning appeal, say, of Shelley, and the waxing magnetic attraction of such figures as Jane Austen, Coleridge, and Newman—to go no further back than the nineteenth century—is probably to be paralleled by the declining interest in Marx and Bakunin.

But if this means a loss to left-wing parties of the younger writer, it is doubtful whether it argues a gain for the right. The late Percy Wyndham Lewis, whose work is now receiving wide critical examination, could have provided the Conservative Party, during its leanest years in the thirties, with entire arsenals of ideas, had its members been ready to receive them. That they did not lend ear, and that their party failed to produce—in the *interbellum* years—one single thinker of notable stature, gives one to wonder if they do not choose to retain the label bestowed upon them by their opponents, who speak of them as "the stupid party." However this may or may not apply to the individual party member, it certainly appears that the Conservative politician places no excessive premium on brains. The younger writer, who votes Conservative (which he may do for a number of reasons) is clearly not tempted by the intellectual brilliance of the party's present program. It is, of course, possible to defend "stupidity" as a factor making for stability in national life. Walter Bagehot and John Henry Newman both made out a case for it: the first, as applying to the electorate; the second, as relating to the strength of the High Church party and its supporters at a time when the Anglican cause was under attack by Whig politicians. But to maintain or promote "stupidity" among the leaders of a party is a rather different thing from defending it, for its psychological assets, as a characteristic of party supporters.

The influence of George Orwell and Arthur Koestler has been another feature in diluting or negating the fervor of Leftist thought among writers. Both of these authors had sounded the entire gamut of Socialist opinion, and the fact that Orwell at his death remained a nominal Socialist, and that Koestler is still thought of as being one, does not minimize their devastating criticism of Socialist orthodoxy. Orwell, in his novel *1984*, emphatically envisaged the villain of the piece as "Big Brother," no True-Blue figure; and, as far back as the last year of World War II, Koestler was saying that he preferred Colonel Blimp to the Kremlin commissar.

Of Orwell, Kingsley Amis has written that "what he did was to become a right-wing propagandist by negation, or at any rate a supremely powerful—though unconscious—advocate of political quietism." One may question that word "unconscious," but certainly as bearing on Orwell's effect, rather than on his intention, Amis's account is substantially valid.

I HAVE SPOKEN of the cultural situation as it relates to left- or right-wing thinking, and as it is likely or unlikely to foster Conservative or Socialist adherents. What, one may ask, are its bearings, if any, upon political liberalism?

According to newspaper reports, the Liberal Party membership, among the students of Oxford and Cambridge, stands today numerically (and proportionally) higher than it has stood for a long period. A taste and vocation for humane arts and knowledge naturally predisposes a person towards that party which claims to uphold the virtues of tolerance and moderation. It is, though, seriously to be questioned whether life at an Ancient University provides a microcosm of the outside modern world; and one may therefore ask whether student liberalism is not likely to prove an interim phase which ends when its holder leaves the university.

The long alliance between liberalism and humanism needs no emphasizing. A university is the natural home of the humanist attitude, but the prevailing temper of the world (especially in political matters) is better described as anti-humanist. This means that those assumptions which the student acquires at the university will often be contradicted or dispelled once he finds himself outside its walls. The following passage from Mr. Frederick Lohr's study *Greek, Roman, and Jew* (1952) sums up, suggestively, the relationship between the liberal-humanist approach and power-politics since 1914. "After the first world-war," writes Lohr, "a book was published entitled *The Strange Death of Liberalism*, and there are still people who are puzzled by the rapid decline of liberal values. They cannot understand why an outlook upon the world which was once so esteemed should now be looked upon as effete. The answer lies in the experience of crisis. Liberal ideas cannot withstand a crisis. The liberal way of life is a compound of tolerance and compromise—Liberalism is a gentleman's creed and neither the facts nor the spirit of our time is gentle. It was one of the flowers that bloomed in a protected area of civilization, and Europe has recently been opened to the harsh realities of history."

The name of Frederick Lohr leads me to remark on a phenomenon outside my present theme, but appropriate as a close to this essay. During the last war, Lohr gave promise of an unusual talent for political thinking in depth with his monograph *The Philoso-*

phy of Anarchism. By 1945, however, he had adopted a religious view of life, and his closest political affiliations were with the Personalist Movement in France.

In Britain we have no influential philosophical-political group-thinking. Neither do we possess any effective Christian political parties. Religion, nonetheless, remains a strong magnetic force for a number of younger writers; and it is possible that the work of not a few might coalesce about religious thought rather than about party or political opinion.

In America, Intellectual Bomb Shelters

by WILLIAM ESTY

A FAST, FLIP, only partly unfair answer to the question "What are the political attitudes of the younger American writers?" would be: there are no younger American writers, and they have no political attitudes. This statement is not, of course, wholly just, and any reviewer intent on justice must set about defining Groups and descrying Tendencies. Let us first survey the "younger" American writing scene teleologically, from on high. We can then traverse selected parts of it on foot and view the phenomena zoologically.

The most obvious, and probably the most important, thing to say is that the political and, more broadly, social attitudes of younger American writers are much like the attitudes of the rest of us. Like us, they are apprehensive and tired, tired especially of politics. This is as true of the writers who put politics explicitly into their work as of those who do not. The politics of most of the "younger" novels is curiously unreal, unfelt—but then, so is the world, so are the people of these novels. American writers, like other intellectuals, have swung between the Scornful-Depressed and the Engaged reactions to public life; insofar as we are now mostly Scornful-Depressed, our period resembles the twenties more closely than the earnest thirties. The American intelligentsia in the twenties felt a contemptuous, frequently amused indifference to the absurdity of public affairs, an attitude typically issuing in theoretical socialism combined with a juvenile brand of hedonism. The intelligent American, in Mencken's metaphor, was a man in a zoo. Well, the zoo is still there, but now it is harder to separate oneself so cozily from the animals, if only because the whole zoo may go up in flames with us inside. The men of the twenties had a gaiety, an energy in their disillusionment, even in their despair, which looks almost idyllic to our envious eyes.

So one cannot be too hard on our young writers if their "politics" is a stammering, rather unconvincing affair: which of us is better? William Styron—the best,

along with Mary McCarthy, of the at-least-tangentially political—tells us in *The Long March* that, "Born into a generation of conformists, even Mannix . . . was aware that his gestures were not symbolic, but individual, therefore hopeless, maybe even absurd, and that he was trapped like all of them in a predicament which one personal insurrection could, if anything, only make worse." Later, Mannix does rebel against The System, and "he only mutilated himself by this perverse and violent rebellion. . . ." Most of us, most of the time, will agree, sighing; it is Our Time. But where is the Stendhal who will make opera out of the time we sigh over? He knew what his time, the *juste-milieu*, did to rebels; and, facing the utter defeat of his yearnings for France, he made honest music out of it, as Yeats in "Lapis Lazuli" did out of our fear of annihilation by bomb.

Below the Styron level of bleakly compassionate, circumscribed honesty we find Allen Ginsburg addressing America "Go——yourself with your atom bomb./ I don't feel good don't bother me./ . . . America stop pushing I know what I'm doing." And below this is Augie March, "hero" of Saul Bellow's novel, summing up his attitude to life: "Meanwhile the clouds, birds, cattle in the water, things, stayed at their distance, and there was no need to herd, account for, hold them in the head . . . occasionally I could look out like a creature." The passionate longing to escape vision and commitment, to trade man's estate for that of the kinkajou or beetle, which breathes through Mr. Bellow's "picaresque comic" novel is the extreme temptation of us all in the fifties: the forsaking of politics and, indeed, life, for an intellectual bomb shelter.

IF LIKE us they are politically rather numb, if they furthermore find the world around them hard even to look at clearly, or at least to present, then our younger writers also betray, explicitly or implicitly, certain deeply-held views about our life today which carry utter conviction, for they are our views too. The credo might be summed up in the closely related

Mr. Esty is a New York critic who contributes frequently to The Commonweal and other magazines.

maxims that Things Are Tough; that Things Are Complicated; and that One Must Be Hep. That is, one must be sophisticated, aware of the complexities—so many more than we used to imagine: not that our awareness will really help us much, but it is a duty, the duty to truth. This idea crops up even in Brendan Gill's flyweight *The Day the Money Stopped;* the novel's hero may be an improvident playboy, but he is redeemed by his devotion to exposing the Full Truth.

The tough-complicated theme runs through Norman Mailer's *The Man Who Studied Yoga* (sex is tough; so is politics: what to do if you're still a radical and hate Nixon's guts but know about the labor camps in Russia?); Bernard Wolfe's slick, readable, superficial Raymond Chandler plus politics-and-psychiatry thriller *In Deep;* Wright Morris's *The Field of Vision,* a sad essay on our powers to transform and, more potently, our aptness to be transformed; and many, many others. The implicit insistence on hepness—part of what Lionel Trilling calls, so rightly, the "secularization of morality" or, more simply, "The Terror"—is strong in the fiction of Dachine Rainer, whose sophistication is the handmaiden of self-pity (one may understand so much and still stiffen in a rented Village room), and J. D. Salinger, whose young mystics are able to reprove the ego of other young mystics who dislike young men who dislike Flaubert in a way that smacks of ego. The gifted Mr. Salinger, the St. Just of the secular quest for purity, has wrenched from an extreme form of The Terror an achievement far more vivid and vertebrate than Bellow's terrible, limp sadness, but one that may be just as much a dead-end. We are a long way from "politics."

The obligation to hepness, knowledge—Seeing Things As They Are—is likely to mean slightly different things, depending on the sex of the writer. To the women, Elizabeth Spencer in *The Voice at the Back Door,* Doris Betts in *Tall Houses in Winter,* H. H. Lynde in *The Adversary,* it means Accepting Responsibility. To the men, it is more likely to mean Know Thyself: "We've got to know who we are" (James Reichly, *The Burying of Kingsmith*). Both Wolfe and Morris use the metaphor of a flawed-heroic "touching the bottom"—skin-diving too deep in Wolfe's novel, an unsuccessful attempt to walk on water in Morris's —to signify failure but also, more importantly, an exploration that is really the exploration of self. Wolfe, very much of his time and place, turns motives on their heads like dolls, asserts that the free man is he who is not "strangled by his [own] diapers," and in general accomplishes the reduction of politics to psychoanalysis. Knowing and Responsibility fuse in the work of Ralph Ellison and James Baldwin, who have achieved the important feat of *seeing* the Negro rather than "the Negro Question." This allows them to produce art,

which is to say create visibility, where before were only the clichés of rage and pity.

OUR YOUNGER writers present us not so much with the anti-hero as the plain un-hero. Saul Bellow's Augie March and Tommy Wilhelm are the type in its full flower, the *schlemiehl,* the poor slob, manipulated by others, aimless, monotonously kicked in the pants, but of course "well-meaning," cherishing his confusion, hugging his good will and "humanity" to his bosom as the Spartan boy his fox. The condition of such mental stumblebums is supposed to be significant and could be made so, but in art a thing must first give us the pleasure of the well-wrought or it signifies nothing to us at all. The danger of using a naive central character who is not treated satirically, who suffers and suffers and will not learn, is that we may laugh instead of cry, especially when we guess his creator means him to stand for Big Things. When the Communists and anti-Communists of Irwin Shaw's *The Troubled Air* finish knocking the "liberal" hero around, we only wish a member of the Mau Mau would come along and finish the poor dope off. Wolfe and, even better, Morris make use of a sort of would-be hero, the hero as fool, implying a rejection of power and "success," and therefore of politics, for politics is power.

We may take leave of the hero in our contemporary fiction by noting that two writers so apparently dissimilar as Saul Bellow and Jack Kerouac both make much use of the term "hung-up," i.e., frustrated, immobilized. And by further noting the musing of Mailer's fictional "hung-up" writer: "One could not have a *hero* today . . . there is only a modern hero damned by no more than the ugliness of wishes whose satisfaction he will never know."

The last General Tendency to note in "younger" American writing is the prevalence of an almost aggressively flat, graceless style. Miss Spencer, Miss Betts, Mr. Reichley are all devotees of this he-went-into-the-bedroom-and-lit-his-pipe-and-scratched-himself-and-kissed-his-wife school. To read twenty-odd recent American novels is to live through a sort of Dark Night of the Taste, to realize how rare is, not the artistic gift, but the mere *narrative* gift, the brute ability to make the ordinary business of life minimally interesting. And these young men and women are so intelligent, so well-educated, they plan and work so seriously, they have all the right attitudes! They will their novels into existence, we will ourselves to read through them, and it is all a labor of virtue in a desert of cacti.

And then there is Shaw's wearisomely "smart" dialogue, and Miss Lynde's insufferable serious-women's-magazine prose, so considerately clear about everything small, so comfortably vague about everything large, withal so suffocatingly cozy. As if with unconscious masochistic intention, many of these writers include in their works embarrassingly self-referential passages about writing. Doris Betts: "Fen said, 'Is it hard to write a novel?' 'Harder for some than others,' Ryan said. 'Very hard to write a good, even a passable novel . . . Maybe the great writers span the gap with something more than work.' Whatever that was, he thought." Jack Kerouac: " 'Man, wow, there's so many things to do, so many things to write! How to even *begin* to get it all down and without modified restraints and all hung-up on like literary inhibitions and grammatical fears . . .' " Allen Ginsberg: "who scribbled all night rocking and rolling over lofty incantations which in the yellow morning were stanzas of gibberish . . ." H. H. Lynde: " 'What I'm talking about now,' he corrected her, 'is fiction. Fiction has fallen on hard days, poor old girl.' 'So much of it is poor stuff now, don't you think?' 'Sure. Pure tripe,' he agreed heartily. 'I seldom read a novel myself.' "

SWITCHING from trends to categories, we should next note a couple of groups or schools. There is the Paul Bowles—Flannery O'Connor cult of the Gratuitous Grotesque. A specimen Bowles story: an American professor of linguistics goes into a remote corner of the North African desert in search of obscure dialects. He is captured by primitive tribesmen who make him into their slave-clown and cut off his tongue (*lingua*—get it?). Flannery O'Connor tells us that she writes out of a "deep Christian concern." The story of hers which, in Allen Tate's view, best exemplifies this concern is the tale of an embittered, virginal Southern bluestocking with a wooden leg who accompanies a young Bible salesman into a barn to seduce him. Her "victim" produces, out of a dummy Bible, whiskey, contraceptives and dirty playing cards. In the end he runs off with her wooden leg in his suitcase. All of these overingenious horrifics are presumably meant to speak to us of the Essential Nature of Our Time, but when the very real and cruel grotesquerie of our world is converted into clever gimmicks for *Partisan Review,* we may be forgiven for reacting with the self-same disgust as the little old lady from Dubuque.

The conscientious zoologist cannot ignore Kerouac-Ginsburg, the literary hoax which San Francisco successfully imposed on the nation last year. This "hip" movement, celebrating sex, jazz, dope, frenetic movement, and *life,* has been hailed by Norman Mailer as the Wave of the Future. *On the Road* is an account (not really a fiction; like James Jones and too many others, Kerouac thinks that writing is Having Experiences and Putting Them Down) of his friends' experiments in the unsystematic derangement of the senses.

It should have been titled *Walt Whitman's Last Gasp* or perhaps *The Chary Ape,* for Kerouac remains a Nice College Boy, a mere fellow-traveler of psychopathy and psychosis, fight his destiny as he will.

The "political" significance of the Kerouac world, whose key words are "holy," "mad," "soul," "wild," and "rush," is simply that it is the Great Bad Place; and poor Kerouac secretly knows it and is ashamed of knowing. As for Ginsberg, his celebrated "Howl" states that the "starving hysterical naked" friends of his who populate the poem are "the best minds of my generation," and are all "holy." If Mr. Ginsberg should be mistaken about this, we are justified in echoing Herbert Gold's farewell in the *Nation* to the booze-and-bop boys: "Hipster, Go Home."

The "politics" of these groups is either invisible or too vasty to be seen. Some very brief notes are in order on the politics of our younger writers who are political, or at least semi-demi-hemi-political. Herman Wouk: the social fabric and all traditional decency are undermined by cowardly irresponsible self-serving intellectuals. Mary McCarthy: conservatives aren't so bad after all, they see the folly of the liberal intellectual's excessive, self-tormenting ethical scruples, and besides, they are all male and rather masterful. Nelson Algren, Jones, Kerouac, Ginsberg: debated Empsonian Pastoral; the outlaw underdogs are better than The System; "the bum's as holy as the seraphim!" Irwin Shaw: be hep, be sad, be good. Elizabeth Spencer: we must accept responsibility for fighting the corruption which flourishes when laziness and the profits of the status quo accommodate evil. James Reichley: we have a wealth of political detail yet everything comes down to the individual, but we're not quite sure how. H. H. Lynde: "Just hang on" and "deal with life and man as they [are]." John Cheever: go bravely into the great crazy world, but take with you as touchstone and amulet the memory of private joys and sane traditional ways. Wolfe, Mailer and Styron as above.

Our younger writers, then, are mostly honest: they reflect the feelings of impotence and fear and hemmed-in weariness that we all share. But, with honorable partial exceptions, they have not yet made art out of our situation. Intelligence, good will, industry are not enough. "We lack the power to imagine what we know." One could work up a Ph.D. thesis on "The Man of Good Will, Alone and Sorely Beset, in the Contemporary American Novel," but it wouldn't really be worth the doing. When we have more good writing, we will have more good political writing. Those who assert that our books must *necessarily* be mediocre because our age is mediocre are merely arguing in a circle; they forget Stendhal. The novelist who will rise above our times has not happened yet; we await him.

Writers and Politics
Stephen Spender

from

Partisan Review, vol. 34, no. 3, 1967.

Stephen Spender

WRITERS AND POLITICS

In England, the circumstances giving rise to poets interfering in politics are special. In their study of Julian Bell's and John Cornford's tragically broken off lives, Peter Stansky and William Abrahams[1] inevitably devote much space to explaining the family background and the personal psychological and intellectual problems which led these young men to anti-Fascism and their deaths in Spain.

If they had been French critics writing about the young Malraux, Aragon or Eluard, there would not have been need of so much explanation. For in France the nineteen thirties was only a recent episode in the long involvement of the French intellectuals with politics since before the French Revolution. As David Caute has pointed out, writers like Romain Rolland, Henri Barbusse, Georges Duhamel and André Gide publicly discussed their attitudes to the Russian Revolution, the League of Nations, war, disarmament, after 1918.

The rightist as well as the leftist French intellectual had centers, organizations, reviews, newspapers, platforms. They regarded imagination and critical intelligence as instruments which could be applied to social problems. In taking sides, the intellectual exploited the legend

1 JOURNEY TO THE FRONTIER. By Peter Stansky and William Abrahams. Constable. 50s.

that, *qua* intellectual, he represented detached intelligence. Stooping from his exalted height, the "clerk" made objective, disinterested judgments.

It is true of course that sometimes a Romain Rolland or a Henri Barbusse, infected with the virus of the International disguised as Internationalism, looked across the channel and appealed to a Shaw or a Wells to attend some international conference or sign some declaration of Human Rights. But if and when they responded, the English "great writers" did not descend as radiant messengers from the realms of pure imagination and impartial intellect. Wells, although priding himself on being a social prophet, cultivated the manner of a traveling salesman for the scientific culture, when he made his public "interventions." Like Shaw, Bennett and Galsworthy he thought of his public personality as antiesthetic, lowbrow. He was forever explaining that he was a journalist who breathed a different air from that in the novels of Henry James.

Eliot, Virginia Woolf, even D. H. Lawrence saw to it that Wells and Bennett should never forget their public streak. When during the thirties E. M. Forster appeared on *"front populaire"* platforms he did so because the time demanded that he should assume a role in which he had no confidence and for which he felt little enthusiasm. His presence at Congresses of the Intellectuals during the anti-Fascist period, and that of young English poets, was extraordinary—like lions walking the streets of Rome on the night preceding the Ides of March, a sign that the artist had become denatured from his function by apocalyptic events.

Until the thirties the younger generation of Oxford and Cambridge were infected by the antipolitics of their parents' generation. Stansky and Abrahams mention that the famous society of Cambridge intellectual undergraduates—the Apostles—which had such a close connection with literary Bloomsbury, agreed in the twenties that "practical politics were beneath discussion." Even more striking, in the early thirties, the Apostles ceased for some years to exist, as the result of the pressure of "too many conflicting political beliefs" among their members. Yet so different was the atmosphere by then that to Julian Bell, no longer then an undergraduate, and to John Cornford, who was one, this must have seemed like saying that having at last something to discuss, the Apostles had decided to discuss nothing.

To the Cambridge and Bloomsbury generation of their parents Bell and Cornford were ducklings hatched out from supposititious hen's eggs, swimming out on to those dirty choppy political waters. Not that

Clive and Vanessa Bell and the Cornford parents disagreed with the younger generation's anti-Fascist politics (they sympathized with them). But they regarded politicians as philistine and the artist in politics as betraying the pure cause of individualist art. Leftish political sympathies were almost a part of the ethos of literary Bloomsbury, but political action seemed vulgar. Art had no connection with political action, nor with the good life of personal relations and refined sensations which could only be enjoyed by the individual in isolation or among friends. J. M. Keynes and Leonard Woolf were, of course, in their different ways, politically involved and influential but they were so without lowering their intellectual values or sacrificing personal relationships.

These attitudes are reflected in Forster's novels, in which the good characters have liberal values but realize them only through the medium of personal relations. Business, power, government for Forster belong to the world of "telegrams and anger." That Margaret or Helen Schlegel should carry their socialism further than a few committees, and those personal relations with Henry Wilcox and Leonard Bast which test their principles, seems unthinkable. And although Fielding, Aziz and the other characters who fight on the side of the angels are opposed to the British Raj, it is difficult to think of them taking any effective political action: they attempt to resolve their problems through personal relations between British and Indians. One of their chief grievances against the British occupiers is that they have made relations perhaps impossible.

Forster's antipolitics, antipower, antibusiness attitude is implicit also in the novels of D. H. Lawrence, Virginia Woolf and Aldous Huxley, which have so little else in common. The fact is that the separation of the world of private values imagined in art from the world of the public values of business, science, politics was an essential part of the victory of the generation for whom "the world changed in 1910" against their elders Shaw, Wells, Bennett and Galsworthy. The accusation leveled against the "Georgian" novelists was that they depicted characters who were the social average of the material circumstances in which they lived. They interpreted human beings as walking functions of the society that conditioned them with body, soul, sensibility and sex, common denominators of the general gritty smog, stabbed through with steely rays of scientific materialist social progress. The aim of D. H. Lawrence and Virginia Woolf was to create characters who were isolated creatures of unique awareness with sensibility transcending their material circumstances.

Of course I do not mean that Lawrence had no political sympathies: still less that he had views in common with the liberal ones of Virginia Woolf and E. M. Forster. In his novels those characters like Birkin and Aaron who are representative of the politically searching Lawrence shop around in the contemporary world of action looking for lords of life who are passional, violent and antidemocratic. Bertrand Russell, after some dealings with him during a few months toward the end of the First World War—when Lawrence toyed with the idea of founding some kind of brain (Bertrand Russell) – and – blood (D. H. Lawrence) political movement—came to the conclusion (stated thirty years afterward) that Lawrence's blood-and-soil view of life was later realized in the horrors of Nazism. My point is though that, apart from this one disastrous attempt to get together with Russell and the Cambridge intelligentsia, and apart from his general sympathy with what might be termed bloody-bodiedness (in Germany, Italy or Mexico), Lawrence found the world of public affairs, business and any kind of social cooperation, utterly antipathetic. He even went so far as to write a letter to Forster (in September, 1922) charging him with "a nearly deadly mistake [in] glorifying those *business* people in *Howards End*," and adding that "business is no good"—a conclusion with which he might have found his correspondent concurred, had he bothered to read Forster's novel.

Different as E. M. Forster, Virginia Woolf and D. H. Lawrence were, they all agreed that the novel should be concerned with awareness of life deeper than the conscious mind of the "old novelistic character" and the computable human social unit. Lawrence in his essay on Galsworthy, and Virginia Woolf in her lecture on Arnold Bennett ("Mr. Bennett and Mrs. Brown") attack Galsworthy and Bennett on similar grounds: that the characters in their books are "social units."

Thus, although the 1910 generation (I call them this to make them immediately distinguishable) sympathized with the anti-Fascism of Julian Bell and John Cornford, they were also horrified at the idea of literature being compromised by politics. Virginia Woolf's *Letter to a Young Poet* (1935) is a subdued but troubled protest at the spectacle of sensitive and talented young Oxford and Cambridge poets echoing public matters with a public voice and not writing out of a Wordsworthian isolation, solitary among the solitary reapers. And E. M. Forster, with politeness and forbearance, indicated the underlying grief of Cambridge friends, when he wrote that the future probably lay with Communism but that he did not want to belong to it.

John Cornford was seven years younger than Julian Bell, who was almost contemporaneous with Auden, Day Lewis, MacNeice and myself. In our speeded-up century, perhaps even those few years marked still another "new generation." For our earlier Oxford and Cambridge one secretly sided with the personalist generation old enough to be our parents. We had, written on our hearts, the motto from *The Orators*:

> *Private faces in public places*
> *Are wiser and nicer*
> *Than public faces in private places.*

But John Cornford's generation of anti-Fascist undergraduate agitators at Cambridge, and of the Oxford October Club, did not cherish our sense of the supreme importance of maintaining the distinction between public and private worlds. This difference of generations comes between Julian Bell and John Cornford.

For Bell, to have to choose between personal loyalties and the public cause was always agonizing. By upbringing antipolitical, his choice would always have been for personal values, if he had not come to think of anti-Fascism as a burning loyalty beyond mere politics. But even so he remained conscious of having to make choices in which one set of loyalties had nearly always to be sacrificed to another. He came to think that the private ones of poetry and of love for his family had to submit to the public ones of anti-Fascism. Yet when he went to Spain, in joining an ambulance unit rather than the International Brigade, he sacrificed his interest in war and strategy to his parents' pacifism.

For Cornford, however, there was no question that personal values had to be sacrificed to the public cause. All that mattered was to defeat Fascism. For him, and for his already "new generation," all choices had to be decided by the Marxist interpretation of history. Subjective motives did not count.

In the jargon of the new activist generation (only five years younger than ours) all our generation's scruples about personal relations and subjective feelings could be consigned to the dustbin of liberal inhibitions. Cornford's conviction of the superiority of the Marxist objective reason over personal consideration is indeed the dominating theme of most of his poetry. Leaving the girl who is mother to his child, the objective reason becomes the image of the surgeon's knife cutting away the soft rot of compassion:

Though parting's as cruel as the surgeon's knife,
It's better than ingrown canker, the rotten leaf.
All that I know is I have got to leave.
There's new life fighting in me to get at the air,
And I can't stop its mouth with the rags of old love.
Clean wounds are easiest to bear.

The adroitness with which he establishes the superiority of the ideological "new life" struggling in him to the real new life—a child—struggling in her, tells a lot about young human nature dominated by an ideology.

To say that Julian Bell could not, except through a distortion of his nature, have discovered such impersonal grounds for apparent callousness is not to say that he might not have behaved just as egotistically to any of his mistresses (whom Stansky and Abrahams list as A, B, C, D, etc., far down the alphabet). The difference is that Bell would have found a personal reason for justifying conduct that Cornford justified by an "objective" one.

To most literary-minded readers, Bell will seem more interesting than Cornford because he is the more self-searching and Hamletian and literary character. Certainly his personality and his relations with his relations make fascinating reading. It is part of the excellence of their book that the authors, having put the reader in possession of some of the facts, often leave him wondering. For instance, when Bell wrote that dissertation *The Good and All That* which, it was hoped, would get him a fellowship at Kings, there were plenty of psychological reasons why he should make a hash of it. On the one hand he wished to please his Cambridge mentors by writing an essay on good and evil in the manner of the discussions of the Apostles, but on the other hand "more perhaps than he himself realized, Julian was in full revolt against his Bloomsbury philosophical background, and its static conception of 'states of mind' as values in themselves, or consequences that might ensue from them." The confusedness was perhaps in part the result of a naïve desire not to shock Roger Fry, to whom the dissertation was sent for a report. This was of course a model of tolerance and fair-mindedness. How *liberal*!

Anna Russell in her famous burlesque exposé of Wagner's operas points out (rightly or wrongly) that Siegfried had the misfortune never to have met a lady who was not his aunt. There was something of such a burlesque Siegfried about the young Julian Bell, who gives one the impression of always encountering very understanding Bloomsbury aunts. He certainly developed something of an anti-aunt complex. But, as with the other Siegfried, we are also left with a further question on our hands—wasn't this Siegfried after all a bit stupid?

John Cornford was priggish but not at all stupid, and it is this which in the end makes him more interesting than Bell. He was a Greek hero rather than a confused Wagnerian one, his specialty being the cutting through of Gordian knots. He dealt with family, school, Cambridge, love affairs, the problems dividing the poet from the man of action, all in the same way—cut right through them with the steel blade of objective action. As between poetry and fighting in Spain, he decidedly chose the latter, after he left Cambridge:

> Poetry had become a marginal activity, and a private one. He never discussed his work with his friends in the party; most of them did not even know until after his death that he had been a poet. . . . In the rare moments when he was free to do so, he wrote both personal and political poems. The latter represents a conscious effort to "objectify" his ideas and attitudes as a revolutionary participator, and to transform them into revolutionary poetry.

Instead of being, like Julian Bell, a poet partly stifled in his work by his need to take action in circumstances which cried out for it, he put poetry aside and immersed himself in the war, but from this, and out of the ideology with which he tempered his will and determination, a hard clear new poetry of the objective will began to emerge. He writes sketchily, tentatively but effectively, as someone dominated by the Communist idea of transforming the dialectic into history—hammered out of his mind and body occupied at the given moment in doing just this:

> *The past, a glacier, gripped the mountain wall,*
> *And time was inches, dark was all.*
> *But here it scales the end of the range,*
> *The dialectic's point of change,*
> *Crashes in light and minutes to its fall.*
>
> *Time present is a cataract whose force*
> *Breaks down the banks even at its source*
> *And history forming in our hands*
> *Not plasticine but roaring sands,*
> *Yet we must swing it to its final course.*

The attempt here is to write a secular Communist poetry corresponding to religious metaphysical poetry. It is blurred perhaps because Marxism, in common with other analytic and scientific systems, cannot be taken outside its own method and terms, and interpreted

imagistically, or converted into a mystique, without appearing to lose
its own kind of precision. Here the Marxist poet is only encountering
the difficulty of other modern poets in a secular world. The precision
of science resists being interpreted into the precision of poetry. But if
one sees beyond the poem, as through a transparent screen, the structure of the dialectic, it is clear that this is an attempt to write Communist poetry. If one does not see this, then one might agree with
Stansky and Abrahams that "the abstractions and metaphors proliferate,
taking us still further from reality and deeper into the visionary world
of the seer." Having lived through the thirties, I can only rub my eyes
reading this. Still—from the Marxist standpoint—all that is wrong is
thinking that "abstractions" (if they are "correct") lead away from reality
instead of penetrating deeper into it. The point is that Cornford was
trying here to be a Marxist visionary and seer. And, but for Stalin and
the Marxists, the attempt would not be a contradiction in terms.

What does seem strange is that the idea of literary Bloomsbury
that literature should be untainted by politics seems to have derived
from France, or rather, from Roger Fry's and Clive Bell's idea of a
France of complete esthetic purism. Probably this went back to de Nerval,
Gautier, Baudelaire, Mallarmé and Flaubert—and to the eighteen-
nineties, reviled and disowned, yet such an influence up till 1930. Art for
art's sake looks sophisticated when metamorphosized into "significant
form," and Oscar Wilde walks again, but unrecognized, through G. E.
Moore's doctrine of the value above all other things of "certain states
of consciousness, which may roughly be described as the pleasures of
human intercourse and the enjoyment of beautiful objects."

But to hold up post-1918 France as the country of pure esthetic
aims is rather as though the French were to point to the work of
Edgar Allen Poe in Baudelaire's translations as the type of recent
American literature.

A young English writer going with eyes unprejudiced by Bloomsbury's view of France to Paris in the late twenties or early thirties
soon discovered that the newspapers and reviews had national parks
freely ranged over by French novelists and poets offering their opinions
on social topics. When Julian Bell was sent in 1927 to Paris, to learn
French at the home of a teacher, he found that his host, as well as
knowing much about French literature and art was a theoretical Communist though "there was nothing of the modern party line about him."

Just as English good taste is often modeled on an idea that France
is the country of perfect elegance (one has only to travel a little in the
provinces to see that the real strength of France lies in its bourgeois bad

taste) so Bloomsbury estheticism was modeled on the idea of French writers and artists devoted to nothing but their art. But France is pre-eminently the country of the *deuxième metier*, of the writer who is also a teacher or journalist, the writer who, though he may be "pure" in his poetry or fiction, yet lives by selling his opinions. Even **Paul Valéry** wrote about politics in the modern world.

It is, indeed, the English who are the real esthetes, failing per-haps to be as pure as they would like to be, but nevertheless upholding a standard of art for art's sake. One has only to mention the names of Kipling, Wells and Shaw to see that these writers, because they published undisguised opinions about politics, damaged their reputa-tions as artists here more than they would have in any other country. And today the writers of the thirties suffer from the odium of their early work being tainted with politics.

All the English or American writer may do with his politics, if he is not to be labeled journalist, is cultivate convictions which show through his work, attitudes basically political, but implicit, not vulgarly declared. The anglicized Americans, Henry James and T. S. Eliot, adapting chameleon-like to England, acquired a traditionalist coloration that, on the rare occasions when it is developed to the point of crude statement, is conservative. But in fact they hardly ever do come into the open.

A point which Mr. John Harrison rather misses in his book *The Reactionaries*,[2] in adding up the sum of Eliot's anti-Semitic and political-ly reactionary observations, is that they are not in character with the Eliot who after all became an English poet. They come rather from another Eliot character, a somberly jaunty young American in Paris, a figure in a cape, almost eighteen-ninetyish. The famous pronounce-ment about being a royalist would do better as a bouquet thrown to the Comte de Paris, than to George V.

The characteristic of the special kind of crisis which persuades the young English or American poet (yesterday Spain, today Vietnam) to take the plunge into politics is one of conscience among sensitive and intelligent young members of the ruling class caused by what they regard as a betrayal of principle on the part of their fathers' genera-tion. The failure is the failure to act according to principles when interests are threatened. Since the principles of democratic and "free" societies are basically liberal and since liberal values are always open to the challenge that those who profess them have refused to pay the

2 THE REACTIONARIES. By John Harrison. Golancz. 35s.

price which they demand, the crisis is one of the liberal conscience. At the time of the French Revolution and in the early nineteenth century the fury of the Romantic poets was against an English governing class which refused to support freedom when revolution threatened English interests. Byron and Shelley were never more the young English aristocrats than in supporting the overthrowers of kings and priests, and in reviling Castlereagh as though he were their delinquent lackey. Their attitude has something in common with that of Robert Lowell to President Johnson.

Likewise in the thirties anti-Fascism was predominantly a reaction of middle-class young men brought up in a liberal atmosphere against the old men in power, of the same class, who while talking about freedom and democracy, were not prepared to denounce Hitler or defend the Spanish Republic. They feared that as the price of doing so they would find themselves on the same side as the Communists. That the old who professed liberal principles should not see the threat of Fascism or, if they did see it, that they did not take action, seemed to the young a betrayal of basic liberal principles by liberals. Cornford and Bell were not just young Oedipuses subconsciously wishing to destroy their father's image. They had conscious reasons for attacking it: Laius was a liberal.

It is only in the circumstances of a moral power vacuum that the English or American writer can justify, to his conscience as an artist, his taking a political stand. But he does so not without qualms. The anti-Fascist writers of the thirties conducted debates, not only in reviews or at meetings, but in their own hearts, between public and isolated artistic conscience. Indeed, ever since the nineteenth century (Shelley, Arnold, Clough, Ruskin, Morris) it has been the case that the English poet mixed up in politics may spend a lifetime divided between two voices: that of social, and that of esthetic, conscience: Shelley calling on the world to dethrone kings, and Keats claiming that his poetry is unshadowed by any trace of public thought.

There is a good deal to be said in support of the English poets' mistrust of overtly taking sides. Only in exceptional historical circumstances do writers here attend the "boring meeting" or read or write the "flat ephemeral pamphlet." Very rarely do they find themselves involved in "the conscious acceptance of guilt in the fact of murder."

The "disgrace" attaching to the "low dishonest decade" of the thirties in England was not the same as that in France of some surrealist turned Communist and currying favor with Stalin by accusing André Gide of being a Fascist because he was critical of the Russia of the Moscow trials. We had the humility to believe that for writers to be involved in politics was itself a fall from grace. To us part of the hideousness of Fascism was that it produced anti-Fascism, involving disinterested artists in interested politics. Reading Auden's poem on the death of Yeats, in 1939, "Intellectual disgrace/Stares from every human face," I think of the whole politically involved intellectual life of that decade, disgraced with ideologies.

However, our English and American idea that the intellectuals should only take political sides in situations providing moral contrasts of inky black and dazzling white has its disadvantages. For one thing there is something unserious about a seriousness which is made conditional on things being so serious.

After all, the shining emergent Causes—Spain, the Bomb, Vietnam—do have chains of further causality stretching before and after. That the intellectuals only have time for them when they have become moral scandals might seem to indicate that they do not have time anyway. The English and American political-unpolitical intellectuals sometime have the look of the gadarene swine hurling themselves down the steepest slope: the gadarene swine being of course in the latest apocalyptic fashion. The cause evaporates when the crisis in its immediate emanation has passed. The long term causes of the Cause find few among the English and American intellectuals to interest them.

In France the intellectuals are, as it were, more or less in continual session like the British House of Lords. They are sometimes irresponsible, nearly always narrowly legalistic in their interpretations of a political line (with that deceptive French "logic") but their concern with politics is sustained and (despite Clive Bell and Roger Fry) not thought to dishonor their art. They do not have to prove that in attending a conference about peace or freedom, they are being serious, whereas the English and Americans are under pressure to show that when they do take up a cause, they do more about it than travel to nice places. His biographers note that Julian Bell dismissed "in a few satirical phrases" the International Writers' Congress which was held in Madrid in the summer of 1937, while he was driving an ambulance on the Brunete front. I happened to attend the Congress of Intellectuals myself and also to have described it satirically (in *World within World*) though without Bell's justification that I was carrying a gun or driving an ambulance. But I don't think any but English and Americans would have thought that a meeting of writers in Madrid when shells were falling was a despicable exercise. The French would have seen it as a useful part of a larger strategy of help for the Republican cause, as useful, in its way, as being at the front, though not so courageous and praiseworthy. They also serve who only sit and talk.

The authors of two books which I have been reading recently seem to me to take the difference between the situation of the French and the Anglo-American intellectuals insufficiently into account: *The Reactionaries* by John Harrison, to which I have already referred, and *Writers and Politics* by Conor Cruise O'Brien.[3]

O'Brien is at his brilliant best when he is discussing French writers: e.g., the shift in Camus' earlier revolutionary position to the resigned pessimism of *La Chute,* written when he refused to take sides over the Algerian War. O'Brien analyzes the relations of Camus with the general current of French-intellectual life with a precision which reads like a description of the modifications caused to some receiving instrument by the electrical impulses passing through it.

O'Brien quite rightly derides those critics who discovered Camus to be "objectively revolutionary," employing what he calls "the convenient principle: 'I know what he thinks: it doesn't matter what he thinks he thinks.' "

Since he has such insight into the fallaciousness of this principle, it seems strange that, on occasion, he employs it himself. In the essay on Dwight Macdonald (*A New Yorker Critic*) he argues that Mr. Macdonald in giving up his "socialist past" and writing about "masscult," "midcult" and the rest for *The New Yorker* in effect (and regardless of what Macdonald may think he thinks) subscribes to the policy of that magazine, which is a projection of the views of its advertisers. This is the "objective" argument squared. *The New Yorker* is as object to its backers, and Dwight Macdonald is as object to *The New Yorker.*

The insidious nonpolitical policy of *The New Yorker* as it operates subliminally on the mind of Dwight Macdonald works like this:

> you could say *almost* anything about Mark Twain, James Joyce, James Agee, Ernest Hemingway, James Cozzens, Colin Wilson, the English or revised Bibles, or Webster's *New International Dictionary*—to list most of Mr. Macdonald's subjects—without causing a *New Yorker* reader or advertiser to wince. If, however, your favourite author happened to be Mao Tse-tung and Fidel Castro and you tried to say so in *The New Yorker*, then you would be going "against the American grain" and you would not be likely to go very far.

3 WRITERS AND POLITICS. By Conor Cruise O'Brien. Alfred A. Knopf. $4.95.

This is really a variant of the "objective" argument: *The New Yorker* is not filled with articles in praise of Mao Tse-tung because of the invisible thought-control of the advertisers. But supposing, after all, that *New Yorker* writers don't admire the prose of the Chinese and Cuban dictators? Should *The New Yorker* nevertheless contain a quota of opinions praising it just to prove to Dr. O'Brien that *The New Yorker* is free from the pressures to which he thinks it is subject? Or supposing that Dr. O'Brien had suggested some different writers whom *New Yorker* writers would praise if they were free agents—say Hitler and Trujillo? One only has to suggest this to see the bias of the argument. Dr. O'Brien is playing on the reader's secret guilt about China and Cuba. There are I think false steps in O'Brien's attack on Dwight Macdonald. In the first place, Macdonald was never a party line socialist revolutionary, he was just a lone rebel all by himself. He was a highly individualist rebel against American capitalism who sought allies among Anarchists, Communists, Trotskyites. In discussing him as though he had reneged from revolutionary socialism (perhaps— because he is such a nice fellow—without realizing he was doing so), Dr. O'Brien fails to mention the important statements made by Macdonald when he gave up his magazine *Politics*, that in the complexity of the postwar situation he no longer found it possible to take up clear positions. He found, as did many other survivors from the simplicist world of the thirties, that politics had become extremely complicated and that it was no longer possible to see them in black and white.

O'Brien's case against Camus seems stronger than that against Macdonald, because the early Camus wrote within the context of the ideas of the left-wing French intellectuals. Camus' attitude toward Algeria certainly separated him from Sartre and his followers. It is plausible then to regard him as abandoning a path followed by leftist French writers. With Macdonald though, all one can say is that an independent thinker whose thoughts when he was young were anarchistic later had other thoughts about other things. The new thoughts were about culture and not about politics. One may or may not agree with them, one may or may not regret that Macdonald stopped having things to say about politics, but to say that he changed the content and the direction of his thinking to suit *The New Yorker* is misleading.

Mr. John Harrison's reactionaries are W. B. Yeats, Wyndham Lewis, Ezra Pound and D. H. Lawrence. Mr. Harrison knows that to prove that they are really reactionary, it is not enough to show that they occasionally labeled themselves so. However he does not altogether avoid the dangers implicit in compiling lists of their reactionary pronouncements without asking how far these really correspond to ideas in their best creative work. His problem is to relate their expressed opinions to convictions of which they themselves may not have been wholly aware, but which do have political implications, in their best writing.

The extent to which we should take a writer's expressed opinions seriously is difficult to ascertain. What I have been suggesting here is that in France it is not so difficult to do this, because there is a tradition of intellectually respect-worthy opinion about politics to which the writer can relate his own views. But in England and America there is no such tradition of the writer in politics. Therefore his interventions tend to be sporadic and occasional and perhaps not consistent with his truest, that is his most imaginative, insights.

This is even more true of the Right than of the Left. For the Left, after all, even in England and America, can merge into the traditions of the French and American Revolutions, the internationalism of nineteenth-century liberals, Marxism, mingling, for the time being, with a world river of continuous thought and energy. During the decade of the Popular Front the English anti-Fascist writers became, as it were, honorary French intellectuals. And this was not altogether absurd because of the international character of the Left. But Fascism, and indeed the European right, so diverse in its manifestations in different countries, although potentially an international threat, was nationalist and local in ideas and performance. Therefore there was something much more esoteric and perverse about the intermittent support which Mr. Harrison's reactionaries gave to right-wing and Fascist movements than about the corresponding political involvements of the anti-Fascists.

The traditionalism which appealed so much to Yeats, Pound, Eliot, Wyndham Lewis and others doubtless had political implications, and given the crucial nature of the period, it was not dishonorable of traditionalists to want to realize these by supporting rightist parties. But a big leap into the near dark had to be made in order to convert the poetic traditionalism of Yeats, Pound or Eliot into support of General O'Duffy, Mussolini or the *Action Française*.

The political attitudes of Yeats, Eliot, Pound, Lewis, Lawrence, consist largely of gestures toward some movement, idea, leadership which *seems* to correspond to the writer's deeply held traditionalism. Such gestures and attitudes are largely rhetorical. For the politics of these writers are secondary effects of their thoughts about the tragedy of culture in modern industrial societies. They are sometimes conscientious, sometimes irresponsible attempts to translate their traditionalist standpoint into programs of action.

Whereas the leftist anti-Fascist writers—believing that the overthrow of Fascism was the most important task of their generation—tended to think that their writing should perhaps be the instrument of the overriding public cause, the reactionaries thought that politics should be the servant of their vision of the high tradition. Wyndham Lewis, for example, never supposed that he should become the mouthpiece of Hitler. What he thought was that as the living representative in the contemporary world of renaissance "genius" perhaps a few renaissance thugs would be helpful to the cause of his art: if this was the role that Hitler and Mussolini had unknowingly cast for themselves, maybe they should be encouraged. Yeats had a not very different attitude toward the soldiers of the Right who could perhaps be given orders by Art, and who also were useful in providing sound effects for the end of a civilization.

The most important thing common to the reactionaries was that they had a kind of shared vision of the greatness of the European past which implied hatred and contempt for the present. It might be said that all their most important work was an attempt to relate their experiences to this central vision. On the secondary level of their attempts to carry forward the vision into action and propaganda there is a good deal of peripheral mess, resulting from their search for political approximations to their love of past intellect, art, discipline and order. Often their politics only shows that they care less for politics than for literature.

Mr. John Harrison takes some remarks of Orwell as his text which he sets out to illustrate with examples drawn from his authors. This text is worth examining:

> The relationship between fascism and the literary intelligentsia badly needs investigating, and Yeats might well be the starting point. He is best studied by someone like Mr. Menon who knows that a writer's politics and religious beliefs are not excrescences to be laughed away, but something that will leave their mark even on the smallest detail of his work.

This sounds sensible enough though it is perhaps too offhand to bear the weight of Mr. Harrison's thesis. Certain objections occur to one. For example, if it were true that a writer's politics and religious beliefs extend from a center outward into every smallest detail of his work, then the converse would also be true that one could deduce his party or creed from an analysis of any smallest detail, whether or not the writer thought that he supported such a party or a creed.

This leads back into the objectivist fallacy of the writer holding certain views whether he thinks he does or not.

What is wrong is Orwell's loose bracketing of religious and political beliefs, and his assumption that it is a comparatively simple matter to know what a writer believes. But it is not simple, since he is writing out of his imagination, his vision of life, and not according to labels which he or others may stick on to him. Orwell appears to think that Yeats's symbolism, mythology, imagery—his poetry in a word— are projections onto the plane of the imagination of his declared political and religious beliefs. It is really the other way round. Yeats's religion and politics are the results of numerous inconsistent attempts to rationalize his central poetic vision, as dogma, politics, action. Whether or not they should be "laughed off," Yeats's Fascism was an excrescence. It grew rather approximately and grossly from the center of his poetic imagination which was neither approximate nor gross. To anyone who reads *A Vision* or his journals and prose, it must be quite clear that his opinions are attempts to systematize the intuitions of his imagination.

Add to this that even when they are stated as prose, one cannot discuss Yeats's beliefs without making many qualifications. Outside of believing in art and in some universe of the spirit in which the visions of art are realistic truth, Yeats himself was extremely approximate about what he believed. He was candid in admitting that he cultivated beliefs and attitudes in himself for the purpose of propping up the symbolism of his poetry. He also had a sharp picture of a materialist world which undermined his world of the poetic imagination: this was Bernard Shaw's Fabian philosophy and belief in material progress. That which to Shaw was superstition and reaction recommended itself as dogma and practice to Yeats.

Dr. O'Brien has drawn up a formidable list of Yeats's pro-Fascist statements, including one or two sympathetic to Hitler. But to the reader who thinks that Yeats's poems and not his opinions matter, it will seem, I think, that he used the political stage properties of the thirties in the same way as he used the assertions of his esoteric system set out in *A Vision*—as a scenario stocked with symbols and metaphors which he could draw on for his poetry. To Yeats writing the tragic-gay poetry of his old age, Hitler had the seductive charm of an apocalyptic cat.

What is distressing about the reactionaries is not that they were occasionally betrayed by intoxication with their own ideas and fantasies into supporting dictators who would, given the opportunity, certainly have disposed very quickly of them, but that in the excess of their hatred of the present and their love of the past, they developed a certain cult of inhumanity. One has to ask though—was not their renaissance vision enormously valuable to us, and could it have been stated without dramatizing the statuesque figures of a visionary past against the twittering ghosts of the disintegrated present?

Eliot's political views, like those of Yeats, are a defense system hastily thrown out with the intention of defending a spiritual world deriving strength from the past, against modern materialism. One suspects that Eliot was convinced intellectually, as a critic, and not with his imagination, as a poet, of the necessity of rationalizing poetic values as politics. Without the example of T. E. Hulme and without some cheer-leading from Ezra Pound and some satiric pushing from Wyndham Lewis, Eliot would scarcely have made those remarks about liberalism and progress, which seem casual asides, and which yet set him up as an authority, defender of the monarchy and the faith. In his role of political commentator in *The Criterion* he must have baffled readers who did not realize that his mind was moving along lines laid down by Charles Maurras. There is also something cloak-and-dagger about the anti-Semitic passages in the Sweeney poems which Mr. Harrison inevitably relies on to demonstrate his thesis:

> The smoky candle end of time
> Declines. On the Rialto once.
>   The rats are underneath the piles.
> The jew is underneath the lot.
>   Money in furs.

Of course this was distasteful caricature even when it was written. In the light of later developments it seems almost criminal. Nevertheless what seems wrong about the Sweeney poems is not that they are reactionary-political but that they use a tawdry view of a conspiratorial capitalism to construct a rather cardboard background to the poetry.

That Eliot, Yeats, Pound and Lawrence were all exiles (and Wyndham Lewis a self-declared outsider—"the Enemy") has a bearing on their politics. The exile is particularly apt to dramatize himself as a metaphor moving through a world of metaphors. Pound and Eliot left what they regarded as barbarous America to come to civilized Europe, where they found, in the First World War:

> *There died a myriad,*
> *And of the best among them,*
> *For an old bitch gone in the teeth,*
> *For a botched civilisation.*

Their poetry exalted the past which they had sought among the Georgian poets and found only embalmed in museums, and it derided the present, the decay of standards. They were, politically, Don Quixotes of the new world armed to rescue the Dulcinea of the old— an old hag. The aim of their polemical criticism was to reinvent the past, shining and modern, and use it as a modern weapon against the arsenals of the dead men stuffed with straw.

Their politics were secondary to the creative and critical attempt. In them, they were drawn to whatever points of view presented social and economic problems as metaphors for their idea of the state of civilization. The appeal of politics in the guise of metaphor is curiously shown in the great attraction—which can only be compared with that of Donne's ideas about time—of Social Credit theories for a number of writers, including not only Eliot and Pound but also Edwin Muir— during the late twenties and thirties. Social Credit is easy to visualize. One sees objects of value being produced on one side of a chart and on the other side money—credit—being printed equal to the value of the objects. Since Schacht and Mussolini actually made adjustments to the German and Italian economies along similar lines, Social Credit seemed to be an idea which could be abstracted from the rest of Fascism and applied to other systems. For reactionaries who could not swallow violence, it was a kind of Fascism without tears.

Students of Ezra Pound's *Cantos* will observe how metaphors of this kind drawn from a reading of economics imagized and then applied to describe the state of the civilization are used by Pound, sometimes to justify inhuman attitudes. A famous example is the passage about usury in which Pound explains that the introduction of usury into the economic system falsifies the line drawn by the painter, causes his hand to err. This justifies a massacre of Jews.

The Left also of course had their metaphors, which by making history appear a poetic act tended to regard human beings as words to be acted upon, deleted if necessary, so that the poem might come right.

In fact, on a level of false rhetoric, so far from there being a separation of politics from poetry, there is a dangerous convergence. Marxism, because it regards history as malleable material to be manipulated by the creative will of the Marxist, is rich in this kind of raw material poetic thinking.

The temptation for the poet is to take over the rhetoric of political will and action and translate it into the rhetoric of poetry without confronting the public rhetoric of politics with the private values of poetry. If there is a sin common to poetry such as Auden's *Spain*, the anti-Semitic passages in Eliot's Sweeney poems, the political passages in Pound's cantos, Wyndham Lewis' adulation of what he calls "the party of genius" (meaning Michelangelo and Wyndham Lewis), Lawrence's worship of the dynamic will of nature's aristocrats (in *The Plumed Serpent*), certain of my own lines, it is that the poet has—if only for a few moments—allowed his scrupulous poet's rhetoric of the study of "minute particulars" to be overwhelmed by his secret yearning for a heroic public rhetoric. Sensibility has surrendered to will, the Keatsian concept of poetic personality to the dominating mode of character.

In a period when poets seemed imprisoned in their private worlds, their occasional acts of surrender to the excitement of a public world of action in the service of what they could pretend to themselves was a civilizing cause is understandable. But the reactionariness of the "reactionaries" is the weakness, not the strength, of their work. William Empson writes in his curious, sympathetic preface to Mr. Harrison's book that he doubts whether the political issues of "their weakness for Fascism" was "the central one." He adds:

> Now that everything is so dismal we should look back with reverence on the great age of poets and fundamental thinkers, who were so ready to consider heroic remedies. Perhaps their gloomy prophecies have simply come true.

We (and here by "we" I mean the thirties' writers) not only look back on them with reverence, but we also revered them at the time. It is important to understand that we thought of them as a greater generation of more devoted artists. That we did so made us reflect that we were a generation less single-minded in our art, but which had perhaps found a new subject—the social situation. We did not think this could lead to better work than theirs, but on the other hand we saw that young poets could not go on writing esoteric poetry about the end of civilization. Yet their endgames were our beginnings. Our generation reacted against the same conventions of Georgian poetry and the novel as did the generation of T. S. Eliot, Virginia Woolf, D. H. Lawrence and E. M. Forster. They were indeed our heroes.

Pound, Wyndham Lewis and Roy Campbell were the only reactionaries whose public attitudes we sometimes attacked: with the mental reservation that we thought them zanies anyway. As for Eliot, Yeats and Lawrence, if one minimized their statements about politics, there was much in their deepest political insights with which we agreed.

> *Things fall apart: the centre cannot hold;*
> *Mere anarchy is loosed upon the world.*

This described our situation. By comparison the fact that Yeats went out and supported General O'Duffy seemed singularly irrelevant. No poem could show better than *The Second Coming* how wrong Orwell was to approach Yeats's poetry as a function of his Fascism. To us, his Fascism seemed a misconception arising from his deep political (and here the word seems quite inadequate) insight.

It is a pity that Mr. Harrison, instead of accepting at their face value labels like "left" and "reactionary," did not compare at a deeper level than that of political parties the social vision of the poets of the thirties and the older generation. He might have found then that the two generations often agreed in their diagnoses: they came to opposite conclusions with regard to remedies. He might also have found that the younger generation, in coming to their revolutionary conclusions, owed their view that we were living in a revolutionary situation to the insights of the reactionaries.

His biographers point out that John Cornford, while he was still a schoolboy, was led to Communism by reading *The Waste Land*. "He believed it to be a great poem, read it not as a religious allegory . . . but as an anatomy of capitalist society in decay; it shaped his style, but more important, it was a preface to his politics."

To the imagination the poetry does not preach party matters. It penetrates into the depths of an external situation and shows what is strange and terrible. Eliot drew conclusions from his own poetic insight with his intellect, with which Cornford disagreed when he wrote:

> *The Waste Land* . . . is of great importance not for the pleasure it gives, but for its perfect picture of the disintegration of a civilisation. . . . But something more than description, some analysis of the situation is needed. And it is here that Eliot breaks down. He refuses to answer the question that he has so perfectly formulated. He retreats into the familiar triangle—Classicism, Royalism, Ango-Catholicism. He has not found an answer to the question of resignation. Rather he has resigned himself to finding no answer.

Here the imagination which can give the "perfect picture of disintegration" is dramatized as posing the question to which the intellect gives the answer—the wrong answer, according to Cornford, but even he, the convinced Communist undergraduate about to go to Spain, cares more that the question should have been posed than that the answer should be "correct," for the question suggests what was to him the "correct" answer.

What was common to modern poets between 1910 and 1930 was their condemnation of a society which they saw as the disintegration of civilization. Given this agreed on line, it was possible to be on the reactionary or the socialist side of it. The reactionaries, on their side asked: "What of the past can be saved?" The socialists, on their side, asked: "How can there be new life?" The awesome achievement of the earlier generation was to have created for their contemporaries a vision of the whole past tradition which had a poignant immediacy: giving shattered contemporary civilization consciousness of its own past greatness, like the legendary glimpse of every act of his life in the eyes of a man drowning. Without the awareness of drowning, of the end of the long game, the apprehended moment could not have been so vivid. Thus the gloomy prophecies of the future, and the consequent weakness for reactionary politics, were the dark side of an intensely burning vision.

The liberals, the progressives, the anti-Fascists could not invest their future with a vision of the values of present civilization as great as the reactionaries' vision of past values. Perhaps though they agreed with the reactionaries that the genius of our civilization which had flickered on since the Renaissance was soon to be extinguished. E. M. Forster, whose work stands midway between the idea of past and present, sees the greatness of England and Europe as over. The past commands his love, though the causes which should ultimately make people better off—freedom of the peoples of the world from the old imperialisms, greater social justice, etc.—command his loyalty. But his loyalty inspires him with little love, and he has no enthusiasm for the liberated materially better world which he felt bound to support.

The anti-Fascists in the end accepted or were influenced by the idea that the struggle for the future meant abandoning nostalgia for a past civilization. They had now to emphasize "new life," a new culture not obsessed with the past. Julian Bell and John Cornford came to feel that in putting the cause before everything they must be prepared even to jettison their own poetry. And they found themselves quite glad to do so. In 1932, when he started becoming interested in politics, John Cornford wrote to his mother: "I have found it a great relief to stop pretending to be an artist" and in the same letter he told her that he had bought "*Kapital* and a good deal of commentary, which I hope to find time to tackle this term. Also *The Communist Manifesto.*" In renouncing being an artist he is also turning back on the world of his mother, Frances Cornford, the poet. Julian Bell experienced an immense sense of relief when he decided to turn away from literature and go to Spain. If Auden and Isherwood had written a play on the theme of Bell and Cornford one can well imagine that their deaths on the battlefield would have been seen as the finale of a dialogue with their art-loving mothers.

Feelings and motives involved here are extremely complex. Uncertainty about their vocations, rebellion against their mothers and against the values of the literary world of Cambridge, Oxford and London, a suppressed anti-intellectualism and an expression of the tendency of the young in that decade to interpret all current issues as a conflict between principles of "life" and "death," the "real" and the "unreal," all enter in. The reader of Stansky and Abrahams cannot help noting that in a decade when people were always being reproached for "escapism" the immersion into the life of action and political choice filled Bell and Cornford with an elation remarkably like that of escape —escape from having to be poets. Escape is wrong only if it means an escape from high standards to lower or more relaxed ones. In their renunciation of those standards of their parents which were, perhaps, too esthetic, Cornford and Bell shared a tendency to escape into accepting means which were perilously close to Fascist ones. Thus Cornford writes:

> The disgraceful part of the German business is not that the Nazis kill and torture their enemies; it is that Socialists and Communists let themselves be made prisoners instead of first killing as many Nazis as they can.

Julian Bell states still more strongly the objection to the liberals. His reaction is all the more striking because it is so much a renunciation of that pacifism which was one of his deepest ties with his parents:

> Most of my friends are utterly squeamish about means; they feel that it would be terrible to use force or fraud against anyone. . . . Even most Communists seem to me to have only a hysterical and quite unrealistic notion about violent methods . . . I can't imagine anyone of the *New Statesman*

doing anything "unfair" to an opponent. . . . Whereas for my own part . . . I can't feel the slightest qualms about the notion of doing anything effective, however ungentlemanly and unchristian, nor about admitting to myself that certain actions would be very unfair indeed. . . .

and he ends the same letter with a sentence that is surely very revealing:

I don't feel, myself, as if I could ever be satisfied to do anything but produce works of art, or even nothing but leading a private life and producing works in the intervals.

I do not quote these passages because I think them characteristic of Cornford and Bell (in fact they are hysterical outbursts out of character) but because of the light which—paradoxically—they throw on the relationship of the thirties generation with an older one. This balances the violence of the reactionaries supporting Fascism in the name of art, against the violence of the leftists prepared to sacrifice art to the cause of anti-Fascism.

The reactionaries cared passionately for past values. Their nostalgia misled them into sympathizing with whatever jack-booted corporal or demagogue set himself up in defense of order. As the history of Ezra Pound shows, the results of this could be tragic. But they did put literature before politics, and their first concern was to preserve the civilization without which, as they thought, neither past nor future literature could survive. They did not, as the anti-Fascist writers did, abandon or postpone their literary tasks. For the anti-Fascists allowed themselves, rightly or wrongly, to be persuaded that civilization could only be saved by action: the logical consequence of this attitude was to put writing at the service of necessity as dictated by political leaders.

There was, then, the paradox that the reactionaries who were on the side of the past, the dead, had to live for the sake of literature, whereas circumstances drove the most sincere anti-Fascists—men like Cornford, Bell, Fox and Caudwell—to death as absolution in a cause which they had made absolute. The reactionaries wrote out of their tragic sense of modern life. The Cornfords and Bells lived and died the tragedy.

Romanticism and Contemporary Poetry
Gabriel Pearson

from

New Left Review, 16, 1962.

Romanticism and Contemporary Poetry

Gabriel Pearson

It is not just antiquarian to assert that any study of contemporary poetry must begin with romanticism. We are talking about English poetry; hence our points of reference will be English Romanticism. I am not concerned with direct historical antecedents. Rather with establishing an astonishing transformation of attitude towards the nature of poetry and of art in general. We are the heirs of this transformation: for this reason we find it difficult to grasp how far reaching it is. It is still working itself out in our own day. At this length treatment must be oblique and illustrative. I hope to show that the romantic conception of poetry is still, in essence, our own. That further, this is the only viable conception today. And beyond even this, that to miss the experience much modern poetry offers, is to risk impoverishing our experience in general. This is so ambitious a programme, that it has seemed worthwhile to group instances, actual contemporary poems, along side this piece. Against these my arguments can be checked. Further, if I fail to make my case, at least there will be poems to read, solidly assembled, as something more than typographical decoration.

Blake, the most urbane as well as the most radical of the Romantics, was indulging in something more than a private joke when he turned his familiar angel into a devil:

> This Angel, who is now become a Devil, is my particular friend; we often read the Bible together in its infernal or diabolical sense, which the world shall have if they behave well.

> I have also the Bible of Hell, which the world shall have whether they will or no.

> One Law for the Lion and Ox is Oppression.

With this one should couple Blake's assertion that "All deities reside in the human breast." For this explains why Blake was not insane to boast of angels and devils among his acquaintance. Nor was Blake the last poet to do so. Rimbaud spends his last season in Hell. Poe visits the ghoul-haunted weir. Rilke's poems are swept through by angelic forms. James Thomson, the atheist poet-friend of Bradlaugh, dwells, like an English Baudelaire, in the City of Dreadful Night. Devils and Angels jostle each other in Goethe, Dostoievsky, Thomas Mann. Even in the early Dickens the demons are at the centre: Fagin,

Quilp. It seems that no sooner had the Enlightenment tidied God up into a remote cause and swept the Devil back into the cesspool of Gothic imagination, than the poets re-adopt them as familiars and intimates.

The reasons are perhaps not far to seek. God and Devil, within religious systems, dramatise and hold in tension the extreme poles of experience. Here religion is imaginatively and psychologically satisfying. In comparison, the joys of Heaven seem tame. Angels and Devils over two thousand years, have assumed a concreteness and firmness of outline that readily fit them for sensuous embodiment. Behind them, remotely, press more primitive presences: local daemons and heroes; fallen and displaced Gods; moral qualities and sensible objects. The great religious systems crumbled; in the ruins the poets—and this is part of the case against them—are seen salvaging the less savoury icons to set up on their own account.

Religion had judged angels and devils, had separated the sheep from the goats. But if the judging and separating deity has fallen out of the centre of his system, then man is left as sole arbiter and judge. To the poet then angels and devils may prove equally interesting. They represent, after all, merely opposed poles of experience. And who is to judge as for interest between devil and angel, between one type of experience and another? No wonder devils and angels interchange their roles. Devils have always been bad and vivid, more comprehensively available to the imagination. Angels by contrast are good and vapid. Vividness has hardly any part to play as a term in a theological system. It is an obvious criterion of success in works of imagination.

Hence the Romantic Artist reads his bible "in its infernal or diabolical sense". He is no longer concerned to uphold moral law, to maintain good against evil. The shift here is of real importance. Pre-Romantic artists had tended to regard their role as directly or deviously pragmatic. Satire taught goodness by lashing vice. Epic showed the great and good man in action on an heroic or epic scale. Tragedy illustrated the vanity of human wishes and the wages of hubris. Actual works of literature continually failed to sustain this role. Johnson worries that Shakespeare appeared to destroy virtue and allow vice to flourish. Satirists showed a suspicious relish in creating the vices they were supposed to castigate. Epic heroes represented only a very limited range of dubious virtues. Clearly, there was always a conflict, sometimes latent, sometimes avowed, between doctrine and embodiment, moral law and artistic creativity, the life enacted and the official positions taken up.

Chaucer at the end of his life-work prayed forgiveness for his "enditynges of worldly vanitees . . . and many a leccherous lay". Such forgiveness a romantic like Blake would never grant. Forgiveness was not the point—gratitude, rather. Unlike most schoolteachers, he could not regard the somonour and pardoner, those two arch-crooks of the Canterbury pilgrimage, as damned souls. Neither really could Chaucer. With empathetic vividness he had made the Pardoner cry out: "That it is joye to se my bisynesse". Surely

Chaucer's voice here: of another character he cries: "But it was joye for to seen him swete (sweat)!" Blake describes the Somonour thus:

His companion, the Somonour, is also a Devil of the first magnitude, grand, terrific, rich and honoured in the rank of which he holds the destiny. The uses to Society are perhaps equal of the Devil and of the Angel, their sublimity, who can dispute.

The difference between Chaucer and Blake is scarcely one of practice. Both, as artists, believe in an almost total availability of experience unmediated by moral judgment. In Blake there is no conflict. In Chaucer, however, the believing man is at odds with the artist. This conflict affects Chaucer's main achievement very little. But this is not the case with other great poets. It is perhaps at its most acute in Milton. *Paradise Lost*, viewed in the Romantic perspective, seems to be virtually about this conflict.

It sets itself the task of justifying the ways of God to Man. This is a famous ambiguity. To justify the-ways-of-God-to-Man is just what any sermon or didactic allegory thought it did. The authority for such justification already pre-existed the poem in revelation or dogma. The poem simply expanded and illuminated a text of divine authenticity. Experience, when it was thought relevant, was generalised, communal experience, not tested, to borrow Keats's phrase, on the pulses. However, Milton's poem becomes something very different when its intention is read as to justify the-ways-of-God to Man. Here the-ways-of-God are themselves being put to the test; man becomes their arbiter. "What difference", Milton seems to ask, "does it make to our trust in divine providence if we re-experience imaginatively the falls of Satan, Adam and Eve, the workings of divine retribution and forgiveness?" And the answer, as Professor Empson argues in his recent *Milton's God*, is a distinctly dusty one, at odds with the official account. God emerges as bullying, vindictive and highly self-contradictory, Adam and Eve as heroically human, Satan's rebellion as perfectly justifiable.

Again Blake transcends Milton's dilemma. If God is being put to the test of imaginative re-creation, and only Gods can judge God, then Milton must be God. All deities reside in the human breast, says Blake. Therefore it is not surprising then that Milton is God: to create imaginatively is to be divine. There had always been difficulties about who to call the hero of *Paradise Lost*. To read the poem as epic involved some such decision. Blake boldly followed through the direction of his dialectic. All deities reside in Milton's breast. Milton is the hero of his own poem. When Blake rewrote the Miltonic epic he called it *Milton*. But by a further dialectical twist, its subject is now not only Milton but Blake himself. For what Blake felt he had in common with Milton was poetic genius, the individual power of creation. This was the only true universal. Hence, by an apparent paradox, individual creativity became the one universal principle to which the romantics adhered.

This brings us near to the crux of Romanticism in its earlier phase, what I would like to call its heroic phase. The total availability of experience is a principle that has gradually won through. Hardly noticing it, we have grown to assume it. Of course, there are taboos. But these are progressively eroded. Some of these taboos take odd forms. Illicit love has always been an accepted theme; whereas marriage is at best an ideal goal, at worst a killing disillusionment. Only at the end of the last century and the beginning of this has marriage been explored in its actual, living completeness. One can see why Meredith's *Modern Love* seemed so revolutionary when it first appeared in the last century. It seemed suddenly to turn a search-light onto one of the most central, dark and private areas of common experience. Previously, marriage tended to be treated either in the novel (though much less directly, in England, and much less often than one would suppose). Or it was treated mythically, as Morris does in *The Defence of Guenevere*. No wonder Meredith's treatment is so tortuous, strained and evasive.

This is just one example of increasing availability. The principle was firmly established by the romantics. Romantic poetry has other characteristics which accompany this new principle and which trans-form the role of the poet and the structure and shape of his poem. First then, the subject of his poem changes. It is not directly about experience itself: or rather the poem reveals the dialectic of a word like experience, which fuses subject and object. (The etymology of experience and experiment is instructive: experimenting is scienti-fically organised experiencing. The words are strongly connected in the eighteenth century. Only in the last do they part company.) The content of a romantic poem then is ultimately the experiencing self.

In a sense, the poem is conceived of as an experiment. But this experiment does not consist in a series of observations about the world. Instead, the poet tries to watch himself observing the world, tries to catch himself in the act of experiencing. This is why so much romantic poetry appears not only entirely egocentric, but also reflexive, as though the poems always wanted to be experiences of experience, or poems about poems. Even in the simplest lyric there often appears the tiny embryo of another poem curled inside the main poem. Frequently, this takes the form of a musical metaphor. Wordsworth's daffodils *dance* to the music of the poem. And the poem is an act of re-call setting the daffodils dancing again. Again the song of the solitary reaper which Wordsworth bears away with him is the music within the music, the experience within the experience.

Much modern poetry retains this reflexive structure. Brownjohn's poem not only *is* a white informal fantasy: it is *about* a white informal fantasy. Jenny Joseph and Snodgrass use their metaphor of cold in a similar way. Thus the structure of romantic poetry is extremely complicated. First of all it is a unique act of experiencing. Secondly this experiencing is a dual process, involving the experiencer and what is experienced. Hence the model for the typical romantic poem would be something like this: a central point which is the originating impulse or occasion of the poem; and then a series of concentric circles generated around this point. The outer circle is the boundary of the total area of experience covered. The inner circles are the reflexive processes going on inside the poem. The observation that the general shape of a romantic poem is circular, rather than linear and progressive, is not of course original. It has been often commented on in Keats. In Keats's *Ode on a Nightingale*, the poet begins with his state of mind. This state is modulated through ever widening circles of involvement with the bird's song which is at the same time the poem he is writing. The circles become so wide that for a moment they seem to embrace the whole of worthwhile human experience: emperor, clown, the sad heart of Ruth, faery lands forlorn. Nevertheless, the poem returns Keats to his sole self; the action of the poem is cyclic.

But it is a dynamic generation of circles rather than a simple curve away into the world and back. The area covered is still held in dynamic tension even when the poem has been tolled back to Keats. So that the poem is only linear, as it were, typographically. Really, once the poem has been heard, any subsequent reading becomes, not a matter of following through the plot of the poem, but of grasping the poem entire in each segment. Thus, I don't think Romantic poems resolve anything in the way for example that *Oedipus Rex* resolves its mystery. The resolution would have to be into some general structure which could offer all sufficing explanations. But the Romantics have lost faith in the possibility of such a structure. Their world is no longer totally explicable: it can only be experienced to the uttermost.

All romantic poetry is really lyrical poetry. It takes over the song without music and melts back all the other forms into it. The song is supposed to be spontaneous and unpremeditated. That at least was the fiction; practice rarely conformed. The romantics seized on this fiction. The lyric was personal, free from conventions, a form adapted to the single voice. Even their long poems, apparent epics and dramas become extended lyrics. Shelley called *Prometheus Unbound* a lyrical drama. Wordsworth's personal epic suggests, by its title, *The Prelude*, not only the introduction to the great philosophical poem that never gets written, but also a piece of music, say like a Chopin prelude, that most personal, egocentric and rhapsodic product of romanticism in music. Above all, romantic poetry is poetry of the individual voice. There is no formal diction to which the poet feels he has to adhere for particular purposes. Actually, personal voice, idiosyncrasy and idiom, are always coming through earlier poetry too. But among the minor writers at least it is often hard to distinguish one voice from another. Minor Elizabethan sonnet-cycles sound much alike: two eighteenth century pastorals are liable to be indistinguishable.

One can see from this why Milton exerted such a charismatic pull on the romantics. Partly, they felt his isolation as a paradigm case of their own solitude. But more than that, Milton's personality is obtrusive and inescapable. *Paradise Lost* is saturated with Milton. Some recent critics (Eliot, Leavis) are bothered by this in the same way as eighteenth century critics were. Johnson thought that Milton wrote "on a perverse and pedantick principle". For the romantics this is just his glory, his sublimity. They would want to say he wrote on an utterly individual and personal principle. Common diction has been cast into the crucible of Milton's imagination: it emerges incandescent and strangely wrought.

The shape of the typical romantic poem derives from the Miltonic precedent. Like Milton, the romantic poet tours the universe under his own steam. He no longer needs divinely appointed guides, such as Dante found in Virgil and Beatrice. Since "all deities reside in the human breast", the tour of the universe is as much internal as external. Typical romantic prototypes are the Ancient Mariner whose really central experience comes when he is "alone on a wide, wide sea": Blake's Mental Traveller: Wordsworth's Wanderer and Recluse—these suggestive names can be reduplicated over and over again from the poetry of the period. At this point the solitary, the mental traveller, is a heroic figure. And it makes sense to call the period 1780–1825 the heroic age of romanticism. This heroism is partly produced by the total commitment of the romantic poet to his internal quest, a commitment that consumes all his life energies. The poetry is a record of the life: the life is shaped by the poetry; the reciprocity between life and poetry seems often almost uncanny. Shelley ends his poem *The Triumph of Life* in the question: Then what is life? I cried . . . and those dots trail out with Shelley himself into his own death by drowning. Shelley's is the most sensational case of this type of coincidence between life and poetry; but parallels abound.

The poet in this heroic phase has not entirely resigned the pragmatic aspirations of earlier poetry. But that aspiration depended upon some more or less publicly available system of belief which the poetry communicated and through which communication could be made. The failure of such a system—Christianity or Deism— meant that the poet felt he had to do its work as well as his own. His poetry aspires towards totality as well as immediacy of experience. The latter has remained one of the criteria of modern romantic poetry; the former has been largely abandoned.

The process of abandonment follows quickly on the initial impulse to evolve a total life philosophy. Blake came nearest succeeding: Coleridge spent a life-time collecting data, Wordsworth got as far as a prelude, Shelley see-sawed between inherently contradictory doctrines (materialist determinism and platonism) and Keats recorded a need. In a sense, this quest for a total life philosophy was inherently doomed to fail. Since such a philosophy would necessarily have to be a philosophy of experience, it would have to be continually reassembled by experience itself. And since the poetry was a record of the experience and was rapidly becoming the process of experiencing itself, any life philosophy could never disentangle itself from the contingency and continuing creation of actual poems. This does not of course mean that nothing worthwhile was produced. It does mean that romantic philosophy in England lived out a curious half life somewhere between poetry and autobiography: Coleridge's notebooks, Keats' and Byrons' letters, Shelley's essays and Wordsworth's autobiographical poems.

But the impulse to universalize could take another direction which is typical of the heroic phase of romanticism: the creation of myths. This itself is a contradictory enterprise. Myths are usually collective acts of imagination which pre-exist doctrinal religion, philosophy and science. They are saturated with communal experience, however, and this, even when their particular social context has evaporated, ensures their continuing vitality. They become large scale structures which, vacated by their original tenants, can be quickly converted to the use of philosophy, religion and art. With the romantics, something new happens. The poet refurbishes old myths or invents new ones to universalize his individual situation. What evaporates away entirely is the old communal content. Now the myths dramatise an individual psychology on which they confer universal status.

The romantic poet has a double attitude towards his self-commitment to his art. Often he is humble, a parasite on other people's real emotions, as Wordsworth implies in his *Preface*, or a kind of vacuum into which reality gushes, as Keats maintains in his letters. Or, like Milton and those who imitated his implicit claims to be arbiter of providence, he is intensely arrogant, almost megalomaniac, in his claims to interpret all experience within the confines of his own nature. The oscillation between humility and arrogance is nicely caught in Shelley's famous description of the poet as "the unacknowledged legislator" of mankind. The failure of acknowledgment indicates the true distance of the romantic poet from universality. His "legislator" implies a constant struggle towards universality.

The poet attempts to make his creative life the supreme illustration and example of processes in the real world. It becomes so by the poet's projection of his inner life outwards into giant figures involved in mythical conflict. The heroic age of romanticism is thronged with such figures. Their drama appears to be cosmic, but is really microcosmic. In fact, Blake's "deities" who dwell in the human breast, assume substance and speech, become deities indeed. There is something paradoxical about this. Blake had conscientiously re-assumed religion as alienated human nature. But this human nature he largely failed to create in specifically human and individual terms. Instead he projects it out again in deified forms acting within a private but systematic quasi-religion. This is what makes him so difficult. Only re-translation into concrete psychological categories, a mastery indeed of a shifting set of correspondences and symbols, enables us to grasp a world where Orc turns into Urizen and Enitharmon into Vala, as the real world contained within individual human consciousness.

Superficially more accessible mythical poems like Shelley's *Prometheus Unbound* offer equal difficulties. By inventing his own names, Blake at least gives fair warning that his mythic figures are really projections of his own experience. *Prometheus Unbound* is equally a projection of Shelley's own experience in universal guise. Again, we have to re-translate, hindered more than aided, by recollections of the original Prometheus myth. These poems always leave a gap between the mythic representation and the individual consciousness represented. What ought to fill this gap is the poet in his purely personal rather than bardic or priestly role. Blake's solution was to prelude his prophecies with gnomic stanzas in a more personal idiom—the *vox humana* in his celestial organ (the hymn, *Jerusalem*, is one such). Shelley is forced weakly back into prefaces. Keats likewise feels the need to project himself through myth. In *Hyperion* the triumph of Olympians over Titans, and particularly of Apollo over Hyperion himself, enact the overthrow of an older order—religious, philosophical, poetic—by one newer, more liberal, more life-enhancing. The epic action, however, still escapes a specifically individual manifestation. Keats himself is only vaguely present as Apollo. Clearly, Keats feels the absence. He writes a second version in which the mythical action becomes specifically his vision, witnessed by a figure who is his prototype.

Romantic poetry, to recapitulate, assumes the total availability of experience. When Blake declared that "Everything that lives is holy," he was not preaching Hinduism or Pantheism, but simply saying what Keats says in another way: that the chameleon poet takes as much delight "in creating an Iago as an Imogen": that Hell and Heaven are simply contrary states of mind: that the true poet unifies his consciousness of the world by marrying them. The romantic poet takes no existing doctrine on trust. His doctrine is continually invented through experience. Proved upon the pulses, authenticated by being lived. (Thus the *Ode on a Grecian Urn* only reaches its famous identification of Beauty with Truth through the poem itself: it ends with it. Whereas doctrinal poetry implicitly or explicitly starts from formulations of doctrine which it unravels and explicates, e.g. "Love, thou art absolute, sole Lord/Of Life and Death"). Further, romantic poetry assumes the shape of the poet's own consciousness in its movement of reflection upon itself, becomes circular, microcosmic, rather than being left like a length lopped off, dependent from some shared and accepted system of values. These articles, I would assert (it has to be assertion: demonstration would take volumes,) implicitly govern all romantic poetry and most art, secular or religious, up to our own time.

The first romantics, however, did not fully realise all the implications of their fundamental stance. They aspire to universality, or, failing that, representativeness, with the result that some of the reality which they claim to be totally accessible to them, doesn't get explored or created in their poetry. Blake had said that "One Law for the Lion and Ox is Oppression". By this he meant, among other things, that what is most valuable in human beings is their uniqueness, that which is specifically the Self. Laws—religious, scientific, artistic, judicial, political—must be formulated generally, not legislate for particulars, and hence perpetually transgress against human uniqueness. Most romantics would agree of course, as indeed would most modern artists. In France early nineteenth century literary history seems mostly taken up by the *avant-garde* revolts against conventional canons: hardly surprising perhaps in a country where the shift of a caesura could rock an Academy. Generally, the search was for a unique voice, a personal idiom and utterance, that could shatter all decorum.

The first romantics often failed, however, to realise their uniqueness through anything but tone of voice, a personal flavour and verbal odour, a choice of vocabulary. And this was because of the absence of a sense of otherness, both of things and of people. When Keats writes "And if thy mistress some rich anger show" he of course means by "thy" a kind of theoretic "my" and any anger (an interpersonal emotion if ever there was one) quickly becomes internalised by its suffusion with a qualitative epithet of a peculiarly expropriative character: such epithets always psychologically tend to absorb objects back into the ascriber. Indeed, despite the common identification of the word "romantic" with erotic, there is very little romantic love poetry. There are scores of poems expressing erotic sentiment, some fine poetry about love situations (Byron and Tennyson) but very little poetry of the intensely interpersonal kind—Sidney, Shakespeare and Donne. (Perhaps love poetry is in any case pretty rare.) The beloved (the supreme other) quickly becomes absorbed into the fantasy life of the romantic poet. (The search for a sister as soul-mate in Shelley, Keats and Wordsworth is very suspect.)

This is just one important instance of the romantic resistance to the actual and other. One could call it a failure to face up to the existential implications of the poet's claim to explore all reality. The world is dissolved back into fantasy rather than being sharply realised. Poets destroy the world of other men and things by individual strategies. Keats devours the world; Shelley whips it up into froth and makes it fly. Later romantics (Tennyson and Arnold) dissolve it in pathos or wistfulness. Later still, "aesthetes" immobilise and gild it, setting it up as a static object of curiosity. What they all, at their worst, try not to realise is its diversity and substantiality, its difference from them. Only by the distinction of things one from another can the uniqueness of the individual be grasped. This may be a commonplace, but it is something the first romantics often failed to do. They raged against judicial and social law: but because they did not present its workings concretely they failed fully to define their rage.

Shelley, for example, set a bad example to more purely political poets by generalising and mythologising the political evils of his day. The result is a curious insubstantiality in his presentation of political struggle. Tyrants can be wished away bloodlessly: the forlorn maid of liberty, simply by waiting to be trampled down by the forces of Anarchy, disperses them. Of course, this is not the entire picture. Romantic poets can produce a fine intimate poetry of address, whose tone is, as it were, printed off the silence of the person addressed. Coleridge does this magnificently in his Dejection Ode (originally, in its more complete and satisfactory form a verse epistle to Sara Hutcheson whom he hopelessly loved). Keats, Shelley, Byron all provide instances.

Often, social actuality and concreteness of situation are accommodated only clumsily through embarrassed periphrasis and exag-

gerated declamation (of the "O my friend" type). This embarrass-
ment persists well into our own century. Even a reputedly "modern"
poet like Hopkins can duck for cover from the actual under frantic
alliteration: "Nor rocket nor lightship shone . . ." This stutter of
slipshod sibilants has no function other than to distract attention
from real lightships and rockets. The latter hardly shine, and if they
do, not in the same way as lightships. Nineteenth century poetry
often evaded actualisation by the most cunning strategy of all: flight
into detail. Hopkins and Browning are full of detailed notation:
poems which by-pass the jagged actuality of things by asserting
a sort of technical descriptive mastery over them. Several Hopkins
sonnets describe men in detail: a plowman say. His muscular
swellings, his handgrip, the fluid strength of body-posture are all set
down. Yet still the man isn't there, but rather a poem about
assembling such a man.

Romantic poetry's temptation to resist personal and hence social
actuality is endemic and inherent. It is basically a defence against
the pain of self-realisation, of that process of soul-making which
Keats, in his Letters, makes the ultimate quest. Religions had
formally assumed the soul as the essential equipment with which
men are born. It was on how you used the equipment that salvation
and damnation depended. Romanticism assumes implicitly what
existentialist morality (itself a romantic life philosophy) makes
explicit: that we are responsible for the shape of our own destinies;
that living is a constant process of self-creation; that the temptation
to evade this responsibility and the anguished consciousness it
involves is almost irresistible; and yet that this consciousness is what
we most want to have.

Projection into myth and flight into detail are only two strategies.
Out of these, running in parallel and series, develop two further
strategies: first, flight into language and, second, diffusion into
multiplicity. Flight into language can take at least two forms. It can
be etymological: each word, each unit of syntax, is assumed to contain its whole historical development. The poem acts as a device for
triggering off the historical charge in the word or phrase, so that each
stage explodes into meaning simultaneously. *Paradise Lost* is an early
and thorough-going use of this procedure. Joyce's *Ulysses* operated
the same device in our own century. Eliot uses it continually. A
sentence like "You are not here . . . to inform curiosity", beyond its
apparent everyday sense, also means: you are not here to find a form
for your artistic powers. The other main form is a development of
imagery, and, on a larger scale, of symbol, independent of the
ostensive argument of the poem. This needs no illustration. Whenever
we try to make a metaphor internally consistent (e.g. "triggering",
"charge", "explosion"), we find ourselves caught up in a kind of
independent logic which often leads away from the arguments it was
supposed to illustrate. Poets are peculiarly liable to submit to this
logic. Theirs is a necessarily heightened linguistic self-consciousness.
The poet's experience tends to become the experience of acts of
composition. He is in constant danger of collapsing the dialectic

between the world given to his senses and his effort to recreate it and hence himself through language. From being poems about the act of composition, they become poems about poetry (two stages held in tension in the best romantic poems) and eventually poems about the language they are being written in. The result may be that language becomes re-invested with the mystery and authority that once belonged to religion. With Mallarmé indeed, language achieves the status of an absolute that transcends every day appearances. We are left with a kind of linguistic platonism. The inherent circularity remains, but now it is a circle contracting and tightening rather than widening and embracing. It forms a kind of running noose which eventually throttles the poem as a unit of experience. We are left with a contorted, opaque thing. All movement inside the poem is jammed and deadlocked. And this deadlocked thing is analogous to the attempt to make ourselves into things rather than endure the anguish of self-creation.

Still, the "eventually" is important. Language is always trying to evolve its separate logics. And the battle between language and the world is precisely what poems are. Anyway, a writer who exploits this self-evolving nature of language really intensively must make discoveries about language as communal self-consciousness. He often succeeds in releasing its latent public content. On a grand scale Joyce pushes his exploitation of linguistic logics to the point where they either take in whole tracts of experience or are seen no longer to apply. By this inside-out procedure he re-discovers the world.

The flight into multiplicity can be more easily defined. It represents an attempt to assemble experience externally, through a simple process of accretion. As such, it is a more developed form of the flight into detail, just as the linguistic circular poem—opaque, auto-telic— is a development of the mythic poem. Obvious instances of poetry by accretion are Whitman and the whole American and European tradition (among which I would include Surrealism, Dadaism and Futurism) that derives from him. The basic form of this poetry is the list. If linguistically self-conscious poetry throttles itself through the tightening of its quasi-logical structures, this kind of poetry smothers under the weight of its own material. (These two kinds correspond very roughly to the usual antithesis between the naturalist and symbolic novel). Often, in Whitman, Sandberg, the Beats and even Rimbaud, structure is imposed by a loose libertarian rhetoric. These poems at their worst become the opposite of clotted opaque things. Rather they swell, threaten to engulf the cosmos, then diffuse and dissipate themselves. Their aspiration is to make a total inventory of the world. In the process the poet loses the distinction of himself against the world. Actuality is no longer a medium through which he defines himself. All that is left is the inventory itself, as arbitrary as such lists usually are.

Such poetry does, however, represent the romantic attempt to come to grips with the phenomenal world. Failure lies in the inability to experience and order it. But romantic poetry is supremely suited for just this endeavour. Its lyrical condensation, its immediacy, the adaptation of its complex structure to the real complexities of consciousness and experience, all these together make up a uniquely flexible and multi-purposed art form. It can move from Words-worth's intense concentration on the measurability of his pond in *The Thorn* through Keatsian sensuousness into the hard declamation of Yeats.

The specific contribution of modern romantic poetry lies in its closer movement towards the actuality of secular, individual existence. It has learned to take in, at its best, the urban landscape, the local anecdote, the particularity of personal relationships. At its highest reach it can still maintain a representative character, imply mythic and universal significance, while not losing its specificity. Take Wilfred Owen's great poem, his last, *Strange Meeting:*

It seemed that out of the battle I escaped
Down some profound, dull tunnel long since scooped
Through granites that titanic wars had groined;
Yet also there encumbered sleepers groaned,
Too fast in thought or death to be be-stirred.
Yet as I probed them, one sprang up and stared,
With hideous recognition in fixed eyes,
Lifting distressful hands as if to bless.
And by that smile I knew that sullen hall;
By his dead smile I knew we stood in Hell.
With a thousand pains that vision's face was grained,
Yet no blood reached there from the upper ground,
And no guns thumped, or down the flues made moan.

Thus the poem begins. It is undoubtedly the Great War, the last of the Titanic wars. The guns are absent yet the poem can accommodate them. The "profound, dull tunnels" are the trenches, but the trenches transfigured. "The encumbered sleepers" are the dead or sleeping soldiers, but again transfigured. The locale, the setting, is un-mistakably that of trench-warfare. Yet the poet's escape from it into sleep is at the same time part of the descent that the all epic poets have made from Homer to Milton into the underworld. The visionary face grained "with a thousand pains" reminds us of Dante's en-counter with the "baked features" of Bruno Latini, the pederast-poet in *The Inferno*, [1] reconstituted in "the familiar, compound ghost" that Eliot encounters during the dawn raid (his version of *The Inferno*). At the same time Keats is appropriately recalled through his Titans in *Hyperion*. Indeed the resemblance between Keats and Owen is striking. Both in last poems anticipated early death. This is the supreme existential experience. To live through your death, really to experience it, is to have taken the measure of secular experience, "to die into life". (Keats' phrase). Both poets move from an intoxication of the senses into a austere, absolutely authentic utterance distilled and purified out of their menaced blood: "But where the dead leaf fell, there did it rest." (Keats) "And no guns thumped or down the

---

[1] The friendly enemy whom Owen meets and whom he has killed is also a poet, but one more damned than even Latini: he is only a poet of the future and for him the future has been abolished.

flues made moan." (Owen) The cadence is almost identical. It is right to call this a purgatorial poetry. It presents experience utterly simplified, utterly controlled and humanised. The only poetry which measures up to this is the virtually pre-religious Homer, the Old Testament, Dante, Shakespeare. And these poets were sustained either by unified social or by religious sanctions. The ultimate heroism is to do without these, to distil a poetry which is purely human, un-evasive, dependant on no deities other than those who dwell in the human breast.

I want to assert then that all worthwhile modern poetry is romantic[2]. Romantic is a big label with lots of names and descriptions scrawled across it. I have tried to trace a number of defining characteristics. No one modern poet displays all these characteristics. Some which I would still like to call romantic poems evade them altogether. I seem, for example, to have defined romantic poetry as principally post-religious. What then does one do with poets like Eliot or R. S. Thomas who are clearly religious poets? But the crucial question is not what beliefs are held but the way the poetry enacts them. Eliot may be a Christian, but his poetry does not depend upon a religious system which pre-exists it. *Four Quartets* is thoroughly aware of the secular world which surrounds it. Its religion is shown in relation to the contemporary world and through a thoroughly accessible appeal to a common psychology (e.g. the loss of childhood oneness with nature). I doubt whether a whole-heartedly Christian poetry is even possible to-day. Perhaps the nearest things to it are the choruses from *The Rock* and *Murder in the Cathedral*. And these works seem to me virtually inaccessible to a non-Christian reader. We just don't credit their doctrinal assertions. When the Knights come down-stage to inform us that we, with our falsely tolerant humanism, are the heirs of the Archbishops' murderers and share their guilt, we just don't believe them. It's the

[2]This, I know, runs counter to the usual account which assumes a basic, qualitative difference between modern poetry and romantic poetry. The criteria which govern this account are two-fold. First, formal differences: free verse, compressed imagery, syntactical dislocation and replacement of diction by the speaking voice. But there are precedents for these formal attributes, so many, that modernist poetry can hardly lay claim to any radical innovations: at best, it is a summation. Second, a thorough-going change in subject-matter. But here there has been not even an evolution so much as an expansion. The principle which justified this expansion had already been firmly established both by romantic theory and practice. There is it seems to me a direct continuity between the first romantics, through Baudelaire, Rimbaud and back into English poetry via Laforgue, Corbière and Eliot—both in formal experimentation and range of communicable experience, including sexual relationships, urban landscapes, cultural allusiveness. (This last I would consider as a renewal of early romantic mythologising, now much less confident, much more defensive.) My view is in any case less bold, more commonly held, than might appear. Recent works, such as Kermode's *The Romantic Image* and Langbaum's *Poetry of Experience* have detailed the continuity between romantic and modern poetry. I have followed them in tracing this distinction *within* poetry itself. I have consciously excluded socio-political connections, important though these are, because a correct account of literary morphology, and the ideological changes which provide its dynamic, ought to precede the attempt to make such connections. I have to plead guilty to a certain ethnocentricity: my account of a development towards a more unassuming, more personally situated poetry holds good only for the Anglo-American scene (though the recent Penguin Yevtushenko makes it look as though something of the sort could be happening in the Soviet Union): clearly, the picture is different in France and Germany.

Parson in disguise trying to pull something over us. One can tell it by his slightly hollow attempts at the colloquial: "You and you must suffer. So must you."

But if my major proposition is to hold good, there must be exceptions which justify my calling modern poetry romantic rather than simply post-eighteenth century, nineteenth century, twentieth century. A paradigm case of non-romantic poetry is so called socialist realist or committed poetry.[3] A good example of this would be Christopher Logue's *To My Fellow Artists* which was reprinted by many socialist magazines. Such poetry I would want to call rhetorical. That is, its justification lies in its audience. Pre-romantic poetry relies heavily on rhetoric and on a decorum which insists that a poem should be judged on the basis of whom it is directed at and the suitability or otherwise of its subject matter. It assumes that literature has a basically pragmatic function, that its end is moral instruction or enlightenment, and that aesthetic pleasure is the means to this end. At least, this is the theory. Practice, as the career and recantation of Chaucer testify, does not always conform. The basic premise is that poetry is directed towards an audience, and its success or failure is judged by its effect on the audience. This assumption looks plausible so long as poet and audience, as they largely will in a religiously centralised society and to some extent still did in the renaissance, share the same central beliefs. Romanticism is precisely the crisis of belief. Men embark on their separate life-histories, regulate themselves by new or revised ideologies. It is a mistake of many socialists that they envisage a socialist society involving an almost religious conformity to certain central regulating principles. The idea that a socialist society could be deeply and humanly satisfying because it liberated the utmost diversity of belief and experience seems deeply alien to them. Socialist-realist poetry or committed poetry of the Logue type it seems to me, tries to re-invest socialist principles or programmes or particular causes with the central, regulating authority once possessed by religion. Accordingly, their poetry directly affronts the kind of romantic assumptions I have described. Certain areas of experience are closed by virtue of their conflict with the central authority. Other areas are obligatory (the modern form of decorum). The criteria for success or failure are crudely affective. This poetry screams for attention and bangs its fists to make you pay heed. It is rhetorical in the bad sense because it only pretends to have an audience at its feet. And it is hollow, because it knows deep-down, that it has no authentic existence in its own right but is utterly

---

[3] I have concentrated on socialist realism as an example of a modern rhetorical poetry, because it seems justified by the most reputable, humanly interesting and complex ideology. But other examples come to mind: imperialist poetry (Kipilng) and patriotic poetry (Brooke) for example. The most reputable socialist poetry has been written outside England, and under conditions that gave rise to the kind of real communal identification with central issues that could justify it: e.g. poetry produced during the Polish crisis and Hungarian revolution (1956). In other socialist poetry, as far as I can judge from translation, there appears to be a confusion between the impulse to communicate personal (which can of course include political) experience and to activate, authorise or enthuse a movement, which may have no true communal existence: (Mayakovsky, Neruda, Nazim Hikhmet).

dependent on some external doctrine which remains inert and unlived.

The nineteenth century poets warred on rhetoric, on poetry as a pragmatic art whose main criterion was effect on audience. This warfare is present in Wordsworth's demand that poetry should be a selection of the language really spoken by men, in Verlaine's brutally direct "take rhetoric and wring its neck". To say "use everyday language" is to say stop trying to move, influence, affect in a calculated way (rhetoric *is* the calculation). Rather the implication is, simply be content to *present*. The effect of your presence is as incalculable as your presence in real life. The pejorative way of saying all this is that the poet and his audience have parted company. He no longer knows whom he is speaking to. Or rather, he is sure of only one person: himself. People sneered at Jack Lindsay for trying to answer Shelley's poem called *The Question* in which the poet having, symbolically, created a vernal paradise of flowers, gathers a posy of them and then tries to find someone to give them to. Shelley had to leave the question in the air. Lindsay's answer is orthodox. The Proletariat had not yet achieved revolutionary consciousness. Hence the society to whom the poet could address himself does not yet exist. Lindsay insists on the primacy of the poet's relationship to his society. Capitalist society, by putting a money value on all activities, has estranged the poet from his society. He becomes either the solitary singer or the professional hack. Only socialist society can restore the poet to his society, can make him once more the honoured rhetorician, one of the vehicles by which society renews its consciousness of itself. Poetry undirected towards its audience must be sick. Lindsay himself has put his position succinctly: "The form and content of a work cannot then be abstracted from the audience to which the work is directed and which must be present one way or another to the writer's consciousness". (Essays on Socialist Realism and the British Cultural Tradition. Arena). [4]

This I take it is the fundamental tenet of socialist realism and the premise of Christopher Logue's type of poem. Socialist realism is the last stronghold of rhetoric; it remains true to the traditional European faith in the primacy of an audience. It holds (waveringly, because of the confusion that Gorky brought into the debate with his notion of "revolutionary romanticism") that the process whereby romanticism overthrew the criterion of audience and substituted for it first the criterion of self-expression and then that of the autonomy of the art-object itself—that this process is not irreversible. As such it reverts to the pre-romantic view of the poet as teacher. Yet the unified audience which this view assumes, has simply disappeared with the old unified system of values. There is no longer a communal ear, only a multiplicity of ears, some switched off, some listen-

---

[4]Yevtushenko in his *Observer* article adopted a similar point of view. "People who come to the Poetry Evenings know that they will hear from the poets the extension of their own thoughts, of their own arguments." But this does not mean the kind of conformity of central beliefs that the rhetorical position demands. Likely enough, Soviet auditors look to these poets to echo their own revolt against mass conformity, to escape the loneliness of modern industrial society, into a shared *solitude*.

ing to different things, sometimes for different things in the same sound. The professors of socialist realism (and its secular varieties like Logue-type political poetry and the Beats) go on using rhetoric: but this rhetoric shriller and emptier.

Socialist realism and Stalinism share a deep going voluntarism. Literature became one of the processes whereby socialist man is to be constructed. Stalin in a famous phrase talked of writers as "engineers of the human soul". This voluntarism lurks perpetually beneath the flat deterministic formulae of socialist realism. Yet to regard Zhdanovite literary criticism as simply philistine and vulgarian is to miss the point. Stalin and Zhdanov if anything over-enhanced the importance of literature. They really expected of it the creative miracle, that it could persuade new men into being. It was this, as much as the lies, surely, that put the huge strain upon writers, that drove them to suicide. The duty of Socialist writers begins to look absolute. Occasional dereliction looks like deliberate opposition. The responsible artists like Mayakovsky crack their voices with shouting. It is the sly ones like Ehrenburg, the utterly independent like Pasternak and Akhmotova and the worst hacks who survive. Stalinism did not simply kill its writers out of hatred. To some extent it hugged them to death out of a perverse excess of love. Because they just could not shout Promethean man into being, they became not only a refractory nuisance to their promoters but a deep disappointment. What then is a poem like Logue's *To My Fellow Artists* up to? Really it is whistling furiously in the dark to keep its and our courage up. Our courage here means our collective longing for political effectiveness. The poem by furious gesturing makes believe that the power of art is harnessed to our cause. In this, it works like a talisman. It is like a megaphone three inches away from the ear of a solitary reader. It gives him a momentary impression that he is sharing a communal ceremony: it destroys the movement of the reader's mind upon the material presented. It does achieve a temporary effect of pseudo-communication. Yet it has produced no meaningful sound: no voice. Only a noise that sounded meaningful. No-one really believes for one moment that the people Logue's poem is aimed at— Eliot, Auden, Wain—will read it or if they did would change their attitude as the result of anything he says. The poem's way of tacitly ignoring this glaring fact is a measure of its complete bad faith.

The rhetoric of earlier poetry brought home to its audience the beliefs by which they collectively lived. The beliefs—religious or secular—held by the community were necessarily the content of the poetry. A poem aimed at an audience which exists only in the poet's mind and not in reality, can have no contact with reality but remains essentially a fantasy. Because it *is* rhetorical it puts forward one set of attitudes and denies or ignores others. Its concern is not to relate disparate areas of experience. Instead it abolishes some areas of experience at the expense of others. Certain areas of experience are closed, "everything that lives" is no longer holy. Some subjects, such as the irreparability of death and the violence of nature lead to possibly undesirable attitudes. They confront a reader with his total reality. Earlier poetry assumed that death was not irreparable and that there was providence in the fall of a sparrow.

What made possible a large range of subject matter to writers without destroying the rhetorical basis of their art was the capaciousness of the containing metaphysic. Puritanism constricted and intensified Christianity. In the process some subjects—such as downright pleasure in warfare—were inhibited. Milton evaded this problem ingeniously by making his Devils into modern soldiers with guns and leaving his angels as old-fashioned warriors with swords. True limitation in the metaphysic sometimes gets rid of subject matter whose presentation for its own sake we would disapprove of now: after the Puritans it was more difficult casually to present torture as the Elizabethan novelist Nashe did in *The Unfortunate Traveller*. But really, once you abandon a systematic scheme of values, all subject matter becomes available again.

Socialist realism establishes its own decorum. Certain themes have definite status. A seasonal scheme of imagery beginning with winter and ending either with Spring or Autumn reassuringly connects programmatic conflict with the forces of nature. (I believe there was a communist anthology of poetry called *Spring Time*. Most socialist poetry backs the natural world heavily). Socialist poetry on the whole avoids winter as a finale because it shows Nature unfriendly and implies pessimism. The great modern theme is the H Bomb as once it was Spain or the working-class. The H Bomb is thought unexceptional. You cannot go wrong with it; it provides vivid, exciting imagery. It can be denounced in utter confidence of rectitude. Personally, I find poems directly about the H Bomb deeply distasteful. Often they seem to me profoundly inauthentic. They don't admit that they are covertly relishing an apocalyptic imagery hitherto the property of religious rhetoric. I would assert that the tendency of poems directly about the H Bomb is to reconcile us, by a kind of verbose numbing, a naming that takes out the sting, to the horror by which we should be continuously outraged and horrified. By our rhetoric about the Bomb we learn to live with it and that could easily spell death. The point of poetry is that it can reilluminate our outrage. (By outrage I do not mean expressions of horror. I mean the undertone of fear that suddenly explodes into realisation and sometimes into action—the realisation that the Bomb will kill me and particular people, not just destroy an abstract humanity). My inclusion of the Peter Redgrove poem indicates that the last thing I want is a taboo on the Bomb. Fear of it is there in

"All the children play at cripples
And cough along with one foot in the gutter"
and in thoughts:
"on fired bones
And body-prints in the charcoal of a house . . ."
But this is not a poem *about* the Bomb: it is not a call to action. Actually, I don't think Redgrove's poem does anything to us, or even organises our attitudes, which is the mature modern way of re-

phrasing the rhetorical position. What it offers is another human presence which mitigates our loneliness. Fear of the Bomb, we might think, has a central but problematic place in this man's feelings. Such shared knowledge makes the universe more human and more habitable. But the poem has not attempted to manipulate and direct our attitudes. It has organised one unit of experience. It doesn't even try to persuade you that its experience is universal. On the contrary, it uniquely, irreduceably happens in the neighbourhood of Chiswick Park. Chiswick as a result becomes a place. The world is less anonymous. I chose *Expectant Father* because it has some of the usual props of socialist rhetoric. But the poem isn't out to squeeze our emotions. It makes no appeal to particular reflexes. The equation of "son" with "sun" isn't made by the poem but by the sister. The poem is about people who naturally use this kind of symbolism. Despite the apparently triumphal flourish at the end of the poem, the glow of pleasure is purely provisional. The new glorious day could easily end in another evening full of "too much death, disaster". This day is one of many in a year when "all the children play at cripples". Similarly the lamps by which the poet undresses, though comforting now, are lit by the same energy which can fire bones and leave "body prints in the charcoal of a house". The flame which sleeps in "the bloodscheme of a house" can be destructive or creative; the shallow print prove that of a corpse or of a sleeper. The pivot of the poem is the "But" that begins the last paragraph. This "but" does not dismiss what has gone before. It suggests new implications that do not cancel the doom-ridden images that precede it. The poet is pleased to make his joke, because jokes dissipate the difficult feeling of the preceding sections, suggest release, are life-confirming, a device that allows the poet to go on enduring contradictory emotions. If the poem is *about* anything, then it is about this joke. It forces us into the poet's own ambivalence towards his coming paternity. His child represents primal human energies. Yet these energies share a common source with the H Bomb that carbonises houses and the electricity that lights them in the sun. The poem makes both the Blakean affirmation that "Energy is eternal delight" and puts its converse. This is something we already know about. The poem makes this knowledge actual and immediate by uniquely re-experiencing it.

Some criteria of value should by now emerge. A poem is an articulated experience. All subject-matter is available: there is no hierarchy of importance or centrality. The poem can appear to be *about* anything it likes. More strictly, it is not a record *of* experience so much as units of experience in their own right. They succeed or fail according to whether the experience is faithfully enacted, personally authenticated and finally ordered. Again, the ordering *is* the poetry.

The criterion of authenticity is a development and complication of the original romantic criterion of sincerity. Sincerity, in turn, displaces pre-romantic criteria such as truth to Nature, Universality, Divine inspiration and Revelation. Such criteria assume an essential truth which poetry, to be valuable, must express. The crisis of belief which gave rise to romanticism also abolished established central Truths or Universals. Nonetheless, romantic critics clung to a more limited essentialism. Poetry ceased to be true to nature; but it remained true to the poet's nature. This was conceived as an essence that predated the poem which expressed it. Truth to such individual nature equals sincerity. Most modern critics reject the criterion of sincerity. It presents too many problems in application. It assumes a dualism of poet and poem, leads to continual recourse from the poems themselves to the psychology of their author. We end up making direct judgments about the man rather than his work. The sincerity criterion is dangerous precisely because it ignores the "made", "worked", "organised" nature of art. On the other hand, "things", "works" are really disguised metaphors for what poems are. Critics are easily tempted into thinking of poems as fabricated objects run by "works". This leaves out of account the degree to which the poet really is in his poem, not just working through it, or ejecting it, but really being it.

The authenticity criterion, by contrast, really puts the emphasis on poems as lived and organised experience. It invites us to judge the sincerity of the poet *within* his poem. We have to judge whether experience is being evaded or "cooked"; whether the poem is a genuine experience or the experience of a wish to have an experience. But how in general does the authenticity criterion work? The answer must inevitably seem unhelpful. It simply doesn't work in general at all. It works only in particular instances. Each critical performance must be as unique and particular as the poem it examines.

This proposition seems less startling if we face up to one fact that we all really know. Critics holding utterly diverse criteria of judgment can arrive at practically identical judgments. Moreover, in most worthwhile critics there is usually a huge gap between their general principles and their particular judgments. Entirely principled critics are either completely uninteresting or interesting by reason of what they reveal of themselves rather than the work (Tolstoy on Shakespeare, for instance). True, my own proposition is a sort of general principle. Some sort of tension between principle and particular judgments is what gives criticism its excitement and value. Its struggle to unify and universalise its proposition, is, as it were, its brand of existential anguish. I am not arguing that there cannot be principled approaches to the judgement of literature nor that we are left with a complete relativism of judgement. A critic can argue us round, but not by the validity of his principles, rather by the depth and authority of his reading of actual works. This reading, of course, might well gain much of its strength and coherence from his choice of concepts.

Authenticity is still difficult to talk about, because we still lack an appropriate critical vocabulary. It is a criterion which we all work instinctively. Modern criticism is simply trying to catch up with instinctual practice. W. D. Snodgrass comes as close to formulating what I would wish to call authenticity as any one. These remarks conclude a very interesting essay appended to *Heart's Needle*, in which he describes the processes of revision by which a glib, tricksy poem gradually assumed what he felt to be its more authentic form:

I am left, then, with a very old-fashioned measure of a poem's worth—the depth of its sincerity. And it seems to me that the poets of our generation—those of us who have gone so far in criticism and analysis that we cannot ever turn back and be innocent again, who have such extensive resources for disguising ourselves from ourselves—that our only hope as artists is to continually ask ourselves, "Am I writing what I *really* think? Not what is acceptable; not what my favourite intellectual would think in this situation; not what I wish I felt. Only what I cannot help thinking". For I believe that the only reality which a man can ever surely know is that self he cannot help being, though he will only know that self through its interactions with the world around it. If he pretties it up, if he changes its meaning, if in short he rejects this reality, his mind will be less than alive. So will his words.

For sincerity I would want to read authenticity. He does make, with great eloquence, a statement of principle which modern criticism needs to follow up. Authenticity would mean for both poet and critic a continuous testing and reappraisal of what we believe. It would concern itself with the fundamental content and direction of our life projects as they appear in art, with the exposure of that self that the self "cannot help being"; and would attack those "extensive resources" that the mind has for disguising itself from itself in art as in life. [5]

The romantic lyric is superbly fitted for a fully authentic rendering of experience. The film has to make its impact at one viewing; it cannot be read back, often only with difficulty reseen. Drama suffers a constant dualism between text and production: the latter suffers by its very nature an overwhelming contingency of property and occasion. The novel dissipates its effects through considerable stretches of time: they can be grasped only by a laborious retrospective effort. The romantic lyric, by contrast, preserves immediacy of impact, evolves patently in time, yet can produce almost simultaneously impressions and permits continual recourse. It is the simplest, least fussy and ought to be the most accessible of all art forms. Yet it has suffered virtual eclipse, become a language grown hieroglyphic.

---

[5]Such a criticism would really have to come to terms, for example, with what is wrong with the Holbrook poems recently published in the Alvarez Penguin anthology. For these really are poems that a favourite intellectual might write for the poet. They are characterised by a kind of hollow wholesomeness as though everything in them were being seen through the eyes of some humanitarian, idealised amalgam of Leavis and Lawrence. The emotional responses are faked up so skilfully and the right comments come so glibly, that it is easy to fall for them at a first reading. They are betrayed by a sense they give of being too right, too respectable. I must say that *Unholy Marriage*, which deals with a fatal motorbicycle crash involving a young couple, made me uneasy even before I read it, when I heard it being recited. Tough yet tender, sophisticated yet simple: it was too good to be true. It manipulated all the machinery for evoking the right kinds of responses a little too conspicuously. Under it, there seemed to be an inner emptiness, something fabricated, some motivations lurking yet unstated which did not square with its subject. *Llarregub Revisited*, Holbrook's recent critical work on Dylan Thomas has confirmed all my unease.

I have chosen these six poems to make one simple point about contemporary poetry. Though these poems vary in difficulty, none is in principle difficult to understand. Alan Brownjohn's poetry speaks in very much a contemporary voice—unassuming, modest, venturing little beyond a quiet notation of the situation. It is a local, tactful voice—one which he shares to some extent with Philip Larkin. The Snodgrass poem emerges as more compelling, more intense, beneath its relaxed surface. Brownjohn's metaphor of snow is one-dimensional, concerned with "saving . . . face", with "hiding" an "unfruitful world". ("Its white informal fantasies" imitate the action of the poem: "informal" is a key word, suggesting not so much informed as form which works without fuss, the poetry being contemporarily "cool", though a little harder than that; "coldish", perhaps). The snow of Snodgrass's poem circles outward in true romantic fashion to embrace the Cold War, the snow blanketing (rather than Brownjohn's "hiding") fertile fields ("bed" serves for sown harvest, love, birth), the purity of American snow which has not yet been fouled like Asia's (or more specifically, Korea's) snow, but which might easily become so, the blank sheet or *tabula rasa* of the child's mind, as well as, lastly, the sheet of paper on which the poem is being written (again, the romantic poem about writing poetry). Every word is noticeably charged with metaphorical energy:

... born
When the new fallen soldiers froze ...

The soldiers are *new-fallen*, because they lie dead or exhausted: they are *new fallen*, because they are very young, almost like the child new fallen out of the womb (and out of eternity) into an icy world, and like the poem which has fallen out of potentiality into form. "Fallen" takes up more remote echoes from a theological fall which mankind endlessly repeats and repents.[6]

The echoes are remote, because the old religious scheme is only felt as a metaphor.

Two separate points. The word "cramped" acts out the pain and difficulty of self-expression in a world thoroughly inattentive to poetry. Such words are common to contemporary idiom, account for much of what is distinctive to its diction: clenched, gripped, clogged, all words which convey contraction, tension, are commonplace. Secondly, all these poems make use of seasonal metaphors but in a thoroughly non-rhetorical way. Jenny Joseph does not covertly twist our emotions when she makes her old woman die in winter. She firmly states that that is the actuality: "It was in the great frost of that year when she died." Any symbolic implications are such as would naturally emerge from the actual situation. The hearts of the burial party stir in the sun, but this does not represent confident dogmatic re-assurance that life goes on. The point of the poem is that life often goes out and that the irreparability of that is unredeemable.

---

[6]Poets from Milton onwards convert the expulsion from Eden theme into an analogue of the transition from innocence into experience. Like Milton, they usually find the fall is eventually "fortunate": they have to, because their poetry is committed to experience, the, theologically speaking, fallen condition, as the only worthwhile enterprise.

Snodgrass uses seasonal imagery too in a wholly personal, convincing way. His "demented summer" is, like Redgrove's, highly ambivalent. It would mean the agony of new love, the Bomb again, the "increase" of life (Snodgrass remembers the biblical imagery of life as a harvest: the Patriarch sinks back to earth "full of years", like a granary full of grain): summer may "deepen" the harvest or simply "bury" it, under the next snow. By this sort of ambiguity, the poem tries to construct a total attitude out of the data which it provides. Of course, it fails to be total: it remains a provisional gesture, the only one possible in any given situation. The situation is indeed a very personal one; the poem part of a sequence about divorce and its effects on a child. There is no fictional guise here. This is explicitly Snodgrass's divorce and child that are being explored. Such an intensely personal, intimately autobiographical poetry is unimaginable before our century. It represents the really unique contribution of our century. Utterly secular, a direct communication without symbolic intermediaries (like Keats's Nightingale) between poet and reader, it becomes something like direct, personal confrontation. Such confrontation is without motive beyond its intrinsic human interest (the fact that poetry doesn't make money is some safeguard of disinterestedness).

All the poems I have used are obsessed by cold weather, culminating in the title of Redgrove's volume, *The Nature of Cold Weather*. One must resist the temptation to make an instant crude reduction to, say, something like the Cold War. My choice has been heavily loaded towards cold weather poetry. Also, each poet makes use of the cold metaphor in a quite distinctive way. For Ted Hughes' *February* is the last untamed month, a violent, wolfish season which reminds us of an implacable nature that by evasion we drive inwards, and make dangerous for ourselves. I do not want to pretty up this poem. It is indeed a grim celebration (over-indulged through a sadistic flogging of the language) of the brute beauty of the raw and primitive. I am not sure who the "he" of the last stanza of *February* is: whether the month or the poet. Perhaps the two are identified. The "making" of "wolf-mask, mouths clamped well onto the world" ("clamped" is another of those typically contemporary words), I read as a kind of sympathetic magic, the poet crying wolf to frighten and alert us. Tom Gunn's cold is the mountain cold of a world of concepts. The abominable snow-man becomes an image of the disincarnated intellect. Hughes goes to winter for a grim, utter stripping down to the primal ferocity of body and nature. Gunn shows the stripping down to the abominable intellect. Hence, they use the image in utterly opposing senses. Yet at another level it becomes the same image, representing the act of stripping down itself, of exposure to a hostile element. Indeed all these poems convey through their differing strategies a condition of exposure, an agonised aloneness in the face of a hostile climate and also a certain icy exultation in enduring it. Even Brownjohn, who seems to show this quality least, who plays with "soft moods" rather than acknowledging that "the abominable endures", takes a cool pleasure in his "white informal fantasies". All these poems let through a knowledge of the cold, affirm that the cold is bracing and killing. They show us what it feels like to be other people living in the world.

The New Poetry of Socialism
David Craig

from

New Left Review, 17, 1962.

Reprinted by permission of *New Left Review*.

The New Poetry of Socialism

David Craig

Gabriel Pearson's recent article[1] on present-day poetry and the trend poetry has followed since the rise of romanticism contained some striking new formulations of a thesis familiar enough from Plekhanov's analysis of the French Romantics in his *Art and Social Life*, T. S. Eliot's essay on Blake, or Marshall McLuhan's essay (in an early number of *Essays in Criticism*) on Tennyson and "picturesque poetry". It seems to be a fact of literary history that romanticism developed out of the breakdown of any culture in Western Europe that felt itself to be (in Pearson's words) "sustained either by unified social or by religious sanctions".

Pearson, however, goes much further than the Twenties or Thirties critics who were preoccupied with this "dissociation of sensibility". He thinks that this split, with its effect of laying an acute stress on the most private emotions, is *still the major factor* in making our poetry what it is. And he will not have it that *any other valid basis for poetry* has yet emerged. Here the challenge to socialism arises. For if socialism, Marxism, communism have not yet brought into being any distinctive forms of literature, in the several generations that have elapsed since the First International or the October Revolution, then indeed we would have to search the heart of our ideology (I say "our" on the assumption that I have a good deal in common with the New Left) and see whether there is something acking in our beliefs and our practice.

1 One of Pearson's key formulations of what romanticism consists of is this: "[The romantic poem] does not consist in a series of observations about the world. Instead, the poet tries to watch himself observing the world, tries to catch himself in the act of experiencing. This is why so much romantic poetry appears not only entirely egocentric, but also reflexive, as though the poems always wanted to be experiences of experiences, or poems about poems." He also asserts that "all worthwhile modern poetry is romantic." When I read this, I at once thought of Bertolt Brecht, and then of Hugh MacDiarmid. Brecht is known for his "alienation effect", his effort to make an art which did not invite the identification of the reader

[1]"Romanticism and Contemporary Poetry": *New Left Review*, 16 (July/August 1962).

or viewer, or tempt him with any emotional luxury, but tried rather to *show*—to demonstrate life as it is, and deliberately to provoke him to form an opinion of the "case" before him. Brecht wanted the audience to say: "I wouldn't have thought that—People shouldn't do things like that—That's extremely odd, almost unbelievable— This has to stop—This person's suffering shocks me, because there might be a way out for him." [2] And MacDiarmid is known for his effort to stretch and transform poetry so that it could take in the complete range of modern knowledge, including Marxism.

The poetry these outstanding writers produced was as different as could be from what Pearson regards, not only as the finest and most typically modern poetry, but almost as the supreme art. "The romantic lyric," he says, "is superbly fitted for a fully authentic rendering of experience." As though this weren't claim enough, he then dismisses in a few sentences the ability of the film, the drama, the novel to do any such thing. And near the end he once again links his touchstone of "authenticity"—"Such an intensely personal, intimately autobiographical poetry is unimaginable before our century"—with his assertion that this is *the* modern literature, "the really unique contribution of our century." The poetry of MacDiarmid and Brecht is not at all intensely personal (in Pearson's sense), they don't offer us their intimate autobiographies, and both were Communists who found their way to a truly Communist poetry. In their work, if anywhere, is the evidence that overturns Pearson's claim for romanticism along with his joint assertion that socialist realism has been, poetically, sterile.

One of the vital factors common to Brecht and MacDiarmid may be approached like this:—F. R. Leavis has published several essays analyzing poems for their "reality", "sincerity", and "emotional quality"—qualities closely akin to Pearson's "authenticity". In the essay " 'Thought' and Emotional Quality" (*Scrutiny*, XIII, 1) one of Leavis's prime examples of a *sound* emotional quality is Scott's little poem "Proud Maisie". He argues that one excellence of this poem (in comparison with Tennyson's "Break, break, break") is that it presents distinct particulars. These generate between them a strong effect, in which emotion plays a part. But the emotion is not injected or larded-on from some unrealized inner feelings of the poet's; it belongs in and to the life that the poet has grasped and presented.

It is significant that it should have been a poem *in a folk mode* that exemplified this soundness. For MacDiarmid and Brecht were both masters of folk modes. They needed them to get beyond the post-romantic impasse in poetry. The romantic lyric, in the hands of Tennyson, Rossetti, Dowson, the early Yeats, had thinned down into the vehicle for a few dim moods. The folk modes had originated in medieval and even earlier times: that is, in an age before the rise of capitalism had brought about that split in the old "unity of social and religious sanctions". The ballad, folk-song, and impersonal narrative

[2] Brecht, "Theatre for Learning": *Tulane Drama Review*, VI, 1 (New Orleans, September 1961), 20-1.

not only offered a stylistic means of getting beyond the late-romantic "slush" (as Pound called it); they also had the special function for Left writers that they could form a fresh link between literature and the people with their still semi-oral culture. [3]

Hugh MacDiarmid came into his own as a poet *via* something close to pastiche. Folk-songs, ballads, flytings, the Burnsian domestic poem—he put all these to use in a lyric verse which is modern in that it is more idiosyncratic or "original" than the typical folk-poem and yet is much less "autobiographical" than the Keatsian type that Pearson has in mind. In a poem such as "Focherty" (from *Penny Wheep*, 1926), about a red-faced brute of a farmer who steals the narrator's girl, we don't sense the least projection of some experience of the poet's. The stress is on the creation of outward character—

> His face is like a roarin' fire
> For love o' the barley-bree.
> . . . Blaefaced afore the throne o' God
> He'll get his fairin' yet,

and on satirical fantasy—

> He'll be like a bull in the sale-ring there,
> And I'll lauch lood to see,
> Till he looks up and canna mak' oot
> Whether it's God—or me!

MacDiarmid then began to use folk modes as the vehicle of themes that were large and public, objective, and at the other pole from the "autobiographical". His major theme became the sense he got from the gathering Slump that the Scottish community had become exhausted and second-rate. For example, this lyric from *A Drunk Man Looks At The Thistle* (1926)—

> O Scotland is
> THE barren fig.
> Up, carles, up
> And roond it jig.
>
> Auld Moses took
> A dry stick and
> Instantly it
> Floo'ered in his hand.
>
> Pu' Scotland up,
> And wha can say
> It winna bud
> And blossom tae.
>
> A miracle's
> Oor only chance.
> Up, carles, up
> And let us dance.

[3]The new dramatists—Wesker, Behan, Delaney, Arden, Osborne—are using folksongs for the same purpose today.

Decidedly there is *emotion* here: a country-dance rhythm is used to suggest a frenzy of frustration, and the folk mode (drawing also on the breezy American-Negro Bible song) is indispensable to the effect, because it leads the poet's own disillusion outwards to the experience of a whole played-out community.

Thus MacDiarmid's earlier work contained a potential of *detachment*—an impersonal style based on folk modes—and of *progressive politics*, concern with Scotland the distressed area. These potentialities were magnificently realized in the poetry of his creative peak, from 1930–35, the years of the two *Hymn to Lenin* volumes. There is no room here for an adequate account of this work.[4] But enough can be said and quoted to show how in this poetry British socialism found an imaginative expression that at the same time took poetry a whole stage beyond the romanticism by which Pearson thinks we are still bound.

Pearson gibes bitterly at the socialist-realist poetry which is "rhetorical in the bad sense, shouting for attention, behaving as though it had an audience at its feet, depending on some external doctrine that remains inert and unlived". MacDiarmid seems to me a master of poetry that draws on public speaking and discusses public subjects. And here is how he writes it ("Another Epitaph for an Army of Mercenaries" from *Second Hymn to Lenin*, 1935):

> It is a God-damned lie to say that these
> Saved, or knew, anything worth any man's pride.
> They were professional murderers and they took
> Their blood money and impious risks and died.
> In spite of all their kind some elements of worth
> With difficulty persist here and there on earth.

The rhythms of this poem are not attuned to delicate vibrations from the poet's inmost feelings. But the rhythms are distinctive, the poem is not characterless, a crude blare from the political loudspeaker. The dry, serious tone, the way in which the phrases of the final sentence seem to measure themselves out scrupulously—such effects combine to suggest (with a precision no less real than the Keatsian sensitivity) an attitude of intentness, a rare dogged toughness, a refusal to compromise. What comes across is the deeply-considered *opinion* that war is utterly anti-human, and avoidable; for, in that feeling of determination logically to state the whole case against war, we sense a grasp of the truth that war is explicable, the rational mind can come to grips with it, and resistance is therefore possible.

Such poetry argues, it condenses ideas (key ideas from Vol. I of *Capital* are visible in the "First Hymn to Lenin"). Such poetry is not mainly concerned to give us the feel of what it is "like to be other people living in the world" (a formulation of Pearson's). All MacDiarmid's passages on Lenin are in this best vein of his. They analyze, and also (by means of that terse, deliberate movement) *make us feel*, the qualities of utter selflessness, utter concentration on the movements of the Russian people and Russian history, that

[4]Such an account is attempted in my "MacDiarmid the Marxist Poet": *Hugh MacDiarmid, A Festschrift*, ed. Duval and Smith (Edinburgh, 1962), 90–94.

gave Lenin his strategic mastery and his grasp of the need for and the process of revolution.

> Lenin was like that wi' the workin'-class life,
>> At hame wi't 'a.
> His fause movements couldna' been fewer
>> The best weaver earth ever saw.
> A' *he'd* to dae wi' moved intact,
>> Clean, clear, and exact.

So must the socialist poet be—

> But as for me in my fricative work
>> I ken fu' weel
> Sic an integrity's what I maun hae,
> Indivisible, real,
> Woven owre close for the point o' a pin
>> Onywhere to win in.[5]

Unless Pearson thinks nothing of such poetry, I don't see how he can deny that socialism here found its voice, and a voice quite new in kind to a literature hitherto bound by romanticism. It might well be said that MacDiarmid's poetry was still wanting in vital respects: it too much evoked only the *attitdes* of seriousness and militancy, and the content of scientific socialism was not there, for example the life of the exploited working-people whose militancy can put an end to exploitation. But this was a lack peculiar to MacDiarmid, who is too much the pure intellectual and too little interested in ordinary lives. This lack was not at all inherent in socialist realism. Brecht filled his poetry more richly with the life of the exploited peoples than any other poet I know, and the new forms he needed drew on an even finer mastery than MacDiarmid's of the folk modes and an equal ability to give us the feel of a serious mind intent on its deepest ideas and beliefs.

Consider the poem "Nannas Lied" from Brecht's play *Round Heads and Pointed Heads* (1931–34). It is a lyric, but not in the Pearson-Keats sense—it is a lyric for the stage. The emotion in it springs not from the presence of the author but from the presentment of a distinct other personality—her speech, her experiences, given for themselves and not because the author can use them to project his own ego. A whore is singing to the audience—

> Good Sirs, at seventeen summers
> I went to Lechery Fair
> And plenty of things it's taught me.
> Many a heartache,
> That's the chance you take.
> But I've wept many times in despair.
> (After all I'm a human being, too.)
> Thank God it's all over with quickly,
> All the love and the grief we must bear.
> Where are the tears of yesterevening?
> Where are the snows of yesteryear?

[5]"The Seamless Garment", from *First Hymn to Lenin* (1931).

As the years pass by it gets easy,
Easy in Lechery Fair.
And you fill your arms with so many.
But tenderness
Grows strangely less
When you spend with so little care.
(For every stock runs out in the end.)
Thank God it's all over with quickly, etc.

And, though you may learn your trade well,
Learn it at Lechery Fair,
Bartering lust for small change
Is a hard thing to do.
Well, it comes to you.
But you don't grow younger there.
(After all you can't stay seventeen forever.)
Thank God it's all over with quickly, etc.[6]

The very speaking manner of the woman comes across: the simplicity, naivety, and pathetic forced jauntiness of the clichés and pop-song phraseology—"After all you can't stay seventeen forever". But although the language, even the rhythm, barely depart from what might actually be said, an extraordinarily wide range of feelings is conveyed—flickerings of desolate self-knowledge, suggested by checks and numbings of the rhythm: "But tenderness Grows strangely less"; sighs of weariness; and then the downright emphasis of the old professional, pulling herself together. It is an achievement precisely comparable with Chaucer's Prologue to the *Wife of Bath's Tale:* artless garrulity, seemingly untransmuted by literary art, is allowed to convey its own mixture of vivacity, homely advice, sudden desolated awareness of its own helplessness—all held together by a stoicism that the poet has been able to respond to and fully to recreate because it so appeals to his own humanity.

This is only one of a hundred effects that Brecht achieves through the use of those folk modes that are rooted in the culture of the people themselves and so are best adapted to express their lives. In the wonderful "Concerning the Infanticide, Marie Farrar" the sufferings of the poor in Slump Germany are presented in full realistic detail:

Between the latrine and her room, she says,
Not earlier, the child began to cry until
It drove her mad so that she says
She did not cease to beat it with her fists
Blindly for some time till it was still.
And then she took the body to her bed
And kept it with her there all through the night:
When morning came she hid it in the shed.
But you, I beg you, check your wrath and scorn
For man needs help from every creature born.

[6]Translated by H. R. Hays: Brecht, *Selected Poems* (New York, 1959), 87.

Marie Farrar, born in April,
An unmarried mother, convicted, died in
The Meissen penitentiary,
She brings home to you all men's sin.
You who bear pleasantly between clean sheets
And give the name "blessed" to your womb's weight
Must not damn the weakness of the outcast,
For her sin was black but her pain was great.
Therefore, I beg you, check your wrath and scorn
For man needs help from every creature born.

It is not only the subject-matter that is socialist, it is the style, with
its iron restraint that yet suggests no chilly aloofness on the poet's
part[7] and does not exclude an outright humanitarian appeal, which
is reserved for the refrain. This style is scientific socialism made over
into fully imaginative terms. The poem has opened with an "un-
emotional" police-record statement of the Marie Farrar case—

Marie Farrar, born in April,
No marks, a minor, rachitic, both parents dead,
Allegedly, up to now without police record,
Committed infanticide, it is said,
As follows: in her second month, she says,
With the aid of a barmaid she did her best
To get rid of her child with two douches,
Allegedly painful but without success . . . [8]

It this were kept up, it would be only a satire on the law and the
courts. But already these perfectly unbeautiful opening phrases,
conveying nothing but facts, have served to show us that we have
here gone beyond the old Charity, which would "relieve" but not
abolish distress. Beatrice Webb tells us in *My Apprenticeship* how
the early socialists detested Charity and all its works. They set
themselves instead to find out, scientifically, the facts of poverty,
ill-health, bad housing, all the forms of inequality. And the facts
served both as evidence of social injustice and as ammunition in the
political fight for a better society. It is in this sense that so many of
Brecht's poems are, in their very style, supreme imaginative products
of socialism.

The rest of his range need only be referred to. There are the workers'
narratives such as "Song of the Railroad Gang of Fort Donald" and
"Coal for Mike"—in these Brecht, the German intellectual, was
able to make himself at home in the tradition of American industrial
folk-poetry. There are the poems written as propaganda for working-
class solidarity in the fight against Nazi fascism ("All of Us or
None", "The United Front Song"). There are ballads that cover the
full range of socialist satire against war-mongering, chauvinism, and
obscurantist religion while giving us, too, the real content of the
soldier's life and the incongruous accidents of warfare ("Legend of
the Dead Soldier", "Children's Crusade 1939"). The common factor
that must be stressed, in answer to Pearson's claims for the "ego-

[7]Compare the very different detachment of T. S. Eliot, e.g. in the passage on
the typist and her lover in section III of *The Waste Land*.
[8]*Selected Poems*, 27, 23.

centric" and the "autobiographical", is that Brecht created a poetry in which the poet's own ego or personality is there only in the sense that, without his mind and experience, the poem could never have been written at all. But, starting from what he knows, the modern people's poet, saturated in socialist struggles and discussions, is able to broaden out, and lose the self-regarding emotions. Without any loss of "authenticity" his poetry is opened to the lives of individuals very different from himself, to whole classes and peoples, and to ideas as such.

Here issue must be joined directly with what Pearson alleges to be the history of socialist literature. For one thing, the *only* socialist poet he discusses in any detail is Christopher Logue. I have never liked Logue's poetry, with its obtrusive undertone of self-justification. Pearson calls his "To my Fellow Artists" "a good example of "socialist realist or committed poetry". Should he not have said that it was the only piece of socialist-realist poetry that happened to be fresh in his mind? If Logue's work to date (with the exception of his fine Homer adaptation) is typical of anything, it is only of the poet who is not unselfconsciously at one with the workers' movement and not saturated in experience of their struggles. He is too "auto-biographical"—and therefore tailor-made for Pearson's case. That is all. To treat one London poet of the Sixties as typical of what is by now a long and experienced tradition is abjectly parochial.

In a footnote, Pearson "pleads guilty to a certain ethnocentricity" —i.e. what he is saying holds good only for poetry in English. Yet on the next page he permits himself this staggering assertion: "The most reputable socialist poetry has been written outside England, and under conditions that gave rise to the kind of real communal identification with central issues that could justify it: e.g. poetry produced during the Polish crisis and Hungarian revolution (1956)." It is the examples that are staggering, for they imply that "real communal identification" between the people and states based on socialism has occurred only during crises in the People's Democracies, and that only this sort of crisis has given rise to "reputable socialist poetry". Only one thing could justify this—a thorough knowledge of *several* socialist literatures; and Pearson has no more knowledge of them (as he admits) than I. But I do know that Becher is esteemed in the German Democratic Republic second only to Brecht, and Becher was the G.D.R.'s Minister of Culture, not a rebel on the fringe of the socialist state. I also know that poetry has remained live enough in the Soviet Union to hold on to a mass audience such as only fiction now commands in Britain. The poetry of Brecht alone gives the lie to Pearson's gross prejudice against the literature of the socialist mainstream. I believe he will come to be seen as the greatest poet of our century. But Pearson never goes near him.

He is even wrong about the socialist poets he does deign to mention. Mayakovsky is said to have suffered from a "confusion between the impulse to communicate personal (which can of course include political) experience and to activate, authorize, or enthuse a movement which may have no true communal existence." But Mayakovsky was writing in the thick of the Civil War and the first desperate years of Soviet power. His posters, articles, and poems went straight into the struggle, and were immensely appreciated. He wrote verse-satires against bureaucracy for *Izvestia*, and Army songs for the soldiers defending Leningrad against Yudenich in the Civil War. If this "movement" which he was trying to "enthuse" had "no true communal existence", then the *subbotniks*, the soviets, and the Red Army didn't exist either.

This point is a key one because Pearson, who denies the existence of any "orthodox" socialist poetry other than agitprop rhetoric, naturally cannot conceive of a new socialist *public* either. He refers to the Soviet open-air poetry readings, where great crowds come to hear the best poets recite their work. Pearson cannot say this audience is only a figment of the poet's with "no true communal existence". It is certainly as tangible a part of the cultural scene as the *New Left Review*. But an ingenious speculation helps him round the difficulty: "Likely enough," he says, "Soviet auditors look to these poets to echo their own revolt against mass conformity, to escape the loneliness of modern industrial society, into a shared *solitude*." Thus the New-Left critic, like any American sociologist alarmed by growing Soviet consumer-affluence, argues that really there is no difference between socialist and bourgeois society: if they're affluent, it must be in the Western way, and if they're decadent, they share our vices. I have not been to the Soviet Union, but descriptions of the poetry readings exist, so does the poetry, and it looks as though literature reaches the people (and the people make their effect on literature) in quite a different, and much more thriving, way than anything we can conceive of in the West. The photo in the *Daily Worker* for 12.5.62 of Yevgeny Yevtushenko reciting his poems at University College, London, poised like a gymnast or a fencer, with his arms flying, is evidence by itself of how natural it is to a Soviet poet to speak out loud to a community. In the *Observer* for 27.5.62 Yevtushenko wrote that on the National Day of Poetry, in many Soviet cities, "all the poets give readings of their verse in the bookshops, and in Moscow in the evening they perform in the Mayakovsky Square, where before an audience of 8,000–10,000 they read their verses for two to three hours, sometimes under falling snow." And it is this public that decides the numbers of copies printed: "They write remarks about the books which it is proposed to publish and in this way the publishers lay down the numbers of copies to be issued." Last year the editors of the *Soviet Literature* monthly were telling me in London how poets like Tvardovsky are used to reciting their poetry at length, on the radio, in halls and lecture-rooms; and I also recall reading in the *NLR's* forebear, the *New Reasoner*, how at a reading given by Pasternak the crowd would jump to their feet after a poem and shout out gleefully the number of the Shakespeare sonnet that they wanted him to read his version of next.[9]

[9] 'Impressions of Pasternak': *New Reasoner*, 4 (Halifax). Spring 1958, 90.

Surely in face of this evidence of a truly communal public it will not do to suggest that the thousands are coming together only to escape into "a shared *solitude*". That would mean that they came to hear their most private emotions evoked for their solitary, introspective response. The poetry itself (such of it as I have found in translation) makes nonsense of this very Western suggestion. Yevtushenko, for example, can write with touches as declamatory as we would expect from his athletic gestures. The poem "Murder!", with its repeated exclamation of "Murder"! and the unashamed use of "I", "I", "I", would be quite impossible for the modern English poet, so cramped and clogged (to use his own typical adjectives) has he become. But this poem of Yevtushenko's is no hysterical appeal for our sentimental or self-righteous horror at a killing. The murder (a shooting for money) becomes, as the poem goes on, the living death of a Party comrade hardened into an automaton by the effort to conform. Again and again Yevtushenko uses seemingly "obvious" styles, sometimes colloquial, sometimes declamatory, to convey at once the enthusiasm and the hardness of Soviet society, in a spirit at once critical and honestly admiring.[10] The balance of feelings is not unsubtle, yet the style is far closer to natural speaking, much less "worked", than what we are now used to in the West. The poet seems to be supported in his way of writing by his knowledge that there is that genuine community of people crowding to hear him. Surely the audience for such poetry are sitting there, not each wrapped in his own introverted "solitude", but in an unforced outgoing consciousness that the common events and habits of their lives together are being rehearsed before them in language that is obscured by no clog or cramp of privacy.

Yevtushenko himself was brought up in Siberia. The Asiatic republics are a large part of the Soviet Union, and it seems that in Kazakhstan, for example, the ancient tradition of minstrels' contests has been kept up and transformed by socialism. On the initiative of the Union of Soviet Writers, national verse contests have been held at the republicam capital, Alma Ata. The songs chanted at the contests are taken down in shorthand, printed, broadcast, translated. The most famous of the minstrels, Jamboul, who died in 1945, aged 99, did his best work after 1917, in long oral poems celebrating the leaders of the new society and great liberals from the past. His funeral was a tremendous public event. The streets were packed and his oldest pupil sang a valedictory song that was taken up and chanted by other minstrels among the crowd.[11]

Such a culture petered out in Britain with the degenerate Victorian street-singers and, perhaps, the reading-aloud of the 18th-century novels in the farmhouse kitchens or Dicken's unique performances of his own works up and down the country. Truer equivalents would be the long oral poems in Gaelic now dying out in the Scottish Islands, or the epics that used to be chanted and played by puppets

[10]See the Penguin ed. of his *Selected Poems*, trans. Milner-Gulland and Levi (1962), esp. "Murder!", "Birthday", and "Party Card".
[11]George Thomson, *Marxism and Poetry* (1945), 57–8 and n. 72.

in medieval Italy. Capitalist society, that drives the nexus of cash-and-profit like an iron wedge between artist and people, cannot sustain such a culture. Socialist society can, for it is already half-freed from the nexus—just as it can "grapple effectively with one of the hardest problems of modern times", "industrializing primitive communities without any signs now of social catastrophe".[12]

The final falsification of socialist literary history comes in Pearson's sentences on Soviet literature: "The duty of Socialist writers begins to look absolute. Occasional dereliction looks like deliberate opposition. The responsible artists like Mayakovsky crack their voices with shouting. It is the sly ones like Ehrenburg, the utterly independent like Pasternak and Akhmatova [who presumably are *ir*responsible?], and the worst hacks who survive." This had been said a thousand times—by Edward Crankshaw in his endless warped hate-affair with Russia, in the *Sunday Times/Life* glossy propaganda book on the Soviet Union, by every sort of publicist in the West who has scarcely opened a book of Soviet literature for himself. It is a Big Lie, and it is given the lie by the shelf-ful of first-class literature that the Soviet writers have produced, from Babel's *Red Cavalry* (hot from the Russo-Polish fighting of 1920), through the Twenties, which saw the first long novels by Fedin and Sholokhov—the Thirties, when Gladkov, Sholokhov, and Leonov reached their prime—the Forties, which saw the award of Stalin Prizes to the first books of Fedin's trilogy, a work equal, I should say, to the best of the Western Slump novels, those of Dos Passos, Farrell, and Steinbeck, and equal, therefore, to the best fiction done in English since the death of Lawrence—right up to the recent period, during which the old masters have still produced excellent works, and new kinds of writer have come to the fore (as Pearson acknowledges in a footnote on Yevtushenko).

How inadequate that last sentence is! I am simply asserting my own tastes! But what is one to say? How is the Big lie to be squashed in half an article? As yet there has been scarcely any *literary criticism* on the Soviet masterpieces. Novels and poems are thrown into the bearpit of cold-war debate and abuse. When Zhdanov or Fadeyev made a statement, there was an outcry. When Dudintsev published *Not By Bread Alone*, there was a burst of applause. And when *Doctor Zhivago* came out, even the angel seemed to join in the chorus of praise. But with a very few honourable exceptions[13] scarcely one literary expert has read, digested, and finally discussed Fedin's trilogy, for example, or the cream of the stories in *Winter's Tales*, 7 (Paustovsky's "The Telegram" and Sholokhov's "One Man's Life"), or Yevtushenko's poems (not his opinions or public appearances). When has Soviet literature (or work from the other socialist countries) ever been given the scrupulous attention that the critics bestow on Faulkner's or Sartre's latest or on a new fragment from some

[12]Nora Beloff, "Exploring the Red Empire": *Observer*, 30.7.62.
[13]For example, Ernest J. Simmons's book on Leonov, Sholokhov, and Fedin (Columbia University Press); or C. P. Snow and Pamela Hansford Johnson's Introduction to their anthology of Soviet short fiction, *Winter's Tales*, 7 (Macmillan, 1961).

monster-work by Robert Musil? If Pearson is content to join this conspiracy of silence, then he, the socialist critic, is no more honest than the ex-Trotskyites of the *Partisan Review*, who seize upon a Soviet story such as Yashin's "The Levers" (good in itself) because it criticizes the Soviet Party, but never dream of reprinting such equally accessible small masterpieces as Sholokhov's "One Man's Life" or the Latvian writer Vilis Lacis's "Four Trips".[14]

The fiction I have mentioned takes us some distance away from the centre of Pearson's attention, which is poetry: "all worthwhile modern poetry is romantic", and the romantic lyric can render experience more "authentically" than the film, the drama, the novel . . . Seen now in the perspective of the later part of his article, with its distortion of socialist literary history, Pearson's fixation on poetry, and especially on the most individual- or ego-centred poetry, shows up all the more clearly as quite typical of most criticism that plays down the novel in favour of the lyric: it is backward-looking, and eccentric. I had half-wondered about bringing such names as Babel, Fedin, Sholokhov against Pearson's travesty of Soviet literature—it was so obvious that he had never even thought of the novelists as belonging in the same world of high art as his chosen poets. But if Pearson wasn't even thinking of the novelists, he should have been. The title given his essay on the cover of the *NLR*—"Poetry in the Ice-Age" with its pun on the Cold War—and his sweeping references to "The most reputable socialist poetry" and "The duty of Socialist writers" claim for the essay an extremely wide application. But in the essay the evidence offered is so scanty (Christopher Logue, and a few minor English and American post-War romantics —no Brecht, no MacDiarmid, and no fiction) that his general case collapses.

Pearson is writing in a socialist journal, and he does say (in one of those footnotes) that socialist realism might seem "justified by the most reputable, humanly interesting and complex ideology". It would be up to him, then, to search the heart of his beliefs and discover how it could have been that so reputable and humane an ideology had given rise to so little literature and then only as an opposition or by-product, not from its core. When I look at socialism and socialist literature for myself, I find that it has given us Brecht and MacDiarmid, the American Slump novelists (plus Lewis Grassic Gibbon in Scotland), the superb Lu Hsun in China, the range of Soviet masters of fiction long and short, the new dramatists in Britain—to say nothing of the new cultures of Hungary, Poland, Czechoslovakia, China and the rest, which to me are still largely unknown territory. How is it that Gabriel Pearson's trust in his own socialist ideology has not led him to the discovery and appreciation of this great modern tradition?

[14]*Soviet Literature*, 1957, 12. These stories are accessible because Soviet publishers invite anyone to re-publish their material without any fee, royalty, or permission.

(*Gabriel Pearson will reply to this article in the next issue.*)

Romanticism and Socialism
Stanley Mitchell

from

New Left Review, 19, 1963.

Reprinted by permission of *New Left Review*.

Romanticism and Socialism

Stanley Mitchell

David Craig is right to challenge Gabriel Pearson where his argument most nearly touches us all, in particular those of us who are socialists, namely: is there a new public basis for poetry ?* Yet this was a small and tardy part of Gabriel Pearson's article, written it would seem in hurried anger after the leisurely, exploratory metaphysics of his main argument. It is a pity that David Craig gave him his thesis on Romanticism, not simply for the sake of literary history, but because Romanticism (a different kind from Gabriel Pearson's) bears very fruitfully on socialist poetry to-day. It is not enough, for instance, to say, as Craig does, that "Brecht created a poetry in which the poet's own ego or personality is there only in the sense that, without his mind or experience, the poem would never have been written at all.". There is a real sense in which the bourgeois socialist poet of the twentieth century does not belong to a stable community with unquestioned values. Brecht, the anarchist troubadour, spent his mature socialist years in exile. Mayakovsky was first a Futurist; Eluard, Aragon, Neruda Surrealists. What are these movements if not a twentieth century Romanticism ? The poet explodes all resurrection, is apocalyptic, blares back at the bourgeoisie a metropolitan clangour, makes loud and lavish the most private fantasies. Let us take this as a metaphor for post-1914. The stance is destructive, cynically or hysterically personal; the verse momentary, wilful, inflammatory. Such a poet is faced with two choices: Fascism or Communism, the one apparently, the other truly an anti-bourgeois revolt. Those who chose Communism grounded themselves in new values, tempered in the case of Mayakovsky by the Civil War and the birth pangs of socialism, in the case of Brecht by the anti-Fascist struggle, in the case of Aragon and Eluard by the Popular Front and the Resistance. Their poetry gained in stature and dignity, but it was no easy growth. It cost Mayakovsky his life.

The mature verse of these poets remains highly individual. Brecht does not use his ballads, folk-songs, hymns in the same naive way in which, say, Bach might have done. They were not part of a warm, stable, day-to-day community life:

> I, Bertolt Brecht, come from the black forests.
> My mother bore me to the cities
> While I lay in her womb. And the cold of the forests
> Will be with me to my dying day.

Rather he *fashions* a new, poetic world out of the modes which

---

*See Gabriel Pearson, *Romanticism And Contemporary Poetry* (NLR.16); David Craig, *The New Poetry of Socialism* (NLR.17).

the city has destroyed. At the same time he is a contemporary, metropolitan poet who exploits the imagery and tempi of the city to the full. To suggest that he became an impersonal bard is both to pretend that a folk-tradition had continued unbroken and to ignore the actual ingenuity and resourcefulness with which Brecht created a poetry whose roots were not immediately visible in the world around him. More important, however, such a description of Brecht or any other socialist poet belittles the intense, personal struggle to which their poetry bears witness. In *To Posterity* 'I' becomes 'we', but through the choric peroration we hear the poet:

> Even anger at injustice
> Makes hoarse the voice.

The picture of the poet on the edge of chaos who finds faith and comradeship in the socialist revolution should recall for us the first Romantics as natural forbears. The French Revolution, with its limitless perspectives, inspired most of them however many later turned their backs on it. How many actually took part in revolutionary movements or regarded themselves as political figures: Byron, Shelley, Pushkin, Mickiewicz, Petöfi, Hugo, Manzoni, Büchner, Heine! David Craig ought to have complained of Gabriel Pearson's parochialism here as much as in modern times. For here it is a much greater sin. With the names of Pushkin, Mickiewicz and Petöfi goes the actual creation of the literatures of modern Russia, Poland and Hungary. If the achievement of a literary language and national classics is simply the projection of the Romantic ego, then these were pretty successful cases.

The Romanticism of Russia, Poland, Hungary, Germany, Italy was primarily concerned to assert the cultural dignity of each of these nations. It was a spiritual expression of national rebirth; it fought a dominating foreign culture: in political terms an aristocracy which spoke a foreign tongue and despised the culture of its own people. In general idèological terms the cry was against the rationalising universalism of French classicism. Romanticism fought for the particular, the nation. It fought a unified culture only where it was cosmopolitan. 'The people' was a warm, living community. This idea runs through the work of all the Slav and German Romantics. It is no accident that Herder should have borrowed so heavily from the English pre-Romantics. The language of the people, their songs and ballads would communicate to young bourgeois writers the vigour wherewith to assail the convenient scepticism which a corrupt nobility had selected from French Enlightenment. Shakespeare and Scott exerted a similar influence in Germany, Poland and Russia.

If English Romanticism played such a part abroad, what was it doing at home? Turning to the people, to myth, folklore, legend, popular imagination, popular epic literature, the Old Testament, Homer (rather than Virgil) was part and parcel of an attack on aristocratic-bourgeois rationalism which the Industrial and later the French Revolution left in mocking ruins. Poets found themselves declassed, isolated, bewildered, and naturally hewed all sorts of harmonious or terrifying wholes out of their disintegrating world. The chaos of the period drove men to the most radical personal solutions. Any rational assurance of the progress of man was gone. On the other hand the potential for human development which the two revolutions opened up was unprecedented. Existential horror alternated with Utopian thrill.

The mistake which Gabriel Pearson makes is to confuse the responses of the Romantics with the actual reality to which they were responding. For instance, he accepts Blake's dictum: "All deities reside in the human breast" as unquestioningly as his own statement: "The great religious systems crumbled." But this needs some demonstration. After all, the great majority of mankind still believes in these systems to-day. Is Gabriel Pearson stating a historical fact or is he telling us about the opinions of a few people like Blake ? The truth of his statement matters greatly, for we are left with the impression that the world itself was systemless, not simply a few human minds, that therefore only the Romantic poem among all the art forms could henceforth adequately render reality, because reality was like the Romantic poem, fragmentary, an agglomeration of unique data, unique experiences. Gabriel Pearson finds the value of Romantic poetry in its authentic rendering of reality. What then is this reality ? To tell us this he must answer all the questions he begs: what caused the religious systems to flower and decline ? Are they true or false ? Is Blake's view any truer or falser ? Is the world knowable ? Gabriel Pearson does not in fact bother himself about the truth of his propositions. One would not mind this so much, did he not present them as the truth. With a series of apparently neutral statements he fashions a reality which he wants us to accept. Thus "God and Devil, within religious systems, dramatize and hold in tension the extreme poles of experience." Or again: "To the poet . . . angels and devils may prove equally interesting. They represent, after all, merely opposed poles of experience." Religion, poetry, presumably every spiritual sphere is then simply a dramatization of experience. What causes religions to flower and decline is their capacity for psychological satisfaction. The reason for this capacity (or lack of it) is never vouchsafed. Truth then can only be subjective, a matter of belief. This is what we are meant to accept.

I submit the very simple case that if the great religious systems failed, originally for a small number of thinking people, this was because they proved unable to cope with the discoveries of science and the rapid evolution of human society. But the crumbling of a religious system, not that it happened as simply as that, does not leave a social and historical void.

The kind of meaning which the Romantics gave to the world derives very specifically from their social situation. If Blake rejected the antithetical absolutes of God and Devil along with Newton's mechanical universe, it was because social change prompted him to think dialectically. That he located the dialectic of Good and Evil in his own breast and then projected it outward into a mythic system does not mean that the Universe or human society was void of laws any more than when the great religions were undisputed. The proper activity of a critic is to examine the ways in which Blake tried to master the complexities of his world, how far his vision corresponded to it. Full-fledged capitalism, because of its unprecedented and unceasing technological change, its rapid and extreme polarization of classes, revealed for the first time the dialectical process of history in a way which could be conceptualized by thinkers. Until then poets had caught it in images, but only during intervals of great social transformation. Blake stood at the beginning of capitalism. Its forms were inchoate. Official Christianity, Deism proved inadequate for his perceptions. He undertook his own imaginative construction of the Universe.

His 'heroism' consisted, not in some kind of mythologising psychotherapy, but in trying to see the world as a whole in a time of confusion and instability. If he starts from his own experience rather than from stale categories, it is to grasp the indivisibility of particular and general:

> To see a world in a grain of Sand
> And a Heaven in a Wild Flower,
> Hold Infinity in the palm of your hand
> And Eternity in an hour.

But Gabriel Pearson will have nothing general. All is particular, and this is the 'essence' (an unresolved generalisation which he evades) of Romanticism; and since Romanticism is the only authentic response to the world this is the 'essence' too of reality. But here is Blake, with all the disadvantages of an epoch of uncertain change, grappling with the Universe. According to Gabriel Pearson, however, he only loses the tangibility of the particular in trying to grasp the general, which in any case does not exist. That the general does not exist is, of course, never argued. As we have noted, when a generalization is needed, it is covertly used, or if not covertly then with a (presumably) unconscious naïveté which is staggering, vide the "total availability of experience" to which we shall return.

The four lines of Blake are a programme for concrete poetry. We do not deny the corroding effects of any closed system, imaginative or conceptual, on the freshness of particular perception. "All theory is grey," wrote Goethe, "only the golden tree of life is green." Yet the heart of Goethe's imaginative and conceptual world is the *Urphänomen*, a kind of original form, a Platonic concrete universal which underlies all morphology. On the other hand, a Romantic poet like Pushkin who stood foursquare on this world, who spurned the fashionable German idealism that trapped his contemporaries, who had no special axe to grind, who is the most tangible, *particular* poet one could wish to meet, whom literary historians call Protean, is so because he was most particular when not himself. And unlike Gabriel Pearson's Romantic archetype, Pushkin was a supreme love poet.

The first Romantics are termed 'heroic' in the sense, I take it, that their heroism was one of grand illusion. The real heroes are our twentieth century toughies who have purged themselves of all metaphysical dross, set their teeth and accepted the world as it is, which means that everybody is like them and therefore they know what it is like to be "other people living in the world". The Romantics blight their liberation of experience with their metaphysics. In contemporary poetry, of which the poems added to Gabriel Pearson's article are quoted as examples, we have unadulterated experience, experience unmediated by moral hierarchies, experience not so much of anything as the act of experience itself.

These acts are unique, the poem is no more than an enactment of an experience, creating a momentary autonomous world, an artefact of particular images sufficient unto themselves.

Let us lay this "total availability of experience" ghost, since it haunts the entire article. Just as a particular is inconceivable without a general which it mediates (however indirectly), so experience is impossible in human beings without some kind of attitude to behaviour; and this would apply even to the youngest children. We are social animals and society inculcates its norms in us before we know where we are. Obviously the Romantics opened up the sluice-gates of decorum, genre, etc. They ravaged the moral codes of their time in every possible way. But to say that experience was made either "totally available" or "equal" is to suggest they had ceased to be human beings. *Don Juan* is a moral critique of contemporary Europe from beginning to end. Or is this not proper poetry but a Romantic 'life-philosophy'? Where does one draw the line between 'life-philosophy' and actual poetry in the Romantics? Let us take some of the main themes which pervade all Romantic poetry: Nature versus Civilization, the passions versus stuffy morality, individual freedom versus abstract social categories, community versus the state. All these counterings are born of a precise historical age, they are alas! generalizations. The Romantic cry for the individual, as with Gabriel Pearson, is a universal appeal. All Romantic poetry is written in the context of such generalizations. Certain values are praised, others rejected, and in no arbitrary manner, but according to a clearly recognizable hierarchy. And what saves the contemporary poems appended to the article is their adherence to a similar hierarchy. One turns with relief from Gabriel Pearson's sophisticated image-divining to the very simple statements which these poems make. Thus Alan Brownjohn: the purity of nature (indeed kindness—'these kind flakes') versus ugly suburbia — a Romantic theme if you like (though not of Gabriel Pearson's variety), since the social problems which gave rise to Romanticism are still with us. Peter Redgrove's poem in the very first line is concerned with 'final things'. 'I saw Eternity the other night,' wrote the Christian Vaughan. 'Final things walk home with me through Chiswick Park,' writes Peter Redgrove. I know nothing of Redgrove's beliefs, but these 'final things' are the prism for all he sees and thinks as he walks home. Apropos of this poem Gabriel Pearson does not persuade me that it is about the H Bomb. Let us for a moment accept that it is. I would agree that a personally felt and conveyed reaction to the H Bomb is preferable to any numbing apocalypse roused up by the wilder of the Beats; though who is to say that the apocalypse is not in its way equally felt by them? We need tools of judgment here with which we are certainly not provided. Otherwise, one simply says: "I like one kind of experiencing better than another"; the rest is grandiloquent obfuscation (and again one exploits a covert hierarchy). The real reason one prefers the personally felt reaction is, as Gabriel Pearson says, that it makes the horror of the H Bomb all the more intense. But this assumes that life is good and worth saving. If all experience is equally available and profitable for art, then why not write a poem in praise of the H Bomb and find it artistically satisfying if it is personally felt. There is no need to list the horrors which one implicitly condemns in judging all art. It is impossible to make an aesthetic judgment without making a moral one, too, though these are not the same. (One is moved by Macbeth while abhorring his crimes.) Gabriel Pearson has his own reasons for preferring one kind of poem about the H Bomb to another, but they are highly moral ones, and not simply of his own choosing: his upbringing, education, a humanist tradition, the political movements in which he has taken part have taught him to think like this. Let us hear him: "I would assert that the tendency of poems directly about the H Bomb is to reconcile us, by a kind of verbal numbing, a naming that takes out the sting, to the horror by which we should be continuously outraged and horrified. By our rhetoric about the Bomb we learn to live with it and that could easily spell death. The point about poetry is that it can reilluminate our outrage."

To continue with the poems. W. O. Snodgrass: the innocence of the child versus the horrors of war. Ted Hughes: the wolf as a symbol of toughness which we (in particular poets) have now lost. Jenny Joseph: life goes on despite individual death. Thom Gunn: against abstractions which shut out real man. There are value judgments implicit, indeed explicit, in each of these poems. This it is that gives their imagery resonance, not the semantic elucubrations which Gabriel Pearson fastens on them.

Let us look at his method. With the old religions all systems have gone. Man or rather individual men have only their individual, unaccommodated selves. Any metaphor therefore must only ripple concentrically round the person. Thus "Brownjohn's metaphor of snow is one-dimensional, concerned with 'saving . . . face', with 'hiding' an unfruitful world. ('Its white informal fantasies' imitate the action of the poem: 'informal' is a key word, suggesting not so much informed as form which works without fuss, the poetry being contemporarily 'cool', though a little harder than that; 'coldish', perhaps)." What does this tell one about the poem ? Instead of getting at its essence, its simple main statement (I am not suggesting that this is all there is to it), Gabriel Pearson draws out as much meaning as he can from words conceived in a purely verbal state, as semantic nuclei, not as references to the real world. The weary punning on 'cold' is fortunately only in the criticism, not in the poems themselves which are almost all about winter and the cold. This choice itself is a crying value judgment as is the title of the essay *Poetry in the Ice Age*. It is an *ex cathedra* judgment on the age we live in. And this judgment in turn determines one's preferences and dislikes. Original Sin is smuggled into Snodgrass's poem under the guise of semantic allusion (see the ripples round 'fallen'). But if this notion is there it has a moral presence; it is more than a word-echo of one of those 'systems'.

A word on "availability of experience" and literary history. Where does Romanticism really begin ? Gabriel Pearson states his aim to establish "an astonishing transformation of attitudes towards the nature of poetry and of art in general" and positions this transformation historically with Blake. However, a little further on we learn that at all times "active works of literature continually failed to sustain" a moral role. "There was always a conflict, sometimes latent, sometimes avowed, between doctrine and embodiment, moral law and artistic creativity, the life enacted and the official positions taken up." No one would wish to deny this. This is simply a description of human progress in every sphere: fresh experience breaks through old forms, creates new ones. It is a process of interchange in which experience is primary. But what do we learn if this process is called Romanticism? Romanticism becomes synonymous with history or more narrowly the history of the arts.

The trouble with these antitheses is that they are not dialectical. Doctrine, moral law appears as an eternal watchdog with which men for some reason have plagued themselves—perhaps in order to play hide-and-seek. Whatever, the fun is in breaking the rules. Breaking the rules or experience is somehow pure, untrammelled, individual. But if rules are broken they will sooner or later be replaced by fresh ones, otherwise Classicism would not have been succeeded by Romanticism or Romanticism (which alas! soon showed that it had rules) by Realism, Realism by Symbolism and so on. The creation, the observance of rules is as much part of experience as the breaking of them.

At one point in his article Gabriel Pearson grapples seriously with the problem of principles. He has just offered a way of judging the Romantic poem: "Each critical performance must be as unique and particular as the poem it examines." A little further on he says: "Entirely principled critics are either completely uninteresting or interesting by reason of what they reveal of themselves rather than the work." He then modifies this by admitting: "my own proposition is a sort of general principle." At last we have him facing up to the difficulties of his argument, namely how do you generalize about the unique; a serious question. How disappointed are we when in the next sentence he slips back into the fun and games of breaking the rules: "Some sort of tension between principle and particular judgment is what gives criticism its excitement and value. Its struggle to unify and universalise its proposition is, as it were, its brand of existential anguish." Again the disdain for truth. It is not the rightness of the proposition that matters, but the existential thrill one elicits from it. He concludes lamely: "I am not arguing that there cannot be principled approaches to the judgment of literature nor that we are left with a complete relativism of judgment. A critic can argue us round, but not by the validity of his principles, rather by the depth and authority of his reading of actual works. This reading, of course, might well gain much of its strength and coherence from his choice of concepts."

Choice of concepts, mark, not validity. He does not consider that depth of reading might modify or reinforce a principle whose, at least partial, validity has been tested over a long period (say Aristotle's view of tragedy). The validity of a concept is not an absolute, unchanging thing, nor is it completely relative, as Gabriel Pearson for a moment admits. But the relationship between its relative and absolute sides is not an existential see-saw inside the breast of a critic; it is the formulation through hard experience of certain recurring facts of social life, which exist independently of the consciousness of any particular individual. Some of these concepts, such as Aristotle's *peripeteion*, hold good almost unmodified to the present day. They hold good because they are largely true; 'largely' because life is more unmanageable than the most subtle formulations of any one individual.

All this brings me back to Romanticism proper. The Industrial and French Revolutions caused perhaps a deeper disturbance to human history than any others. Looking back on the period we may say that the ideological conflict to which they gave rise, or rather which they immeasurably extended, lay between religion and science. However, science was subject to the social interests of a rising bourgeois class, which concluded Deistic agreements with the nobility or weighed religion and science on separate scales. The poets and writers, that is the most radical, the most temperamentally extreme of them, rejected the new society along with the old. They fell back on themselves. They recreated the world in their own image. Yet at its best this image embraced the immense vistas which social and scientific revolution had thrown open. It is no accident that some of the most mystical Romantics, like Shelley or Novalis, were scientific enthusiasts. Shelley "see-sawed" between "materialist determinism and platonism" (Pearson) in attempting to give philosophical unity to a still mechanical scientific outlook. How unjust and impoverishing to describe *Prometheus Unbound* as simply "a projection of Shelley's own experience in universal guise"! Shelley conjured into a lyrical drama the liberating potentialities of his epoch. The myth of Prometheus reassumed flesh in the Greek Independence struggle. Prometheus, who stole fire from Heaven and broke his chains, was an appropriate enough figure in this age of revolutions. Only in the sense that his age did not fulfil his dreams is Shelley wish-fulfilling. His use of allegory, myth, abstraction does not necessarily make his political poetry insubstantial. The political verse of Lebrun, de Lisle, Schiller, Hölderlin, Pushkin is full of abstraction and allegory. But this did not detract from their rhetorical force. The *Marseillaise* after all led people into revolt. The personifications of political verse matched the abstractions of political thought. Liberty, Equality, Fraternity were inscribed in blood upon the banner of the French Revolution. The abstractions, imaginative or conceptual, were real enough: they sprang from actual struggles, not from isolated egos declaiming into a void. The poetry captured new audiences. Byron and Shelley nourished the Chartists. A line of Pushkin, from a poem addressed to a group of exiled and humiliated Decembrists, became the epigraph to Lenin's newspaper *Iskra* ('the spark')— in the context of the poem an allegorical rather than visual image.

The universality of the Romantics is therefore not a phantom, but an aspiration to something real which their age seemed to promise them. In our own time the promise begins to yield a harvest. Gabriel Pearson himself talks of the poet's attempt "to make his creative life the supreme illustration and example of processes in the real world"—and thereby betrays his whole thesis (the world, he suggests, is after all truly real and knowable). This is why we appreciate, even if we do not love, the many reactionary Utopias of the Romantics. Of course, given their isolation and rejection, this universality often shot into arrogance, megalomania, or toppled into penitence and despair. But from this we should not conclude that the Romantics were vainly replacing the irredeemable religious systems, that reality was henceforth as fragmentary as the fragmented systems, that poets should therefore concentrate on their own persons in their particularity rather than their universality. This is not Romanticism, but its arch-enemy Philistinism. Indeed, Blake is most vivid and particular when he turns the fierce light of his vision on to contemporary London. He would not write like this without such vision.

I would not wish to deny the damage which this personally achieved universality did to some of the poetry of some of the Romantics, in the sense of blurring their *actual* personalities and the *actual* world they lived in. But this would depend largely on whether or not a poet could extend his imaginative orbit beyond himself. Pushkin, for instance, achieved a marvellously unmisted universality by entrenching himself in Russian history and the popular language and culture, not in an antiquarian way, but by learning from a failed revolution, pondering the problem of serfdom, comparing Russia's development with that of the West, embodying in his work both the elemental poetry as well as the simple strengths of the Russian people. In Pushkin we watch a delightfully uninhibited development from the early poet who projects a Romantic image of himself, in various guises, or of some Romantic theme (be it a plea for seclusion or a challenge to tyranny), using imagery that is emotive rather than actual, to the mature poet who is either unashamedly his real self or who creates characters quite unlike himself. (And 'quite unlike' means more than opposite: they are neither alter egos nor dialogue partners, though he has these as well.) He can still play the game of Romantic disguises, but it is now a conscious masquerade which he uses to dramatise different aspects of himself, different attitudes. He still remains a lyric poet who is unabashedly there in his work (if not in person then in intonation). In *Eugene Onegin* he may not hold infinity in the palm of his hand, but he gives us very personally 'an encyclopedia of Russian life' (Belinsky). And this is not just a random metaphor. Pushkin's felicitous brevity, born of the French Enlightenment (he grew up on its literature), avoids the prolixity of much Romantic poetry. He touches the principal phenomena of contemporary Russia with a significant brush-stroke and they glow into life. Russian conditions were propitious to Pushkin's genius. In the post-Decembrist period, in the dark reign of Nicholas, the antagonisms in Russian social life became too severe, and the personal development of Pushkin's own class, or rather its most intelligent, progressive, idealistic members, became too problematic for a poet to compass them in a simple, harmonious whole. The analytical novel was born out of the poetic (*Eugene Onegin* is a novel in verse) and this in turn strove for a new synthesis. But that is another story.

Yet it is worth dwelling on the novel for a bit. Gabriel Pearson's literary history, ostensibly about poetry, implicitly subsumes all good literature after Blake under Romanticism. The Romantic lyric renders experience more 'authentically' than the film, the drama, the novel. The novel rebels against such a blanket interpretation. Pushkin may serve as an example of where the novel inherits Romanticism and goes beyond it, where it makes sense to talk of a shift to Realism, a new artistic outlook. The Romantic hero from a figure of lyrical protest, very much a projection of his author (in Pushkin's lyrical long poems), becomes a social phenomenon. The protest does not disappear, but the emphasis shifts to the social circumstances which produced such a hero. It is a criticism not merely of the society, but of the demonic, individualist reaction to it. Criticism of this kind requires explanation, analysis; it goes beyond lyricism. Naturally, this is only one kind of novel. There is, too, the Romantic novel, but this would take me too far. I want to establish simply that it was the social novel which determined the main development of European literature after Romanticism proper and which gave birth to the concept of Realism. To speak schematically, the nineteeth century social novel resumes the social novel of the eighteenth, but it has absorbed all the intervening experience of Romanticism as well as the sense of history which the French Revolution and its wars left on men's minds and pulses. The relationship between individual and society is therefore infinitely more complex. The universality for which the Romantics strove is not lost. In Balzac and Tolstoy it assumes more epic forms. Gogol or Dickens work round a centripetal imagery which is strongly reminiscent of the Romantics. Gogol indeed called *Dead Souls* a poem.

I would agree more narrowly with Gabriel Pearson's account of the development of lyric poetry. But here again one must distinguish between different kinds of Romanticism, between say the revolutionary potential of a Rimbaud and the private 'platonism' (Pearson) of a Mallarmé. Once the Rimbaud kind of Romantic poetry can take root in a social movement, it becomes charged with public energies, its imagery becomes more stable, its tone more confident. Compare from this point of view *Le Bateau Ivre* with Mayakovsky's *Atlantic Ocean*. The strength of the Mallarmé poet, too, as Gabriel Pearson himself tells us, lies in releasing the "latent public content of language": "a writer who exploits this self-evolving nature of language really intensively must make discoveries about language as communal self-consciousness."

What one likes about the poems appended to the article is their social and moral awareness, not in the sense that they are committed to any big cause: one respects the tentativeness and quietness of tone which is true of most of them. But in what way are they Romantic? If it is because they are series of semantic convolutions, which is dubious, one certainly does not admire them for that and this in any case is a questionable and exclusive definition. They may be Romantic in the sense that all art created in a society where the artist feels himself and his values shut off must betray a private and nostalgic strain. But here again that "battle between language and the world" (Pearson) can lend strength to this Romanticism, prevent it from becoming escapist. I think this is what gives the present poems their sturdiness. But we must be sure that we are talking about a "battle", that is an active engagement with the world and not a kind of inbred punning on words which does service for imagery and generalization.

A final word on rhetoric. Why should socialist realism (not Logue's kind, but one with a real audience as in the socialist countries or such as Brecht enjoyed internationally) entail rhetorical manipulation? If one is fortunate enough to have an audience, one will enjoy the relaxation of writing unrhetorical poetry. Why hunt down the most private lines of Yevtushenko to prove that he is a Romantic? Is his 'private' verse more authentic than his public simply for being private? Why should one demand of a Socialist poet that he behaves quite differently from any other poet? For by suggesting that the only type of socialist poet (i.e. a poet holding socialist beliefs) is Christopher Logue, Gabriel Pearson exposes himself to David Craig's charge that he reduces socialist poetry to *agitprop*; the Socialist poet can thus only behave as propagandist. If Brecht found that politics made his voice hoarse, then he would also write verse like this:

> The little house among trees on the lake,
> From the roof rises smoke,
> Were there none,
> How desolate would be
> House, trees and lake.

Only the malice of a Martin Esslin would regard this as an escape from politics. This little poem is imbued with the same values as Brecht's political verse. On the other hand it has nothing which many a pre-socialist, humanist poet would not write. But then neither socialism nor socialist culture has ever set itself up as something *absolutely* new in human affairs: only late-bourgeois art forms do this. It is here that I would criticize David Craig for labouring scientific socialism in Brecht's poetry. He has got a point (see such didactic poems as *In Praise of the Party*), but it is one which applies more to the novel than to the lyric poem which is both more intimate and more universal. Where it is specific, it is to a particular emotion, rather than to a particular social reality, though I would not want to deny the underground connections between these two.

Let me quote some political verse of Heine.

> I shall sing you now a sweeter song,
> A different song, my friends;
> We shall not wait for the Kingdom of God
> But build it ourselves on this earth.
>
> On this earth we shall find our happiness
> We shall no longer starve,
> Nor idle bellies stuff themselves
> With the toil of diligent hands.

He is sympathising with the poor, attacking the hypocrisy of the prelates and suggesting a revolutionary way to have done with them. The spiritual link with Brecht is obvious ("First comes food and then morality"). But is this therefore scientific socialism? (A novel by Sholokhov or Fedin on the construction of socialism is a ideology presents many tricky problems. If it is good art it is likely to be one step ahead of ideology.) One must distinguish between poems such as *In Praise of the Party*, which is straight scientific socialism, political parables like *The Legend of how the Book Taoteking was written during Lao Tse's Journey into Emigration*, different matter, though even here the relationship between art and the ballads and songs, and finally poems like the one I have quoted. I suggest that the more specifically political are the least permanent, not because they are too political, but because they are not sufficiently universal. This is not a fault, because they were not intended to be anything else. But they are the only ones where one can talk about straight scientific socialism. The others, though imbued with socialist values, are more permanent because they have more in common with all lyric poetry, they are more universal. For this same reason I would hazard that Brecht's poetry will outlast most of his theatre. Here again it is unwise to identify Brecht's 'alienation effect' with Marxism without further discussion as David Craig appears to do. The idea itself originates among the Russian Formalists, and indeed there has been much Marxist criticism of it (e.g. Lukács) before the recent cult of Brecht. The idea is to operate by technical surprise, jolts, breaks, upon some piece of conventional artistic material and make it appear strange and interesting (Shklovsky's *ostranenie*). Brecht invests the technique with greater social content. Yet if one is to change the world one needs to be emotionally identified with it as well as critically detached. Too many of Brecht's subjects are remote, or 'alienated' versions of other people's plays. Does it really work for instance to link the *Caucasian Chalk Circle* with our own day by prefacing it with the collective farm scene?

I noted at the beginning of this article that Gabriel Pearson got angry as soon as he came to speak of politics. Significantly, he only talks about politics in modern times. He scarcely mentions them in relation to Romanticism. It was possible to ignore them under cover of an existentialist literary history. I have deliberately stressed the relationship between the two to show how much we, as socialists, have in common with the Romantic heritage. I would however add here the caution that we must not make a socialist literary history in the same way as an existentialist one. The history of literature is neither a metaphysical nor a political playground where we indulge our present-day adherences. To avoid this danger we must strive to think *historically*. Before, for instance, we accept the idea of a unified culture and its breakdown, either as existentialists or Marxists, we must examine actual history. How many cultures are unified in the way Gabriel Pearson suggests? Did Chaucer and Milton, two highly conscious and individual poets, write within a unified culture? It would be better to examine this question rather than conclude without further ado that they were Romantics *ante rem*. I do not want to dismiss the idea of a unified culture. I have been at pains to stress the watershed of the Industrial and French Revolutions, the development of the natural and social sciences and their challenge to the hegemony of religion. But Heaven knows there were enough religious conflicts before modern science appeared; there was a bourgeois revolution in England fought in the name of religion. These bear as importantly on Milton as Blake's or Gabriel Pearson's appropriation of him.

In the same way I do not wish to look upon the Romantics as socialists *ante rem*, though with some of them there is justice enough for doing so: the early socialist movements of modern times sprang directly from the French Revolution. But this was precisely a Utopian Socialism. The tragedy of the radical Romantics was that the revolutions of their time failed them: these were either crushed, or cruelly disappointing. As Gabriel Pearson suggests, there was almost a deliberateness about the early deaths of some of the Romantics (sometimes it was actual suicide): this rather than face the shipwreck of their ideals. The revolutions of the twentieth century, despite their failures, continue to live and propagate. They have held most of the twentieth century 'Romantics' who joined them, though they have dealt tragically enough with others. They have raised their own poets. They have appealed to the non-committed: "In the people's communes in China I saw poems written by peasants and pinned up on the notice-board in the village hall; no doubt not very good poems, but *millions of* them are written among the pigs and the water buffaloes and from such a ferment an essence will remain." (Herbert Read, *Encounter 109*.)

The uncompromisingness of the first Romantics should inspire us. For how far are we still from Shelley's vision of 'man unaccommodated'? The success of the revolutions of our century has involved so much unromantic compromise. Brecht as usual gives us both sides of the argument:

> O, we
> Who wished to prepare the ground for friendliness,
> Could not ourselves be friendly.
> But you, when at last
> Man can truly help his fellow man,
> Think of us
> With forbearance.
> (Brecht, *To Posterity*.)